THE PELICAN FREUD LIBRARY

General Editor: Angela Richards

VOLUME 6

JOKES AND THEIR RELATION TO THE UNCONSCIOUS

Sigmund Freud

Sigmund Freud was born in 1856 in Moravia; between the ages of four and eighty-two his home was in Vienna: in 1938 Hitler's invasion of Austria forced him to seek asylum in London, where he died in the following year. His career began with several years of brilliant work on the anatomy and physiology of the nervous system. He was almost thirty when, after a period of study under Charcot in Paris, his interests first turned to psychology, and another ten years of clinical work in Vienna (at first in collaboration with Breuer, an older colleague) saw the birth of his creation, psychoanalysis. This began simply as a method of treating neurotic patients by investigating their minds, but it quickly grew into an accumulation of knowledge about the workings of the mind in general, whether sick or healthy. Freud was thus able to demonstrate the normal development of the sexual instinct in childhood and, largely on the basis of an examination of dreams, arrived at his fundamental discovery of the unconscious forces that influence our everyday thoughts and actions. Freud's life was uneventful, but his ideas have shaped not only many specialist disciplines, but the whole intellectual climate of the last half-century.

THE PELICAN FREUD LIBRARY
VOLUME 6

•

JOKES AND THEIR RELATION TO THE UNCONSCIOUS

Sigmund Freud

•

*Translated from the German and
Edited by James Strachey*

*The present edition revised
by Angela Richards*

PENGUIN BOOKS

Penguin Books Ltd, Harmondsworth, Middlesex, England
Penguin Books, 625 Madison Avenue, New York, New York
10022, U.S.A.
Penguin Books Australia Ltd, Ringwood, Victoria, Australia
Penguin Books Canada Ltd, 41 Steelcase Road West, Markham,
Ontario, Canada
Penguin Books (N.Z.) Ltd, 182–190 Wairau Road, Auckland 10,
New Zealand

—

Der Witz und seine Beziehung zum Unbewussten first published 1905
First English translation by A. A. Brill, under the title *Wit and
its Relation to the Unconscious*, published 1916

Present English translation (by James Strachey) first published in
*The Standard Edition of the Complete Psychological Works of Sigmund
Freud*, Volume VIII, by the Hogarth Press and the Institute of Psycho-
Analysis, by arrangement with Routledge & Kegan Paul, London, 1960
Published by Routledge & Kegan Paul Ltd, 1960
Published as a Routledge Paperback 1966
Published in Pelican Books 1976

Translation and Editorial Matter copyright © Angela Richards and
the Institute of Psycho-Analysis, 1960
Additional Editorial Matter copyright © Angela Richards, 1976

—

Made and printed in Great Britain by
Cox & Wyman Ltd,
London, Reading and Fakenham
Set in Monotype Bembo

CONTENTS

JOKES AND THEIR RELATION TO THE UNCONSCIOUS
(1905)

CONTENTS

C. THEORETIC PART

INTRODUCTION TO
THE PELICAN FREUD LIBRARY

The Pelican Freud Library is intended to meet the needs of the general reader by providing all Freud's major writings in translation together with an appropriate linking commentary. It is the first time that such an edition has been produced in paperback in the English language. It does not supplant *The Standard Edition of the Complete Psychological Works of Sigmund Freud*, translated from the German under the general editorship of James Strachey in collaboration with Anna Freud, assisted by Alix Strachey and Alan Tyson, editorial assistant Angela Richards (Hogarth Press, twenty-four volumes, 1953–74). The *Standard Edition* remains the fullest and most authoritative collection published in any language. The present edition does, however, provide a large enough selection to meet the requirements of all but the most specialist reader – in particular it aims to cater for students of sociology, anthropology, criminology, medicine, aesthetics and education, all of them fields in which Freud's ideas have established their relevance.

The texts are reprinted unabridged, with corrections, from the *Standard Edition*. The editorial commentary – introductions, footnotes, internal cross-references, bibliographies and indexes – is also based upon the *Standard Edition*, but it has been abridged and where necessary adapted to suit the less specialized scope and purposes of the *Pelican Freud Library*. Some corrections have been made and some new material added.

Selection of Material

This is not a complete edition of Freud's psychological works – still less of his works as a whole, which included important contributions to neurology and neuropathology dating from the early part of his professional life. Of the psychological writings, virtually all the major works have been included. The arrangement is by subject-matter, so that the main contributions to any particular theme will be found in one volume. Within each volume the works are, for the main part, in chronological sequence. The aim has been to cover the whole field of Freud's observations and his theory of psychoanalysis: that is to say, in the first place, the structure and dynamics of human mental activity; secondly, psychopathology and the mechanism of mental disorder; and thirdly, the application of psychoanalytic theory to wider spheres than the disorders of individuals which Freud originally, and indeed for the greater part of his life, investigated – to the psychology of groups, to social institutions and to religion, art and literature.

In his 'Sigmund Freud: A Sketch of his Life and Ideas' (p. 11 ff. below), James Strachey includes an account of Freud's discoveries as well as defining his principal theories and tracing their development.

Writings excluded from the Edition

The works that have been excluded are, (1) The neurological writings and most of those very early works from the period before the idea of psychoanalysis had taken form. (2) Writings on the actual technique of treatment. These were written specifically for practitioners of psychoanalysis and for analysts in training and their interest is correspondingly specialized. Freud never in fact produced a complete text on psychoanalytic treatment and the papers on technique only deal with selected points of difficulty or theoretical interest. (3) Writings which cover the same ground as other major works which have been included; for example, since the *Library* includes the *Introductory Lectures on Psychoanalysis* and the *New Lectures*, it was decided to leave out several of the shorter expository works in which Freud surveys the whole subject. Similarly, because *The Interpretation of Dreams* is included, the shorter writings on this topic have been omitted. (4) Freud's private correspondence, much of which has now been published in translation.[1] This is not to imply that such letters are without interest or importance though they have not yet received full critical treatment. (5) The numerous short writings such as reviews of books, prefaces to other authors' works, obituary notices and little *pièces d'occasion* – all of which lose interest to a large extent when separated from the books or occasions to which they refer and which would often demand long editorial explanations to make them comprehensible.

Editorial Commentary

The bibliographical information, included at the beginning of the Editor's Note or Introduction to each work, gives the title of the German (or other) original, the date and place of its first publication and the position, where applicable, of the work in Freud's *Gesammelte Werke*, the most complete edition at present available of the works in German (published by S. Fischer Verlag, Frankfurt am Main). Details of the first translation of each work into English are also included, together with the *Standard Edition* reference. (Full details of all German editions published in Freud's lifetime and of all English editions prior to the *Standard Edition* are included in the *Standard Edition*.)

The date of original publication of each work has been added to the half-title page, with the date of composition included in square brackets wherever it is different from the former date.

Further background information is given in introductory notes and in footnotes to the text. Apart from dealing with the

1. [See the list, p. 24 *n*. below, and the details in the Bibliography, p. 305 ff.]

time and circumstances of composition, these notes aim to make it possible to follow the inception and development of important psychoanalytic concepts by means of systematic cross-references. Most of these references are to other works included in the *Pelican Freud Library*. A secondary purpose is to date additions and alterations made by Freud in successive revisions of the text and in certain cases to provide the earlier versions. No attempt has been made to do this as comprehensively as in the *Standard Edition*, but variants are given whenever they indicate a definite change of view. Square brackets are used throughout to distinguish editorial additions from Freud's text and his own footnotes.

It will be clear from this account that I owe an overwhelming debt to the late James Strachey, the general editor and chief translator of the *Standard Edition*. He indeed was mainly responsible for the idea of a *Pelican Freud Library*, and for the original plan of contents. I have also had the advantage of discussions with Miss Anna Freud and the late Mrs Alix Strachey both of whom gave advice of the greatest value. I am grateful to the late Mr Ernst Freud for his support and to the Publications Committee of the Institute of Psycho-Analysis for help in furthering preparations for this edition.

ANGELA RICHARDS, 1976

SIGMUND FREUD

A SKETCH OF HIS LIFE AND IDEAS

SIGMUND FREUD was born on 6 May 1856 in Freiberg, a small town in Moravia, which was at that time a part of Austria-Hungary. In an external sense the eighty-three years of his life were on the whole uneventful and call for no lengthy history.

He came of a middle-class Jewish family and was the eldest child of his father's second wife. His position in the family was a little unusual, for there were already two grown-up sons by his father's first wife. These were more than twenty years older than he was and one of them was already married, with a little boy; so that Freud was in fact born an uncle. This nephew played at least as important a part in his very earliest years as his own younger brothers and sisters, of whom seven were born after him.

His father was a wool-merchant and soon after Freud's birth found himself in increasing commercial difficulties. He therefore decided, when Freud was just three years old, to leave Freiberg, and a year later the whole family settled in Vienna, with the exception of the two elder half-brothers and their children, who established themselves instead in Manchester. At more than one stage in his life Freud played with the idea of joining them in England, but nothing was to come of this for nearly eighty years.

In Vienna during the whole of Freud's childhood the family lived in the most straitened conditions; but it is much to his father's credit that he gave invariable priority to the charge of Freud's education, for the boy was obviously intelligent and was a hard worker as well. The result was that he won a place in the 'Gymnasium' at the early age of nine, and for the last six of the eight years he spent at the school he was regularly top of his class. When at the age of seventeen he passed out of school his career was still undecided; his education so far had been of the most general kind, and, though he seemed in any case destined for the University, several faculties lay open to him.

Freud insisted more than once that at no time in his life did he feel 'any particular predilection for the career of a doctor. I was moved, rather,' he says, 'by a sort of curiosity, which was, however, directed more towards human concerns than towards natural objects.'[1] Elsewhere he writes: 'I have no knowledge of having had any craving in my early childhood to help suffering humanity ... In my youth I felt an over-powering need to understand something of the riddles of the world in which we live and perhaps even to contribute something to their solution.'[2] And in yet another passage in which he was discussing the sociological studies of his last years: 'My interest, after making a lifelong *détour* through the natural sciences, medicine, and psychotherapy, returned to the cultural problems which had fascinated me long before, when I was a youth scarcely old enough for thinking.'[3]

What immediately determined Freud's choice of a scientific career was, so he tells us, being present just when he was leaving school at a public reading of an extremely flowery essay on 'Nature', attributed (wrongly, it seems) to Goethe. But if it was to be science, practical considerations narrowed the choice to medicine. And it was as a medical student that Freud enrolled himself at the University in the autumn of 1873 at the age of seventeen. Even so, however, he was in no hurry to obtain a medical degree. For his first year or two he attended lectures on a variety of subjects, but gradually concentrated first on biology and then on physiology. His very first piece of

1. [*An Autobiographical Study* (1925*d*), near the opening of the work.]
2. ['Postscript to *The Question of Lay Analysis*' (1927*a*).]
3. ['Postscript (1935) to *An Autobiographical Study*' (1935*a*).]

research was in his third year at the University, when he was deputed by the Professor of Comparative Anatomy to investigate a detail in the anatomy of the eel, which involved the dissection of some four hundred specimens. Soon afterwards he entered the Physiological Laboratory under Brücke, and worked there happily for six years. It was no doubt from him that he acquired the main outlines of his attitude to physical science in general. During these years Freud worked chiefly on the anatomy of the central nervous system and was already beginning to produce publications. But it was becoming obvious that no livelihood which would be sufficient to meet the needs of the large family at home was to be picked up from these laboratory studies. So at last, in 1881, he decided to take his medical degree, and a year later, most unwillingly, gave up his position under Brücke and began work in the Vienna General Hospital.

What finally determined this change in his life was something more urgent than family considerations: in June 1882 he became engaged to be married, and thenceforward all his efforts were directed towards making marriage possible. His fiancée, Martha Bernays, came of a well-known Jewish family in Hamburg, and though for the moment she was living in Vienna she was very soon obliged to return to her remote North-German home. During the four years that followed, it was only for brief visits that he could have glimpses of her, and the two lovers had to content themselves with an almost daily interchange of letters. Freud now set himself to establishing a position and a reputation in the medical world. He worked in various departments of the hospital, but soon came to concentrate on neuroanatomy and neuropathology. During this period, too, he published the first inquiry into the possible medical uses of cocaine; and it was this that suggested to Koller the drug's employment as a local anaesthetic. He soon formed two immediate plans: one of these was to obtain an appointment as *Privatdozent*, a post not unlike that of a university lecturer in England, the other was to gain a travelling bursary which would enable him to spend some time in Paris where the reigning figure was the great Charcot. Both of these aims, if they were realized, would, he felt, bring him real advantages, and in 1885, after a hard struggle, he achieved them both.

The months which Freud spent under Charcot at the Salpêtrière (the famous Paris hospital for nervous diseases) brought another change in the course of his life and this time a revolutionary one. So far his work had been concerned entirely with physical science and he was still carrying out histological studies on the brain while he was in Paris. Charcot's interests were at that period concentrated mainly on hysteria and hypnotism. In the world from which Freud came these subjects were regarded as barely respectable, but he became absorbed in them, and, though Charcot himself looked at them purely as branches of neuropathology, for Freud they meant the first beginnings of the investigation of the mind.

On his return to Vienna in the spring of 1886 Freud set up in private practice as a consultant in nervous diseases, and his long-delayed marriage followed soon afterwards. He did not, however, at once abandon all his neuropathological work: for several more years he studied in particular the cerebral palsies of children, on which he became a leading authority. At this period, too, he produced an important monograph on aphasia. But he was becoming more and more engaged in the treatment of the neuroses. After experimenting in vain with electrotherapy, he turned to hypnotic suggestion, and in 1888 visited Nancy to learn the technique used with such apparent success there by Liébeault and Bernheim. This still proved unsatisfactory and he was driven to yet another line of approach. He knew that a friend of his, Dr Josef Breuer, a Vienna consultant considerably his senior, had some ten years earlier cured a girl suffering from hysteria by a quite new procedure. He now persuaded Breuer to take up the method once more, and he himself applied it to several fresh cases with promising results. The method was based on the assumption that hysteria was the product of a psychical trauma which had been forgotten by the patient; and the treatment consisted in inducing her in a hypnotic state to recall the forgotten trauma to the accompaniment of appropriate emotions. Before very long Freud began to make changes both in the procedure and in the underlying theory; this led eventually to a breach with Breuer, and to the ultimate development by Freud of the whole system of ideas to which he soon gave the name of psychoanalysis.

From this moment onwards – from 1895, perhaps – to the very end of his life, the whole of Freud's intellectual existence revolved around this development, its far-reaching implications, and its theoretical and practical repercussions. It would, of course, be impossible to give in a few sentences any consecutive account of Freud's discoveries and ideas, but an attempt will be made presently to indicate in a disconnected fashion some of the main changes he has brought about in our habits of thought. Meanwhile we may continue to follow the course of his external life.

His domestic existence in Vienna was essentially devoid of episode: his home and his consulting rooms were in the same house from 1891 till his departure for London forty-seven years later. His happy marriage and his growing family – three sons and three daughters – provided a solid counterweight to the difficulties which, to begin with at least, surrounded his professional career. It was not only the nature of his discoveries that created prejudice against him in medical circles; just as great, perhaps, was the effect of the intense anti-semitic feeling which dominated the official world of Vienna: his appointment to a university professorship was constantly held back by political influence.

One particular feature of these early years calls for mention on account of its consequences. This was Freud's friendship with Wilhelm Fliess, a brilliant but unbalanced Berlin physician, who specialized in the ear and throat, but whose wider interests extended over human biology and the effects of periodic phenomena in vital processes. For fifteen years, from 1887 to 1902, Freud corresponded with him regularly, reported the development of his ideas, forwarded him long drafts outlining his future writings, and, most important of all, sent him an essay of some forty thousand words which has been given the name of a 'Project for a Scientific Psychology'. This essay was composed in 1895, at what might be described as the watershed of Freud's career, when he was reluctantly moving from physiology to psychology; it is an attempt to state the facts of psychology in purely neurological terms. This paper and all the rest of Freud's communications to Fliess have, by a lucky chance, survived: they throw a fascinating light on the development of Freud's ideas and show how much of the later findings of psychoanalysis were already present in his mind at this early stage.

Apart from his relations with Fliess, Freud had little outside support to begin with. He gradually gathered a few pupils round him in Vienna, but it was only after some ten years, in about 1906, that a change was inaugurated by the adhesion of a number of Swiss psychiatrists to his views. Chief among these were Bleuler, the head of the Zurich mental hospital, and his assistant Jung. This proved to be the beginning of the first spread of psychoanalysis. An international meeting of psycho-analysts gathered at Salzburg in 1908, and in 1909 Freud and Jung were invited to give a number of lectures in the United States. Freud's writings began to be translated into many languages, and groups of practising analysts sprang up all over the world. But the progress of psychoanalysis was not without its set-backs: the currents which its subject-matter stirred up in the mind ran too deep for its easy acceptance. In 1911 one of Freud's prominent Viennese supporters, Alfred Adler, broke away from him, and two or three years later Jung's differences from Freud led to their separation. Almost immediately after this came the First World War and an interruption of the international spread of psychoanalysis. Soon afterwards, too, came the gravest personal tragedies – the death of a daughter and of a favourite grandchild, and the onset of the malignant illness which was to pursue him relentlessly for the last sixteen years of his life. None of these troubles, however, brought any interruption to the development of Freud's observations and inferences. The structure of his ideas continued to expand and to find ever wider applications – particularly in the sociological field. By now he had become generally recognized as a figure of world celebrity, and no honour pleased him more than his election in 1936, the year of his eightieth birthday, as a Corresponding Member of the Royal Society. It was no doubt this fame, supported by the efforts of influential admirers, including, it is said, President Roosevelt, that protected him from the worst excesses of the National Socialists when Hitler invaded Austria in 1938, though they seized and destroyed his publications. Freud's departure from Vienna was nevertheless essential, and in June of that year, accompanied by some of his family, he made the journey to London, and it was there, a year later, on 23 September 1939, that he died.

It has become a journalistic cliché to speak of Freud as one of the revolutionary founders of modern thought and to couple his name with that of Einstein. Most people would, however, find it almost as hard to summarize the changes introduced by the one as by the other.

Freud's discoveries may be grouped under three headings – an instrument of research, the findings produced by the instrument, and the theoretical hypotheses inferred from the findings – though the three groups were of course mutually interrelated. Behind all of Freud's work, however, we should posit his belief in the universal validity of the law of determinism. As regards physical phenomena this belief was perhaps derived from his experience in Brücke's laboratory and so, ultimately, from the school of Helmholtz; but Freud extended the belief uncompromisingly to the field of mental phenomena, and here he may have been influenced by his teacher, the psychiatrist Meynert, and indirectly by the philosophy of Herbart.

First and foremost, Freud was the discoverer of the first instrument for the scientific examination of the human mind. Creative writers of genius had had fragmentary insight into mental processes, but no systematic method of investigation existed before Freud. It was only gradually that he perfected the instrument, since it was only gradually that the difficulties in the way of such an investigation became apparent. The forgotten trauma in Breuer's explanation of hysteria provided the earliest problem and perhaps the most fundamental of all, for it showed conclusively that there were active parts of the mind not immediately open to inspection either by an on-looker or by the subject himself. These parts of the mind were described by Freud, without regard for metaphysical or terminological disputes, as the unconscious. Their existence was equally demonstrated by the fact of post-hypnotic suggestion, where a person in a fully waking state performs an action which had been suggested to him some time earlier, though he had totally forgotten the suggestion itself. No examination of the mind could thus be considered complete unless it included this unconscious part of it in its scope. How was this to be accomplished? The obvious answer seemed to be: by means of hypnotic suggestion; and this was the instrument used by Breuer and, to begin with, by Freud. But it soon turned out to be an imperfect one, acting irregularly and un-certainly and sometimes not at all. Little by little, accordingly, Freud abandoned the use of suggestion and replaced it by an entirely fresh instrument, which was later known as 'free association'. He adopted the unheard-of plan of simply asking the person whose mind he was investigating to say whatever came into his head. This crucial decision led at once to the most

SIGMUND FREUD: HIS LIFE AND IDEAS   19

startling results; even in this primitive form Freud's instrument produced fresh insight. For, though things went along swimmingly for a while, sooner or later the flow of associations dried up: the subject would not or could not think of anything more to say. There thus came to light the fact of 'resistance', of a force, separate from the subject's conscious will, which was refusing to collaborate with the investigation. Here was one basis for a very fundamental piece of theory, for a hypothesis of the mind as something dynamic, as consisting in a number of mental forces, some conscious and some unconscious, operating now in harmony now in opposition with one another.

Though these phenomena eventually turned out to be of universal occurrence, they were first observed and studied in neurotic patients, and the earlier years of Freud's work were largely concerned with discovering means by which the 'resistance' of these patients could be overcome and what lay behind it could be brought to light. The solution was only made possible by an extraordinary piece of self-observation on Freud's part – what we should now describe as his self-analysis. We are fortunate in having a contemporary first-hand description of this event in his letters to Fliess which have already been mentioned. This analysis enabled him to discover the nature of the unconscious processes at work in the mind and to understand why there is such a strong resistance to their becoming conscious; it enabled him to devise techniques for overcoming or evading the resistance in his patients; and, most important of all, it enabled him to realize the very great difference between the mode of functioning of these unconscious processes and that of our familiar conscious ones. A word may be said on each of these three points, for in fact they constitute the core of Freud's contributions to our knowledge of the mind.

The unconscious contents of the mind were found to consist wholly in the activity of conative trends – desires or wishes – which derive their energy directly from the primary physical instincts. They function quite regardless of any consideration other than that of obtaining immediate satisfaction, and are thus liable to be out of step with those more conscious elements in the mind which are concerned with adaptation to reality and the avoidance of external dangers. Since, moreover, these primitive trends are to a great extent of a sexual or of a destructive nature, they are bound to come in conflict with the more social and civilized mental forces. Investigations along this path were what led Freud to his discoveries of the long-disguised secrets of the sexual life of children and of the Oedipus complex.

In the second place, his self-analysis led him to an inquiry into the nature of dreams. These turned out to be, like neurotic symptoms, the product of a conflict and a compromise between the primary unconscious impulses and the secondary conscious ones. By analysing them into their elements it was therefore possible to infer their hidden unconscious contents; and, since dreams are common phenomena of almost universal occurrence, their interpretation turned out to be one of the most useful technical contrivances for penetrating the resistances of neurotic patients.

Finally, the painstaking examination of dreams enabled Freud to classify the remarkable differences between what he termed the primary and secondary processes of thought, between events in the unconscious and conscious regions of the mind. In the unconscious, it was found, there is no sort of organization or coordination: each separate impulse seeks satisfaction independently of all the rest; they proceed uninfluenced by one another; contradictions are completely inoperative, and the most opposite impulses flourish side by side. So, too, in the unconscious, associations of ideas proceed along lines without any regard to logic: similarities are treated as identities, negatives are equated with positives. Again, the objects to which the conative trends are attached in the unconscious are extraordinarily changeable – one may be replaced by another along a whole chain of associations that have no rational basis. Freud perceived that the intrusion into conscious thinking of mechanisms that belong properly to the primary process accounts for the oddity not only of dreams but of many other normal and pathological mental events.

It is not much of an exaggeration to say that all the later part of Freud's work lay in an immense extension and elaboration of these early ideas. They were applied to an elucidation of the mechanisms not only of the psychoneuroses and psychoses but also of such normal processes as slips of the tongue, making jokes, artistic creation, political institutions, and religions; they played a part in throwing fresh light on many applied sciences – archaeology, anthropology, criminology, education; they also served to account for the effectiveness of psychoanalytic therapy. Lastly, too, Freud erected on the basis of these elementary observations a theoretical superstructure, what he named a 'metapsychology', of more general concepts. These, however, fascinating as many people will find them, he always insisted were in the nature of provisional hypotheses. Quite late in his life, indeed, influenced by the ambiguity of the term 'unconscious' and its many conflicting uses, he proposed a new structural account of the mind in which the uncoordinated instinctual trends were called the 'id', the organized realistic part the 'ego', and the critical and moralizing function the 'super-ego' – a new account which has certainly made for a clarification of many issues.

This, then, will have given the reader an outline of the external events of Freud's life and some notion of the scope of his discoveries. Is it legitimate to ask for more? to try to penetrate a little further and to inquire what sort of person Freud was? Possibly not. But human curiosity about great men is insatiable, and if it is not gratified with true accounts it will inevitably clutch at mythological ones. In two of Freud's early books (*The Interpretation of Dreams* and *The Psycho-*

pathology of Everyday Life) the presentation of his thesis had forced on him the necessity of bringing up an unusual amount of personal material. Nevertheless, or perhaps for that very reason, he intensely objected to any intrusion into his private life, and he was correspondingly the subject of a wealth of myths. According to the first and most naïve rumours, for instance, he was an abandoned profligate, devoted to the corruption of public morals. Later fantasies have tended in the opposite direction: he has been represented as a harsh moralist, a ruthless disciplinarian, an autocrat, egocentric and unsmiling, and an essentially unhappy man. To anyone who was acquainted with him, even slightly, both these pictures must seem equally preposterous. The second of them was no doubt partly derived from a knowledge of his physical sufferings during his last years; but partly too it may have been due to the unfortunate impression produced by some of his most widespread portraits. He disliked being photographed, at least by professional photographers, and his features on occasion expressed the fact; artists too seem always to have been overwhelmed by the necessity for representing the inventor of psychoanalysis as a ferocious and terrifying figure. Fortunately, however, alternative versions exist of a more amiable and truer kind – snapshots, for instance, taken on a holiday or with his children, such as will be found in his eldest son's memoir of his father (*Glory Reflected*, by Martin Freud [1957]). In many ways, indeed, this delightful and amusing book serves to redress the balance from more official biographies, invaluable as they are, and reveals something of Freud as he was in ordinary life. Some of these portraits show us that in his earlier days he had well-filled features, but in later life, at any rate after the First World War and even before his illness, this was no longer so, and his features, as well as his whole figure (which was of medium height), were chiefly remarkable for the impression they gave of tense energy and alert observation. He was serious but kindly and considerate in his more formal manners, but in other circumstances could be an entertaining talker with a pleasantly ironical sense of humour. It was easy to discover his devoted fondness for his family and to recognize a man who would inspire affection. He had many miscellaneous interests – he was fond of travelling abroad, of country holidays, of mountain walks – and there were other, more engrossing subjects, art, archaeology, literature. Freud was a very well-read man in many languages, not only in German. He read English and French fluently, besides having a fair knowledge of Spanish and Italian. It must be remembered, too, that though the later phases of his education were chiefly scientific (it is true that at the University he studied philosophy for a short time) at school he had learnt the classics and never lost his affection for them. We happen to have a letter written by him at the age of seventeen to a school friend.[1] In it he describes his varying success in the different papers of his school-leaving examination: in Latin a passage from Virgil, and in Greek thirty-three lines from, of all things, *Oedipus Rex*.

In short, we might regard Freud as what in England we should consider the best kind of product of a Victorian up-bringing. His tastes in literature and art would obviously differ from ours, his views on ethics, though decidedly liberal, would not belong to the post-Freudian age. But we should see in him a man who lived a life full of emotion and of much suffering without embitterment. Complete honesty and directness were qualities that stood out in him, and so too did his intellectual readiness to take in and consider any fact, however new or extraordinary, that was presented to him. It was perhaps an inevitable corollary and extension of these qualities, combined with a general benevolence which a surface misanthropy failed to disguise, that led to some features of a surprising kind. In spite of his subtlety of mind he was essentially unsophisticated, and there were sometimes unexpected lapses in his critical faculty –

1. [Emil Fluss. The letter is included in the volume of Freud's correspondence (1960a).]

a failure, for instance, to perceive an untrustworthy authority in some subject that was off his own beat such as Egyptology or philology, and, strangest of all in someone whose powers of perception had to be experienced to be believed, an occasional blindness to defects in his acquaintances. But though it may flatter our vanity to declare that Freud was a human being of a kind like our own, that satisfaction can easily be carried too far. There must in fact have been something very extraordinary in the man who was first able to recognize a whole field of mental facts which had hitherto been excluded from normal consciousness, the man who first interpreted dreams, who first accepted the facts of infantile sexuality, who first made the distinction between the primary and secondary processes of thinking – the man who first made the unconscious mind real to us.

[Those in search of further information will find it in the three-volume biography of Freud by Ernest Jones, an abridged version of which was published in Pelican in 1964, in the important volume of Freud's letters edited by his son and daughter-in-law, Ernst and Lucie Freud (1960a), in several further volumes of his correspondence, with Wilhelm Fliess (1950a), Karl Abraham (1965a), C. G. Jung (1974a), Oskar Pfister (1963a), Lou Andreas-Salomé (1966a) and Arnold Zweig (1968a), and above all in the many volumes of Freud's own works.]

CHRONOLOGICAL TABLE

This table traces very roughly some of the main turning-points in Freud's intellectual development and opinions. A few of the chief events in his external life are also included in it.

1856. 6 May. Birth at Freiberg in Moravia.

1860. Family settles in Vienna.

1865. Enters Gymnasium (secondary school).

1873. Enters Vienna University as medical student.

1876–82. Works under Brücke at the Institute of Physiology in Vienna.

1877. First publications: papers on anatomy and physiology.

1881. Graduates as Doctor of Medicine.

1882. Engagement to Martha Bernays.

1882–5. Works in Vienna General Hospital, concentrating on cerebral anatomy: numerous publications.

1884–7. Researches into the clinical uses of cocaine.

1885. Appointed *Privatdozent* (University Lecturer) in Neuropathology.

1885 (October)–1886 (February). Studies under Charcot at the Salpêtrière (hospital for nervous diseases) in Paris. Interest first turns to hysteria and hypnosis.

1886. Marriage to Martha Bernays. Sets up private practice in nervous diseases in Vienna.

1886–93. Continues work on neurology, especially on the cerebral palsies of children at the Kassowitz Institute in Vienna, with numerous publications. Gradual shift of interest from neurology to psychopathology.

1887. Birth of eldest child (Mathilde).

1887–1902. Friendship and correspondence with Wilhelm Fliess in Berlin. Freud's letters to him during this period, published posthumously in 1950, throw much light on the development of his views.

1887. Begins the use of hypnotic suggestion in his practice.

c. 1888. Begins to follow Breuer in using hypnosis for cathartic treatment of hysteria. Gradually drops hypnosis and substitutes free association.

1889. Visits Bernheim at Nancy to study his suggestion technique. Birth of eldest son (Martin).

1891. Monograph on Aphasia. Birth of second son (Oliver).

1892. Birth of youngest son (Ernst).

1893. Publication of Breuer and Freud 'Preliminary Communication': exposition of trauma theory of hysteria and of cathartic treatment. Birth of second daughter (Sophie).

1893–8. Researches and short papers on hysteria, obsessions, and anxiety.

1895. Jointly with Breuer, *Studies on Hysteria*: case histories and description by Freud of his technique, including first account of transference.

1893–6. Gradual divergence of views between Freud and Breuer. Freud introduces concepts of defence and repression and of neurosis being a result of a conflict between the ego and the libido.

1895. *Project for a Scientific Psychology*: included in Freud's letters to Fliess and first published in 1950. An abortive attempt to state psychology in neurological terms; but foreshadows much of Freud's later theories. Birth of youngest child (Anna).

1896. Introduces the term 'psychoanalysis'. Death of father (aged 80).

1897. Freud's self-analysis, leading to the abandonment of the trauma theory and the recognition of infantile sexuality and the Oedipus complex.

1900. *The Interpetation of Dreams*, with final chapter giving first full account of Freud's dynamic view of mental processes, of the unconscious, and of the dominance of the 'pleasure principle'.

1901. *The Psychopathology of Everyday Life*. This, together with the book on dreams, made it plain that Freud's theories applied not only to pathological states but also to normal mental life.

1902. Appointed Professor Extraordinarius.

1905. *Three Essays on the Theory of Sexuality*: tracing for the first time the course of development of the sexual instinct in human beings from infancy to maturity.

c. 1906. Jung becomes an adherent of psychoanalysis.

1908. First international meeting of psychoanalysts (at Salzburg).

1909. Freud and Jung invited to the USA to lecture.

Case history of the first analysis of a child (Little Hans, aged five): confirming inferences previously made from adult analyses, especially as to infantile sexuality and the Oedipus and castration complexes.

c. 1910. First emergence of the theory of 'narcissim'.

1911–15. Papers on the technique of psychoanalysis.

1911. Secession of Adler.

Application of psychoanalytic theories to a psychotic case: the autobiography of Dr Schreber.

1913–14. *Totem and Taboo*: application of psychoanalysis to anthropological material.

1914. Secession of Jung.

'On the History of the Psycho-Analytic Movement'. Includes a polemical section on Adler and Jung.

Writes his last major case history, of the 'Wolf Man' (not published till 1918).

1915. Writes a series of twelve 'metapsychological' papers on basic theoretical questions, of which only five have survived.

1915–17. *Introductory Lectures*: giving an extensive general account of the state of Freud's views up to the time of the First World War.

1919. Application of the theory of narcissism to the war neuroses.

1920. Death of second daughter.

Beyond the Pleasure Principle: the first explicit introduction of the concept of the 'compulsion to repeat' and of the theory of the 'death instinct'.

1921. *Group Psychology*. Beginnings of a systematic analytic study of the ego.

1923. *The Ego and the Id*. Largely revised account of the structure and functioning of the mind with the division into an id, an ego, and a super-ego.

First onset of cancer.

1925. Revised views on the sexual development of women.

1926. *Inhibitions, Symptoms, and Anxiety*. Revised views on the problem of anxiety.

1927. *The Future of an Illusion*. A discussion of religion: the first of a number of sociological works to which Freud devoted most of his remaining years.

1930. *Civilization and its Discontents*. This includes Freud's first extensive study of the destructive instinct (regarded as a manifestation of the 'death instinct').

Freud awarded the Goethe Prize by the City of Frankfurt.

Death of mother (aged 95).

1933. Hitler seizes power in Germany: Freud's books publicly burned in Berlin.

1934–8. *Moses and Monotheism*: the last of Freud's works to appear during his lifetime.

1936. Eightieth birthday. Election as Corresponding Member of Royal Society.

1938. Hitler's invasion of Austria. Freud leaves Vienna for London. *An Outline of Psycho-Analysis*. A final, unfinished, but profound, exposition of psychoanalysis.

1939. 23 December. Death in London.

JOKES AND THEIR RELATION
TO THE UNCONSCIOUS
(1905)

Acknowledgement by James Strachey included in the Routledge & Kegan Paul edition, 1960.

The Editor would like to thank his wife, Miss Anna Freud and
Mr Alan Tyson for their help in preparing the translation. He
is also especially indebted to Miss Angela Richards for her
invaluable work in tracing and verifying the numerous references as well as for her assistance in seeing the book through the
press.

X

EDITOR'S INTRODUCTION

DER WITZ UND SEINE BEZIEHUNG
ZUM UNBEWUSSTEN

1905   First German edition: Leipzig and Vienna: Deuticke.
1912   Second Edition (with a few small additions).
1940   *Gesammelte Werke*, **6**.
1916   First English translation (by A. A. Brill), under the title *Wit and its Relation to the Unconscious*: New York: Moffat, Yard.
1917   London (same as above): T. Fisher Unwin.
1960   *Standard Edition*, **8** (trans. James Strachey).
1960   London: Routledge & Kegan Paul (reprint of above).

In the course of discussing the relation between jokes and dreams, Freud mentions his own 'subjective reason for taking up the problem of jokes' (p. 231 below). This was, put briefly, the fact that when Wilhelm Fliess was reading the proofs of *The Interpretation of Dreams* in the autumn of 1899, he complained that the dreams were too full of jokes. The episode had already been reported by Freud in a footnote to the first edition of *The Interpretation of Dreams* itself (1900a) *P.F.L.*, **4**, 405–6n.

This occurrence acted, no doubt, as a precipitating factor, and led to Freud's giving closer attention to the subject; but it cannot possibly have been the origin of his interest in it. There is ample evidence that it had been in his mind for several years earlier. For one thing, this is shown by the reference to the mechanism of 'comic' effects, which appears on a later page of *The Interpretation of Dreams* (*P.F.L.*, **4**, 765ff.) and which forestalls one of the main points in the final chapter of the present work. It was, of course, inevitable that as soon as Freud began his close investigation of dreams he would be struck by the frequency with which structures resembling jokes figure in the dreams themselves or their associations. *The Interpretation of Dreams* is full of examples of this, but perhaps the earliest one recorded is the punning hallucination of Frau Cäcilie M., reported in a footnote at the end of the case history of Fräulein Elisabeth von R. in the *Studies on Hysteria* (1895d), *P.F.L.*, **3**, 255n.

For another thing, quite apart from dreams, there is evidence of Freud's early theoretical interest in jokes in his letters to Fliess (Freud, 1950a). On 12 June 1897 (Letter 65), he wrote: 'I must confess that for some time past I have been putting together a collection of Jewish anecdotes of deep significance.' Freud mentions his 'collection' more than once and quotes several Jewish stories from it in the Fliess correspondence; a number also appear in *The Interpretation of Dreams*. It was from this collection, of course, that he derived the many examples of such anecdotes on which his theories are so largely based.

Another influence which was of some importance to Freud at about this time was that of Theodor Lipps. Lipps (1851–1914) was a Munich professor of philosophy who wrote on psychology and aesthetics, and who is accredited with having introduced the term *'Einfühlung'* ('empathy'). Freud's interest in him was probably first attracted by a paper on the unconscious which he read at a psychological congress in 1897. It is the basis of a long discussion in the last chapter of *The Interpretation of Dreams* (*P.F.L.*, **4**, 771 ff.). We know from the Fliess letters that in August and September, 1898, Freud was reading an earlier book by Lipps on *The Basic Facts of Mental Life* (1883) and was again struck by his remarks on the unconscious. But in 1898 there appeared yet another work from Lipps and this time on a more specialized subject – *Komik und Humor*. And it was this work, as Freud tells us at the very beginning of the present study, which encouraged him to embark upon it.

It was on ground thus prepared that the seed of Fliess's critical comment fell, but even so several more years were to elapse before the moment of fruition.

Freud published three major works in 1905: the 'Dora' case history, which appeared in the autumn though it was written for the most part four years earlier, the *Three Essays on the Theory of Sexuality* and *Jokes and their Relation to the Unconscious*. Work on the last two books proceeded simultaneously: Ernest Jones (1955, 13) tells us that Freud kept the two manuscripts on adjoining tables and added to one or the other according to his mood. The books were published almost simultaneously; it is not entirely certain which was the earlier, but *Jokes* must have appeared before the beginning of June, for a long and favourable review was printed in the Vienna daily paper *Die Zeit* on 4 June.

The later history of the book was very different from that of Freud's other major works of this period. *The Interpretation of Dreams*, *The Psychopathology of Everyday Life* and the *Three Essays* were all of them expanded and modified almost out of recognition in their later editions. Half-a-dozen small additions were made to the *Jokes* when it reached its second edition in 1912, but no further changes were ever made in it.[1]

It seems possible that this is related to the fact that this book lies somewhat apart from the rest of Freud's writings. He himself may have taken this view of it. His references to it in other works are comparatively few; in the *Introductory Lectures* (1916–1917) Lecture 15, *P.F.L.*, **1**, 274, he speaks of its having temporarily led him aside from his path; and in the *Autobiographical Study* (1925*d*), Chapter VI, there is even what looks like a slightly depreciatory reference to it. Then, unexpectedly, after an interval of more than twenty years, he picked up the thread again with his short paper on 'Humour' (1927*d*), in

1. In the present edition the sections into which the author divided the long chapters have been numbered for convenience of reference.

which he used his newly propounded structural view of the mind to throw a fresh light on an obscure problem.

Ernest Jones describes this as the least known of Freud's works, and that is certainly, and not surprisingly, true of non-German readers.

'Traduttore – Traditore!' The words – one of the jokes discussed by Freud below (p. 67) – might appropriately be emblazoned on the title-page of the present volume. Many of Freud's works raise acute difficulties for the translator, but this presents a special case. Here, as with *The Interpretation of Dreams* and *The Psychopathology of Everyday Life*, and perhaps to a greater extent, we are faced by large numbers of examples involving a play upon words that is untranslatable. And here, as in these other cases, we can do no more than explain the rather uncompromising policy adopted in this edition. There are two methods one or other of which has usually been adopted in dealing with such intractable examples – either to drop them out altogether or to replace them by examples of the translator's own. Neither of these methods seems suitable to an edition which is intended to present English readers with Freud's own ideas as accurately as possible. Here, therefore, we have to be content with giving the critical words in the original German and explaining them as shortly as possible in square brackets or footnotes. Inevitably, of course, the joke disappears in the process. But it must be remembered that, by either of the alternative methods, what disappears are portions, and sometimes most interesting portions, of Freud's arguments. And, presumably, these, and not a moment's amusement, are what the reader has in view.

There is, however, a much more serious difficulty in translating this particular work – a terminological difficulty which runs through the whole of it. By a strange fatality (into whose causes it would be interesting to inquire) the German and English terms covering the phenomena discussed in these pages seem never to coincide: they seem always too narrow or too wide – to leave gaps between them or to overlap. A major problem faces us with the very title of the book, '*Der Witz*'. To translate it 'Wit' opens the door to unfortunate misapprehensions. In ordinary English usage 'wit' and 'witty' have a highly restricted meaning and are applied only to the most refined and intellectual kind of jokes. The briefest inspection of the examples in these pages will show that '*Witz*' and '*witzig*' have a far wider connotation.[1] 'Joke' on the other hand seems itself to be too wide and to cover the German '*Scherz*' as well. The only solution in this and similar dilemmas has seemed to be to adopt one English word for some corresponding German one, and to keep to it quite consistently and invariably even if in some particular context it seems the wrong one. In this way the reader will at least be able to form his own conclusion as to the sense in which Freud is using the word. Thus, throughout the book '*Witz*' has been rendered 'joke' and '*Scherz*' 'jest'. There is great trouble with the adjective '*witzig*', which is used here in most cases simply as the qualifying adjective to '*Witz*'. The *Concise Oxford Dictionary* actually gives, without comment, an adjective 'joky'. The word would have saved the translator innumerable clumsy periphrases, but he confesses that he had not the nerve to use it. The only places in which '*Witz*' has been translated 'wit' are two or three (e.g. on p. 191) in which the German word is used (as explained in the last footnote) for the mental function and not for the product, and where there seemed no possible English alternative.

There are other, though less severe, difficulties over the German '*das Komische*' and '*die Komik*'. An attempt to differentiate between these, and to use 'the comic' for the first and 'comic-

---

1. '*Der Witz*', incidentally, is used both for the mental faculty and for its product – for 'wittiness' and 'the witticism', to use renderings that have been rejected here. The German word can be used besides in a much vaguer sense, for 'ingenuity'; but the English 'wit', for the matter of that, also has its wider usages.

A. ANALYTIC PART

I

INTRODUCTION

[1]

ANYONE who has at any time had occasion to inquire from the literature of aesthetics and psychology what light can be thrown on the nature of jokes and on the position they occupy will probably have to admit that jokes have not received nearly as much philosophical consideration as they deserve in view of the part they play in our mental life. Only a small number of thinkers can be named who have entered at all deeply into the problems of jokes. Among those who have discussed jokes, however, are such famous names as those of the novelist Jean Paul (Richter) and of the philosophers Theodor Vischer, Kuno Fischer and Theodor Lipps. But even with these writers the subject of jokes lies in the background, while the main interest of their inquiry is turned to the more comprehensive and attractive problem of the comic.

The first impression one derives from the literature is that it is quite impracticable to deal with jokes otherwise than in connection with the comic.

According to Lipps (1898),[1] a joke is 'something comic which is entirely subjective' – that is, something comic 'which *we* produce, which is attached to action of ours as such, to which we invariably stand in the relation of subject and never of object, not even of voluntary object' (ibid., 80). This is explained further by a remark to the effect that in general we call a joke 'any conscious and successful evocation of what is comic, whether the comic of observation or of situation' (ibid., 78).

Fischer (1889) illustrates the relation of jokes to the comic

1. It is this book that has given me the courage to undertake this attempt as well as the possibility of doing so.

with the help of caricature, which in his account he places between them. The comic is concerned with the ugly in one of its manifestations: 'If it [what is ugly] is concealed, it must be uncovered in the light of the comic way of looking at things; if it is noticed only a little or scarcely at all, it must be brought forward and made obvious, so that it lies clear and open to the light of day . . . In this way caricature comes about' (ibid., 45). – 'Our whole spiritual world, the intellectual kingdom of our thoughts and ideas, does not unfold before the gaze of external observation, it cannot be directly imagined pictorially and visibly; and yet it too contains its inhibitions, its weaknesses and its deformities – a wealth of ridiculous and comic contrasts. In order to emphasize these and make them accessible to aesthetic consideration, a force is necessary which is able not merely to imagine objects directly but itself to reflect on these images and to clarify them: a force that can illuminate thoughts. The only such force is *judgement*. A joke is a judgement which produces a comic contrast; it has already played a silent part in caricature, but only in judgement does it attain its peculiar form and the free sphere of its unfolding' (ibid., 49–50).

It will be seen that the characteristic which distinguishes the joke within the class of the comic is attributed by Lipps to action, to the active behaviour of the subject, but by Fischer to its relation to its *object*, which he considers is the concealed ugliness of the world of thoughts. It is impossible to test the validity of these definitions of the joke – indeed, they are scarcely intelligible – unless they are considered in the context from which they have been torn. It would therefore be necessary to work through these authors' accounts of the comic before anything could be learnt from them about jokes. Other passages, however, show us that these same authors are able to describe essential and generally valid characteristics of the joke without any regard to its connection with the comic.

The characterization of jokes which seems best to satisfy Fischer himself is as follows: 'A joke is a *playful* judgement' (ibid., 51). By way of illustration of this, we are given an analogy: 'just as aesthetic freedom lies in the playful contemplation of things' (ibid., 50). Elsewhere (ibid., 20) the aesthetic attitude towards an object is characterized by the condition that we do not ask anything of the object, especially no satisfaction of our serious needs, but content ourselves with the enjoyment of contemplating it. The aesthetic attitude is *playful* in contrast to work. – 'It might be that from aesthetic freedom there might spring too a sort of judging released from its usual rules and regulations, which, on account of its origin, I will call a "playful judgement", and that in this concept is contained the first determinant, if not the whole formula, that will solve our problem. "Freedom produces jokes and jokes produce freedom," wrote Jean Paul. "Joking is merely playing with ideas"' (ibid., 24).[1]

A favourite definition of joking has long been the ability to find similarity between dissimilar things – that is, hidden similarities. Jean Paul has expressed this thought itself in a joking form: 'Joking is the disguised priest who weds every couple.' Vischer [1846–57, **1**, 422] carries this further: 'He likes best to wed couples whose union their relatives frown upon.' Vischer objects, however, that there are jokes where there is no question of comparing – no question, therefore, of finding a similarity. So he, slightly diverging from Jean Paul, defines joking as the ability to bind into a unity, with surprising rapidity, several ideas which are in fact alien to one another both in their internal content and in the nexus to which they belong. Fischer, again, stresses the fact that in a large number of joking judgements *differences* rather than similarities are found, and Lipps points out that these definitions relate to joking as an ability possessed by the joker and not to the jokes which he makes.

Other more or less interrelated ideas which have been brought up as defining or describing jokes are: 'a contrast of

1. [Jean Paul Richter, 1804, Part II, Paragraph 51.]

ideas', 'sense in nonsense', 'bewilderment and illumination'.

Definitions such as that of Kraepelin[1] lay stress on contrasting ideas. A joke is 'the arbitrary connecting or linking, usually by means of a verbal association, of two ideas which in some way contrast with each other'. A critic like Lipps had no difficulty in showing the total inadequacy of this formula; but he does not himself exclude the factor of contrast, but merely displaces it elsewhere. 'The contrast remains, but it is not some contrast between the ideas attached to the words, but a contrast or contradiction between the meaning and the meaninglessness of the words' (Lipps, 1898, 87). He gives examples to show how this is to be understood. 'A contrast arises only because ... we grant its words a meaning which, again, we nevertheless cannot grant them' (ibid., 90).

If this last point is developed further, the contrast between 'sense and nonsense' becomes significant. 'What at one moment has seemed to us to have a meaning, we now see is completely meaningless. That is what, in this case, constitutes the comic process ... A remark seems to us to be a joke, if we attribute a significance to it that has psychological necessity and, as soon as we have done so, deny it again. Various things can be understood by this "significance". We attach *sense* to a remark and know that logically it cannot have any. We discover *truth* in it, which nevertheless, according to the laws of experience or our general habits of thought, we cannot find in it. We grant it logical or practical consequences in excess of its true content, only to deny these consequences as soon as we have clearly recognized the nature of the remark. In every instance, the psychological process which the joking remark provokes in us, and on which the feeling of the comic rests, consists in the immediate transition, from this attaching of sense, from this discovering of truth, and from this granting of consequences, to the consciousness or impression of relative nothingness' (ibid., 85).

1. [Kraepelin, 1885, 143.]

However penetrating this discussion may sound, the question may be raised here whether the contrast between what has meaning and what is meaningless, on which the feeling of the *comic* is said to rest, also contributes to defining the concept of the *joke* in so far as it differs from that of the comic.

The factor of 'bewilderment and illumination', too, leads us deep into the problem of the relation of the joke to the comic. Kant[1] says of the comic in general that it has the remarkable characteristic of being able to deceive us only for a moment. Heymans (1896) explains how the effect of a joke comes about through bewilderment being succeeded by illumination. He illustrates his meaning by a brilliant joke of Heine's, who makes one of his characters, Hirsch-Hyacinth, the poor lottery-agent, boast that the great Baron Rothschild had treated him quite as his equal – quite 'famillionairely'. Here the word that is the vehicle of the joke appears at first simply to be a wrongly constructed word, something unintelligible, incomprehensible, puzzling. It accordingly bewilders. The comic effect is produced by the solution of this bewilderment, by understanding the word. Lipps (1898, 95) adds to this that this first stage of enlightenment – that the bewildering word means this or that – is followed by a second stage, in which we realize that this meaningless word has bewildered us and has then shown us its true meaning. It is only this second illumination, this discovery that a word which is meaningless by normal linguistic usage has been responsible for the whole thing – this resolution of the problem into nothing – it is only this second illumination that produces the comic effect.

Whether the one or the other of these two views seems to us to throw more light on the question, the discussion of bewilderment and enlightenment brings us closer to a particular discovery. For if the comic effect of Heine's 'famillionairely' depends on the solution of the apparently meaningless word, the 'joke' must no doubt be ascribed to the formation of that

1. [Kant, *Kritik der Urteilskraft*, Part I, Section 1, 54.]

word and to the characteristics of the word thus formed.

Another peculiarity of jokes, quite unrelated to what we have just been considering, is recognized by all the authorities as essential to them. '*Brevity* is the body and the soul of wit, it is its very self,' says Jean Paul (1804, Part II, Paragraph 42), merely modifying what the old chatterbox Polonius says in Shakespeare's *Hamlet* (Act II, Scene 2):

> 'Therefore, since brevity is the soul of wit,
> And tediousness, the limbs and outward flourishes,
> I will be brief.'

In this connection the account given by Lipps (1898, 90) of the brevity of jokes is significant: 'A joke says what it has to say, not always in few words, but in *too* few words – that is, in words that are insufficient by strict logic or by common modes of thought and speech. It may even actually say what it has to say by not saying it.'

We have already learnt from the connection of jokes with caricature that they 'must bring forward something that is concealed or hidden' (Fischer, 1889, 51). I lay stress on this determinant once more, because it too has more to do with the nature of jokes than with their being part of the comic.

[2]

I am well aware that these scanty extracts from the works or writers upon jokes cannot do them justice. In view of the difficulties standing in the way of my giving an unmistakably correct account of such complicated and subtle trains of thought, I cannot spare curious inquirers the labour of obtaining the information they desire from the original sources. But I am not sure that they will come back fully satisfied. The criteria and characteristics of jokes brought up by these authors and collected above – activity, relation to the content of our thoughts, the characteristic of playful judgement, the coupling of dissimilar things, contrasting ideas, 'sense in nonsense', the succession of bewilderment and enlightenment, the bringing forward of what is hidden, and the peculiar brevity of wit – all this, it is true, seems to us at first sight so very much to the point and so easily confirmed by instances that we cannot be in any danger of underrating such views. But they are *disjecta membra*, which we should like to see combined into an organic whole. When all is said and done, they contribute to our knowledge of jokes no more than would a series of anecdotes to the description of some personality of whom we have a right to ask for a biography. We are entirely without insight into the connection that presumably exists between the separate determinants – what, for instance, the brevity of a joke can have to do with its characteristic of being a playful judgement. We need to be told, further, whether a joke must satisfy *all* these determinants in order to be a proper joke, or need only satisfy *some*, and if so which can be replaced by others and which are indispensable. We should also wish to have a grouping and classification of jokes on the basis of the characteristics considered essential. The classification that we find in the literature rests on the one hand on the technical methods employed in them (e.g. punning or play upon words) and on the other hand on the use made of them in speech (e.g. jokes used for the purposes of caricature or of characterization, or joking snubs).

We should thus find no difficulty in indicating the aims of any new attempt to throw light on jokes. To be able to count on success, we should have either to approach the work from new angles or to endeavour to penetrate further by increased attention and deeper interest. We can resolve that we will at least not fail in this last respect. It is striking with what a small number of instances of jokes recognized as such the authorities are satisfied for the purposes of their inquiries, and how each of them takes the same ones over from his predecessors. We must not shirk the duty of analysing the same instances that have already served the classical authorities on jokes. But it is our intention to turn besides to fresh material so as to obtain a broader foundation for our conclusions. It is natural then that we should choose as the subjects of our investigation examples of jokes by which we ourselves have been most struck in the course of our lives and which have made us laugh the most.

Is the subject of jokes worth so much trouble? There can, I think, be no doubt of it. Leaving on one side the personal motives which make me wish to gain an insight into the problems of jokes and which will come to light in the course of these studies, I can appeal to the fact that there is an intimate connection between all mental happenings – a fact which guarantees that a psychological discovery even in a remote field will be of an unpredictable value in other fields. We may also bear in mind the peculiar and even fascinating charm exercised by jokes in our society. A new joke acts almost like an event of universal interest; it is passed from one person to another like the news of the latest victory. Even men of eminence who have thought it worth while to tell the story of their origins, of the cities and countries they have visited, and of the important people with whom they have associated, are not ashamed in their autobiographies to report their having heard some excellent joke.[1]

1. Von Falke's *Memoirs*, 1897.

II

THE TECHNIQUE OF JOKES

[1]

LET us follow up a lead presented to us by chance and consider the first example of a joke that we came across in the preceding chapter.

In the part of his *Reisebilder* entitled 'Die Bäder von Lucca [The Baths of Lucca]' Heine introduces the delightful figure of the lottery-agent and extractor of corns, Hirsch-Hyacinth of Hamburg, who boasts to the poet of his relations with the wealthy Baron Rothschild, and finally says: 'And, as true as God shall grant me all good things, Doctor, I sat beside Salomon Rothschild and he treated me quite as his equal – quite famillionairely.'[1]

Heymans and Lipps used this joke (which is admittedly an excellent and most amusing one) to illustrate their view that the comic effect of jokes is derived from 'bewilderment and illumination' (see above [p. 43]). We, however, will leave that question on one side and ask another: 'What is it that makes Hirsch-Hyacinth's remark into a joke?' There can be only two possible answers: either the thought expressed in the sentence possesses in itself the character of being a joke or the joke resides in the expression which the thought has been given in the sentence. In whichever of these directions the character of being a joke may lie, we will pursue it further and try to lay hands on it.

A thought can in general be expressed in various linguistic forms – in various words, that is – which can represent it with equal aptness. Hirsch-Hyacinth's remark presents his thought in a particular form of expression and, as it seems to us, a

1. [*Reisebilder* III, Part II, Chapter VIII.]

specially odd form and not the one which is most easily intelligible. Let us try to express the same thought as accurately as
possible in other words. Lipps has already done so, and in that
way has to some extent explained the poet's intention. He
writes (1898, 87): 'Heine, as we understand it, means to say
that his [Hyacinth's] reception was on familiar terms – of the
not uncommon kind, which does not as a rule gain in agreeable-
ness from having a flavour of millionairedom about it.' We
shall not be altering the sense of this if we give it another shape
which perhaps fits better into Hirsch-Hyacinth's speech:
'Rothschild treated me quite as his equal, quite familiarly –
that is, so far as a millionaire can.' 'A rich man's condescension,'
we should add, 'always involves something not quite pleasant
for whoever experiences it.'[1]

Whether, now, we keep to the one or the other of the two
equally valid texts of the thought, we can see that the question
we asked ourselves is already decided. In this example the
character of being a joke does not reside in the thought. What
Heine has put into Hirsch-Hyacinth's mouth is a correct and
acute observation, an observation of unmistakable bitterness,
which is understandable in a poor man faced by such great
wealth; but we should not venture to describe it as in the nature
of a joke. If anyone is unable in considering the translation to get
away from his recollection of the shape given to the thought by
the poet, and thus feels that nevertheless the thought in itself is
also in the nature of a joke, we can point to a sure criterion of the
joking character having been lost in the translation. Hirsch-
Hyacinth's remark made us laugh aloud, whereas its accurate
translation by Lipps or our own version of it, though it may

1. We shall return to this same joke later on [p. 191]; and we shall
then have occasion to make a correction in the translation of it given by
Lipps which our own version has taken as its starting-point. This, however, will not affect the discussion that follows here. [It may be remarked that '*familiär*' can also have the meaning of 'belonging to the
family'.]

please us and make us reflect, cannot possibly raise a laugh.

But if what makes our example a joke is not anything that resides in its thought, we must look for it in the form, in the wording in which it is expressed. We have only to study the peculiarity of its form of expression to grasp what may be termed the verbal or expressive technique of this joke, something which must stand in an intimate relation with the essence of the joke, since, if it is replaced by something else, the character and effect of the joke disappear. Moreover, in attributing so much importance to the verbal form of jokes we are in complete agreement with the authorities. Thus Fischer (1889, 72) writes: 'It is in the first place its sheer *form* that makes a judgement into a joke, and we are reminded of a saying of Jean Paul's which, in a single aphorism, explains and exemplifies this precise characteristic of jokes – "Such is the victorious power of sheer position, whether among warriors or words."'

In what, then, does the 'technique' of this joke consist? What has happened to the thought, as expressed, for instance, in our version, in order to turn it into a joke that made us laugh so heartily? Two things – as we learn by comparing our version with the poet's text. First, a considerable *abbreviation* has occurred. In order to express fully the thought contained in the joke, we were obliged to add to the words 'R. treated me quite as his equal, quite familiarly' a postscript which, reduced to its shortest terms, ran 'that is, so far as a millionaire can'. And even so we felt the need for a further explanatory sentence.[1] The poet puts it far more shortly: 'R. treated me quite as his equal – quite famillionairely.' In the joke, the whole limitation added by the second sentence to the first, which reports the familiar treatment, has disappeared.

But not quite without leaving a substitute from which we can reconstruct it. For a second change has also been made.[2] The

1. This is equally true of Lipps's translation.
2. [Although this example has so far borne translation into English comparatively well, what follows can only make its precise effect if the

word '*familiär* [familiarly]' in the unjoking expression of the thought has been transformed in the text of the joke into '*famillionär* [famillionairely]'; and there can be no doubt that it is precisely on this verbal structure that the joke's character as a joke and its power to cause a laugh depend. The newly constructed word coincides in its earlier portion with the '*familiär*' of the first sentence, and in its final syllables with the '*Millionär* [millionaire]' of the second sentence. It stands, as it were, for the '*Millionär*' portion of the second sentence and thus for the *whole* second sentence, and so puts us in a position to infer the second sentence that has been omitted in the text of the joke. It can be described as a 'composite structure' made up of the two components '*familiär*' and '*Millionär*', and it is tempting to give a diagrammatic picture of the way in which it is derived from those two words:[1]

FAMILI ÄR
MILIONÄR
FA**MILIONÄR**

The process which has converted the thought into a joke can then be represented in the following manner, which may at first sight seem fantastic, but nevertheless produces precisely the outcome that is really before us:

'R. treated me quite *familiär*,
that is, so far as a *Millionär* can.'

Let us now imagine that a compressing force is brought to bear

German words are given. The main point of difference is that in German the adverbial form does not require the addition of 'ly' to the adjective.]

1. The two words are printed one in Roman and the other in Italic type, and the syllables common to them both are printed in bold type. The second 'l', which is scarcely pronounced, could of course be left out of account. It seems probable that the fact of the two words having several syllables in common offered the joke-technique the occasion for constructing the composite word.

on these sentences and that for some reason the second is the less resistant one. It is thereupon made to disappear, while its most important constituent, the word '*Millionär*', which has succeeded in rebelling against being suppressed, is, as it were, pushed up against the first sentence, and fused with the element of that sentence which is so much like it – '*familiär*'. And the chance possibility, which thus arises, of saving the essential part of the second sentence actually favours the dissolution of its other, less important, constituents. The joke is thus generated:

'R. treated me quite *famili on är.*'

(*mili*) (*är*)

If we leave out of account any such compressing force, which indeed is unknown to us, the process by which the joke is formed – that is, the joke-technique – in this instance might be described as 'condensation accompanied by the formation of a substitute'; and in the present example the formation of the substitute consists in the making of a 'composite word'. This composite word '*famillionär*', which is unintelligible in itself but is immediately understood in its context and recognized as being full of meaning, is the vehicle of the joke's laughter-compelling effect – the mechanism of which, however, is not made in any way clearer by our discovery of the joke-technique. In what way can a linguistic process of condensation, accompanied by the formation of a substitute by means of a word, give us pleasure and make us laugh? This is evidently a different problem, whose treatment we may postpone till we have found a way of approaching it. For the present we will keep to the technique of jokes.

Our expectation that the technique of jokes cannot be a matter of indifference from the point of view of discovering their essence leads us at once to inquire whether there are other examples of jokes constructed like Heine's '*famillionär*'. There are not very many of them, but nevertheless enough to make up a small group which are characterized by the formation of composite words. Heine himself has derived a second joke from the word '*Millionär*' – copying from himself, as it were. In Chapter XIV of his 'Ideen'[1] he speaks of a '*Millionarr*', which is an obvious combination of '*Millionär*' and '*Narr*'[2] and, just as in the first example, brings out a suppressed subsidiary thought.

Here are some other examples I have come upon. – There is a certain fountain [*Brunnen*] in Berlin, the erection of which brought the Chief Burgomaster Forckenbeck into much disfavour. The Berliners call it the '*Forckenbecken*', and there is certainly a joke in this description, even though it was necessary to replace the word '*Brunnen*' by its obsolete equivalent '*Becken*' in order to combine it into a whole with the name of the Burgomaster. – The voice of Europe once made the cruel joke of changing a potentate's name from Leopold to Cleopold, on account of the relations he had at one time with a lady with the first name of Cleo. This undoubted product of condensation keeps alive an annoying allusion at the cost of a single letter. – Proper names in general fall easy victims to this kind of treatment by the joke-technique. There were in Vienna two brothers named Salinger, one of whom was a *Börsensensal* [stockbroker; *Sensal* = broker]. This provided a handle for calling him 'Sensalinger', while his brother, to distinguish him, was given the unflattering name of 'Scheusalinger'.[3] This was convenient, and certainly a joke; I cannot say whether it was justified. But jokes do not as a rule inquire much into that.

I have been told the following condensation joke. A young man who had hitherto led a gay life abroad paid a call, after a considerable absence, on a friend living here. The latter was surprised to see an *Ehering* [wedding-ring] on his visitor's hand. 'What?' he exclaimed, 'are you married?' 'Yes,' was the reply, '*Trauring* but true.'[4] The joke is an excellent one. The word

---

1. [*Reisebilder* II.]   2. [The German for 'fool'.]
3. ['*Scheusal*' means 'monstrous creature'.]
4. ['*Traurig*' would have meant 'sad'. '*Trauring*' is a synonym for '*Ehering*'.]

'*Trauring*' combines both components: '*Ehering*' changed into '*Trauring*' and the sentence '*traurig, aber wahr* [sad but true]'. The effect of the joke is not interfered with by the fact that here the composite word is not, like '*famillionär*', an unintelligible and otherwise non-existent structure, but one which coincides entirely with one of the two elements represented.

In the course of conversation I myself once unintentionally provided the material for a joke that is once again quite analogous to '*famillionär*'. I was talking to a lady about the great services that had been rendered by a man of science who I considered had been unjustly neglected. 'Why,' she said, 'the man deserves a monument.' 'Perhaps he will get one some day,' I replied, 'but *momentan* [for the moment] he has very little success.' '*Monument*' and '*momentan*' are opposites. The lady proceeded to unite them: 'Well, let us wish him a *monumentan*[1] success.'

I owe a few examples in foreign languages,[2] which show the same mechanism of condensation as our '*famillionär*', to an excellent discussion of the same subject in English by A. A. Brill (1911).

The English author De Quincey, Brill tells us, somewhere remarked that old people are inclined to fall into their 'anecdotage'. This word is a fusion of the partly overlapping words

ANECDOTE

and   DOTAGE.

In an anonymous short story Brill once found the Christmas season described as 'the alcoholidays' – a similar fusing of

ALCOHOL

and   HOLIDAYS.

1. [A non-existing word. '*Monumental*' (as in English) would have been expected.]

2. [This paragraph and the three examples that follow were added in 1912.]

After Flaubert had published his celebrated novel *Salammbô*, the scene of which is laid in ancient Carthage, Sainte-Beuve laughed at it, on account of its elaboration of detail, as being 'Carthaginoiserie';

CARTHAGINOIS
CHINOISERIE.

But the best example of a joke of this group originated from one of the leading men in Austria, who, after important scientific and public work, now fills one of the highest offices in the State. I have ventured to make use of the jokes which are ascribed to him, and all of which in fact bear the same impress, as material for these researches,[1] above all because it would have been hard to find any better.

Herr N.'s attention was drawn one day to the figure of a writer who had become well known from a series of undeniably boring essays which he had contributed to a Vienna daily paper. All of these essays dealt with small episodes in the relations of the first Napoleon with Austria. The author had red hair. As soon as Herr N. heard his name mentioned he asked: 'Is not that the *roter Fadian*[2] that runs through the story of the Napoleonids?'

1. Have I the right to do so? At least I have not obtained my knowledge of these jokes through an indiscretion. They are generally known in this city (Vienna) and are to be found in everyone's mouth. A number of them have been given publicity by Eduard Hanslick [the famous music critic] in the *Neue Freie Presse* and in his autobiography. As regards the others, I must offer my apologies for any possible distortions, which, in the case of oral tradition, are scarcely to be avoided. [It seems likely that Herr N. was Josef Unger (1828–1913), Professor of Jurisprudence and from 1881 President of the Supreme Court.]

2. ['*Roter*' means 'red', 'scarlet'. '*Fadian*' means 'dull fellow'. The termination '-*ian*' is occasionally added to an adjective, giving the somewhat contemptuous sense of 'fellow'. Thus '*grob*' means 'coarse', '*Grobian*' means 'coarse fellow': '*dumm*' means 'stupid', '*Dummian*' means 'stupid fellow'. The adjective '*fade*' or '*fad*' means (like its French equivalent) 'insipid', 'dull'. Finally, '*Faden*' means 'thread'. If all this is borne in mind, what follows will be intelligible.]

In order to discover the technique of this joke, we must apply to it the process of reduction[1] which gets rid of the joke by changing the mode of expression and instead introducing the original complete meaning, which can be inferred with certainty from a good joke. Herr N.'s joke about the '*roter Fadian*' proceeds from two components – a depreciatory judgement upon the writer and a recollection of the famous simile with which Goethe introduces the extracts 'From Ottilie's Diary' in the *Wahlverwandtschaften*.[2] The ill-tempered criticism may have run: 'So this is the person who is for ever and ever writing nothing but boring stories about Napoleon in Austria!' Now this remark is not in the least a joke. Nor is Goethe's pretty analogy a joke, and it is certainly not calculated to make us laugh. It is only when the two are brought into connection with each other and submitted to the peculiar process of condensation and fusion that a joke emerges – and a joke of the first order.[3]

The linking of the disparaging judgement upon the boring historian with the pretty analogy in the *Wahlverwandtschaften* must have taken place (for reasons which I cannot yet make intelligible) in a less simple manner than in many similar cases. I shall try to represent what was probably the actual course

1. [Here and elsewhere in this work Freud uses the word 'reduction' in the sense of taking something back to its original form. He had already carried out this process in the case of the Heine joke above, p. 47f. Similarly with the verb 'to reduce': see, for instance, p. 59.]

2. 'We hear of a peculiar practice in the English Navy. Every rope in the king's fleet, from the strongest to the weakest, is woven in such a way that a *roter Faden* [scarlet thread] runs through its whole length. It cannot be extracted without undoing the whole rope, and it proves that even the smallest piece is crown property. In just the same way a thread of affection and dependence runs through Ottilie's diary, binding it all together and characterizing the whole of it' (Goethe [*Elective Affinities*], Sophienausgabe, 20, 212).

3. I need hardly point out how little this observation, which can invariably be made, fits in with the assertion that a joke is a playful judgement [p. 40].

of events by the following construction. First, the element of the constant recurrence of the same theme in the stories may have awoken a faint recollection in Herr N. of the familiar passage in the *Wahlverwandtschaften*, which is as a rule wrongly quoted: 'it runs like a *roter Faden* [scarlet thread]'. The '*roter Faden*' of the analogy now exercised a modifying influence on the expression of the first sentence, as a result of the chance circumstance that the person insulted was also *rot* [red] – that is to say had red hair. It may then have run: 'So it is that red person who writes the boring stories about Napoleon!' And now the process began which brought about the condensation of the two pieces. Under its pressure, which had found its first fulcrum in the sameness of the element '*rot*', the 'boring' was assimilated to the '*Faden* [thread]' and was changed into '*fad* [dull]'; after this the two components were able to fuse together into the actual text of the joke, in which, in this case, the quotation has an almost greater share than the derogatory judgement, which was undoubtedly present alone to begin with.

'So it is that *red* person who writes this *fade* stuff about N[apoleon]. The   red   Faden that runs through everything.'

'Is not that the *red Fadian* that runs through the story of the N[apoleonids]?'

In a later chapter [p. 148] I shall add a justification, but also a correction, to this account, when I come to analyse this joke from points of view other than purely formal ones. But whatever else about it may be in doubt, there can be no question that a condensation has taken place. The result of the condensation is, on the one hand, once again a considerable abbreviation; but on the other hand, instead of the formation of a striking composite word, there is an interpenetration of the constituents of the two components. It is true that '*roter Fadian*' would be capable of existing as a mere term of abuse but in our instance it is certainly a product of condensation.

If at this point a reader should become indignant at a method of approach which threatens to ruin his enjoyment of jokes without being able to throw any light on the source of that enjoyment, I would beg him to be patient for the moment. At present we are only dealing with the technique of jokes; and the investigation even of this promises results, if we pursue it sufficiently far.

The analysis of the last example has prepared us to find that, if we meet with the process of condensation in still other examples, the substitute for what is suppressed may be not a composite structure, but some other alteration of the form of expression. We can learn what this other form of substitute may be from another of Herr N.'s jokes.

'I drove with him *téte-à-bête*.' Nothing can be easier than the reduction of this joke. Clearly it can only mean: 'I drove with X *tête-à-tête*, and X is a stupid ass.'

Neither of these sentences is a joke. They could be put together: 'I drove with that stupid ass X *tête-à-tête*', and that is not a joke either. The joke only arises if the 'stupid ass' is left out, and, as a substitute for it, the 't' is turned into a 'b'. With this slight modification the suppressed 'ass' has nevertheless once more found expression. The technique of this group of jokes can be described as 'condensation accompanied by slight modification', and it may be suspected that the slighter the modification the better will be the joke.

The technique of another joke is similar, though not without its complication. In the course of a conversation about someone in whom there was much to praise, but much to find fault with, Herr N. remarked: 'Yes, vanity is one of his four Achilles heels.'[1] In this case the slight modification consists in the fact that, instead of the *one* Achilles heel which the hero himself must have possessed, *four* are here in question. Four heels – but

1. [*Footnoted added* 1912:] It seems that this joke was applied earlier by Heine to Alfred de Musset.

only an ass[1] has four heels. Thus the two thoughts that are condensed in the joke ran: 'Apart from his vanity, Y is an eminent man; all the same I don't like him – he's an ass rather than a man.'[2]

I happened to hear another similar, but much simpler, joke *in statu nascendi* in a family circle. Of two brothers at school, one was an excellent and the other a most indifferent scholar. Now it happened once that the exemplary boy too came to grief at school; and their mother referred to this while expressing her concern that it might mean the beginning of a lasting deterioration. The boy who had hitherto been overshadowed by his brother readily grasped the opportunity. 'Yes,' he said, 'Karl's going backwards on all fours.'

The modification here consists in a short addition to the assurance that he too was of the opinion that the other boy was going backwards. But this modification represented and replaced a passionate plea on his own behalf: 'You mustn't think he's so much cleverer than I am simply because he's more successful at school. After all he's only a stupid ass – that's to say, much stupider than I am.'

Another, very well-known joke of Herr N.'s offers a neat example of condensation with slight modification. He remarked of a personage in public life: 'he has a great future behind him'. The man to whom this joke referred was comparatively young, and he had seemed destined by his birth, education and personal qualities to succeed in the future to the leadership of a great political party and to enter the government at its head. But times changed; the party became inadmissible as a govern-

---

1. [In this and in the previous example the actual term of abuse in German is '*Vieh*', whose literal meaning is more generally 'animal'.]

2. One of the complications in the technique of this example lies in the fact that the modification by which the omitted insult is replaced must be described as an *allusion* to the latter, since it only leads to it by a process of inference. For another factor that complicates the technique here, see below [p. 147].

ment, and it could be foreseen that the man who had been pre-destined to be its leader would come to nothing as well. The shortest reduced[1] version by which this joke could be replaced would run: 'The man has had a great future before him, but he has it no longer.' Instead of the 'had' and the second clause, there was merely the small change made in the principal clause of replacing 'before' by its contrary, 'behind'.[2]

Herr N. made use of almost the same modification in the case of a gentleman who became Minister for Agriculture with the sole qualification of being himself a farmer. Public opinion had occasion to recognize that he was the least gifted holder of the office that there had ever been. When he had resigned his office and retired to his farming interests, Herr N. said of him, 'Like Cincinnatus, he has gone back to his place before the plough.'

The Roman, however, who had also been called away to office from the plough, returned to his place *behind* the plough. What went *before* the plough, both then and today, was only – an ox.[3]

Karl Kraus[4] was responsible for another successful condensa-tion with slight modification. He wrote of a certain yellow-press journalist that he had travelled to one of the Balkan States by '*Orienterpresszug*'.[5] There is no doubt that this word combines two others: '*Orientexpresszug* [Orient Express]' and '*Erpressung* [blackmail]'. Owing to the contest, the element

1. [See footnote 1, p. 55.]
2. There is another factor operating in the technique of this joke which I reserve for later discussion. It concerns the actual nature of the modification (representation by the opposite [p. 109 ff.] or by something absurd [p. 93 ff.]). There is nothing to prevent the joke-technique from simultaneously employing several methods; but these we can only get to know one by one.
3. ['*Ochs*' in German has much the same meaning as 'ass' in English.]
4. [In the 1905 edition only, this read 'A witty writer'. Karl Kraus was a celebrated Viennese journalist and editor. See also below, p. 118 ff.]
5. [A non-existent word, explained by what follows.]

'*Erpressung*' emerges only as a modification of the '*Orient-expresszug*' – a word called for by the verb ['travelled']. This joke, which presents itself in the guise of a misprint, has yet another claim on our interest.[1]

This series of examples could easily be further increased; but I do not think we require any fresh instances to enable us to grasp clearly the characteristics of the technique in this second group – condensation with modification. If we compare the second group with the first, whose technique consisted in condensation with the formation of composite words, we shall easily see that the difference between them is not an essential one and that the transitions between them are fluid. Both the formation of composite words and modification can be subsumed under the concept of the formation of substitutes; and, if we care to, we can also describe the formation of a composite word as a modification of the basic word by a second element.

[2]

But here we may make a first stop and ask ourselves with what factor known to us from the literature of the subject this first finding of ours coincides, wholly or in part. Evidently with the factor of brevity, which Jean Paul describes as 'the soul of wit' (p. 44 above). But brevity does not in itself constitute a joke, or otherwise every laconic remark would be one. The joke's brevity must be of a particular kind. It will be recalled that Lipps has tried to describe this particular brevity of jokes more precisely (p. 44). Here our investigation contributes something and shows that the brevity of jokes is often the outcome of a particular process which has left behind in the wording of the joke a second trace – the formation of a substitute. By making use of the procedure of reduction, which seeks to undo

1. [As being on the borderline between a joke and a parapraxis. Cf. *The Psychopathology of Everyday Life* (1901*b*), Chapter VI (B), Examples 19 ff., *P.F.L.*, **5**, 178 ff.]

the peculiar process of condensation, we also find, however, that the joke depends entirely on its verbal expression as established by the process of condensation. Our whole interest now turns, of course, to this strange process, which has hitherto scarcely been examined. Nor can we in the least understand how all that is valuable in a joke, the yield of pleasure that the joke brings us, can originate from that process.

Are processes similar to those which we have described here as the technique of jokes known already in any other field of mental events? They are – in a single field, and an apparently very remote one. In 1900 I published a book which, as its title (*The Interpretation of Dreams*) indicates, attempted to throw light on what is puzzling in dreams and to establish them as derivatives of our normal mental functioning. I found occasion there to contrast the *manifest*, and often strange, *content of the dream* with the *latent*, but perfectly logical, *dream-thoughts* from which the dream is derived; and I entered into an investigation of the processes which make the dream out of the latent dream-thoughts, as well as of the psychical forces which are involved in that transformation. To the totality of these transforming processes I gave the name of the 'dream-work'; and I have described as a part of this dream-work a process of condensation which shows the greatest similarity to the one found in the technique of jokes – which, like it, leads to abbreviation, and creates substitute-formations of the same character. Everyone will be familiar, from a recollection of his own dreams, with the composite structures both of people and of things which emerge in dreams.[1] Indeed, dreams even construct them out of words, and they can then be dissected in analysis. (For instance, 'Autodidasker' = 'Autodidakt' + 'Lasker'.)[2] On other occasions – much more often, in fact – what the work of condensation in dreams produces is not composite structures but pictures which exactly resemble one thing or one person except for an

1. [Cf. *The Interpretation of Dreams* (1900a), *P.F.L.*, **4**, 400.]
2. ibid., **4**, 406 ff.

addition or alteration derived from another source – modifications, that is, just like those in Herr N.'s jokes. We cannot doubt that in both cases we are faced by the same psychical process, which we may recognize from its identical results. Such a far-reaching analogy between the technique of jokes and the dream-work will undoubtedly increase our interest in the former and raise an expectation in us that a comparison between jokes and dreams may help to throw light on jokes. But we will refrain from entering upon this task, for we must reflect that so far we have investigated the technique of only a very small number of jokes, so that we cannot tell whether the analogy by which we are proposing to be guided will in fact hold good. We will therefore turn away from the comparison with dreams and go back to the technique of jokes, though at this point we shall, as it were, be leaving a loose end to our inquiry, which at some later stage we may perhaps pick up once more.

[3]

The first thing that we want to learn is whether the process of condensation with substitute-formation is to be discovered in every joke, and can therefore be regarded as a universal characteristic of the technique of jokes.

Here I recall a joke which has remained in my memory owing to the special circumstances in which I heard it. One of the great teachers of my young days, whom we thought incapable of appreciating a joke and from whom we had never heard a joke of his own, came into the Institute one day laughing, and, more readily than usual, explained to us what it was that had caused his cheerful mood. 'I have just read an excellent joke,' he said. 'A young man was introduced into a Paris *salon*, who was a relative of the great Jean-Jacques Rousseau and bore his name. Moreover he was red-haired. But he behaved so awkwardly that the hostess remarked critically to the gentleman who had introduced him: "Vous m'avez fait connaître un jeune homme *roux* et *sot*, mais non pas un *Rousseau*."[1] And he laughed again.

By the nomenclature of the authorities this would be classed as a '*Klangwitz*',[2] and one of an inferior sort, with a play upon a proper name – not unlike the joke, for instance, in the Capuchin monk's sermon in *Wallensteins Lager*, which, as is well known, is modelled on the style of Abraham a Santa Clara:

> Lässt sich nennen den *Wallenstein*,
> ja freilich ist er uns *allen* ein *Stein*
> des Anstosses und Ärgernisses.[3]

But what is the technique of this joke? We see at once that the characteristic that we may have hoped to be able to prove was a universal one is absent on the very first fresh occasion. There is no omission here, and scarcely an abbreviation. The lady herself says straight out in the joke almost everything that we can attribute to her thoughts. 'You had raised my expectations about a relative of Jean-Jacques Rousseau – perhaps a spiritual relative – and here he is: a red-haired silly young man, a *roux et sot*.' It is true that I have been able to make an interpolation; but this attempt at a reduction had not got rid of the joke. It remains, and is attached to the identity of sound of the words $\dfrac{\text{ROUSSEAU}}{\text{ROUX SOT}}$. It is thus proved that condensation

---

1. ['You have made me acquainted with a young man who is *roux* (red-haired) and *sot* (silly), but not a Rousseau.' '*Roux-sot*' would be pronounced exactly like '*Rousseau*'.]

2. ['Sound-joke.' A joke depending on sound. See below p. 81.]

3. [Schiller's *Wallensteins Lager*, Scene 8. Literally: 'He gets himself called Wallenstein, and indeed he is for *allen* (all) of us a *Stein* (stone) of offence and trouble.' – Abraham a Santa Clara was a celebrated Austrian popular preacher and satirist (1644–1709).] – Nevertheless, as a result of another factor, this joke [the Rousseau joke] deserves to be more highly thought of. But this can only be indicated later on [p. 115].

with substitute-formation has no share in the production of this joke.

What besides? Fresh attempts at a reduction can teach me that the joke remains resistant until the name 'Rousseau' is replaced by another. If, for instance, I put 'Racine' instead of it, the lady's criticism, which remains just as possible as before, loses every trace of being a joke. I now know where I have to look for the technique of this joke, though I may still hesitate over formulating it. I will try this: the technique of the joke lies in the fact that one and the same word – the name – appears in it *used in two ways*, once as a whole, and again cut up into its separate syllables like a charade.

I can bring up a few examples which have an identical technique.

An Italian lady[1] is said to have revenged herself for a tactless remark of the first Napoleon's with a joke having this same technique of the double use of a word. At a court ball, he said to her, pointing to her fellow countrymen: 'Tutti gli Italiani danzano si male.' To which she made the quick repartee: 'Non tutti, ma buona parte.[2] (Brill, 1911).

Once when the *Antigone* [of Sophocles] was produced in Berlin, the critics complained that the production was lacking in the proper character of antiquity. Berlin wit made the criticism its own in the following words: '*Antik? Oh, nee*'[3] (Vischer [1846–57, I, 429] and Fischer, 1889 [75]).

An analogous dividing-up joke is at home in medical circles. If one inquires from a youthful patient whether he has ever had anything to do with masturbation, the answer is sure to be: 'O na, nie!'[4]

1. [This example was added in 1912.]

2. ['All Italians dance so badly!' 'Not all, but *buona parte* (a good part)' – the original, Italian version of Napoleon's surname.]

3. ['Antique? Oh, no.' The words, in Berlin dialect, approximate in pronunciation to 'Antigone'.]

4. ['Oh, no, never!' '*Onanie* (onanism)' is the common German word for 'masturbation'.]

In all three[1] of these examples, which should suffice for this species, we see the same joke-technique: in each of them a name is used twice, once as a whole and again divided up into its separate syllables, which, when they are thus separated, give another sense.[2]

The multiple use of the same word, once as a whole and again in the syllables into which it falls, is the first instance we

1. [This should by rights have been changed to 'four' in 1912, but was left unaltered.]

2. The goodness of these jokes depends on the fact that another technical method of a far higher order is simultaneously brought into use (see below [p. 115]). – At this point I may also draw attention to a connection between jokes and riddles. The philosopher Brentano composed a kind of riddle in which a small number of syllables had to be guessed which when they were put together into words gave a different sense according as they were grouped in one way or another. For instance: '. . . liess mich das Platanenblatt ahnen' ['the plane-tree leaf (Platanenblatt) led me to think (ahnen)', where 'Platanen' and 'blatt ahnen' sound almost the same]. Or: 'wie du dem Inder hast verschrieben, in der Hast verschrieben' ['when you wrote a prescription for the Indian, in your haste you made a slip of the pen', where 'Inder hast (have to the Indian)' and 'in der Hast (in your haste)' sound the same. An English parallel may perhaps make the point clearer: 'he said he would solicit her solicitor'.]

The syllables to be guessed were inserted into the appropriate place in the sentence under the disguise of the repeated sound 'dal'. [Thus the English example would be stated: 'he said he would daldaldaldal daldaldaldal'.] A colleague of the philosopher's took a witty revenge on him when he heard of the elderly man's engagement. He asked: 'Daldaldal daldaldal?' – 'Brentano brennt-a-no?' ['Brentano – does he still burn?']

What is the difference between these daldal riddles and the jokes in the text above? In the former the technique is given as a precondition and the wording has to be guessed; while in the jokes the wording is given and the technique is disguised.

[The Brentano in question was Franz Brentano (1838–1917) whose lectures on philosophy Freud had attended during his first year as a student at the University of Vienna. A fuller explanation of these riddles is given below in an appendix, p. 303.]

have come across of a technique differing from that of condensation. But the profusion of examples that have met us must convince us after a little reflection that the newly-discovered technique can scarcely be limited to this one method. There are a number of possible ways – how many it is as yet quite impossible to guess – in which the same word or the same verbal material can be put to multiple uses in one sentence. Are all these possibilities to be regarded as technical methods of making jokes? It seems to be so. And the examples of jokes which follow will prove it.

In the first place, one can take the same verbal material and merely make some alteration in its *arrangement*. The slighter the alteration – the more one has the impression of something different being said in the same words – the better is the joke technically.

'Mr and Mrs X live in fairly grand style. Some people think that the husband has earned a lot and so has been able to lay by a bit [*sich etwas zurückgelegt*]; others again think that the wife has lain back a bit [*sich etwas zurückgelegt*] and so has been able to earn a lot.'[1]

A really diabolically ingenious joke! And achieved with such an economy of means! 'Earned a lot – lay by a bit [*sich etwas zurückgelegt*]; lain back a bit [*sich etwas zurückgelegt*] – earned a lot.' It is merely the inversion of these two phrases that distinguishes what is said about the husband from what is hinted about the wife. Here again, by the way, this is not the whole technique of the joke. [See below, pp. 75 and 115.][2]

A wide field of play lies open to the technique of jokes if we

1. Daniel Spitzer, 1912 [1, 280]. [Spitzer, Viennese journalist, 1835–1893.]

2. [*Footnote added* 1912:] This is also true of the excellent joke reported by Brill [1911] from Oliver Wendell Holmes: 'Put not your trust in money, but put your money in trust.' Here there is promise of an antithesis but it does not materialize. The second part of the sentence cancels the antithesis. Incidentally, this is a good instance of the untranslatability of jokes with this technique.

extend the 'multiple use of the same material' to cover cases in which the word (or words) in which the joke resides may occur once unaltered but the second time with a slight modification. Here, for instance, is another of Herr N.'s jokes:

He heard a gentleman who was himself born a Jew make a spiteful remark about the Jewish character. 'Herr Hofrat,' he said, 'your ante*semitism* was well known to me; your anti*semitism* is new to me.'

Here only a single letter is altered, whose modification could scarcely be noticed in careless speech. The example reminds us of Herr N.'s other modification jokes (on p. 57 f.), but the difference is that here there is no condensation; everything that has to be said is said in the joke itself: 'I know that earlier you were yourself a Jew; so I am surprised that *you* should speak ill of Jews.'

An admirable example of a modification joke of this kind is the well-known cry: '*Traduttore – Traditore!*'[1] The similarity, amounting almost to identity, of the two words represents most impressively the necessity which forces a translator into crimes against his original.[2]

The variety of possible slight modifications in such jokes is so great that none of them exactly resembles another.

Here is a joke that is said to have been made during an examination in jurisprudence. The candidate had to translate a passage in the Corpus Juris: '"Labeo ait" . . . I fall, says he.' 'You fail, say I,' replied the examiner, and the examination was at an end.[3] Anyone who mistakes the name of the great jurist for a verbal form, and moreover one wrongly recalled,

1. ['Translator – traitor!']

2. [*Footnote added* 1912:] Brill [1911] quotes a quite analogous modification joke: *Amantes amentes* (lovers are fools).

3. [This is neater in German, since exactly the same word '*fallen*' is used for both 'to fall' and 'to fail in an examination'. Labeo is in fact the name of a famous Roman jurist (*c.* 50 B.C.–A.D. 18), and the Latin words should really have been translated 'Labeo says'. The candidate took '*labeo*' for '*labeor*', a Latin word which does mean 'I fall'.]

no doubt deserves nothing better. But the technique of the joke lies in the fact that almost the same words which proved the ignorance of the candidate were used to pronounce his punishment by the examiner. The joke is, moreover, an example of 'ready repartee', the technique of which, as we shall see [p. 107], does not differ greatly from what we are illustrating here.

Words are a plastic material with which one can do all kinds of things. There are words which, when used in certain connections, have lost their original full meaning, but which regain it in other connections. A joke of Lichtenberg's carefully singles out circumstances in which the watered-down words are bound to regain their full meaning:

'"How are you getting along?"[1] the blind man asked the lame man. "As you see," the lame man replied to the blind man.'

There are, too, words in German that can be taken, according as they are 'full' or 'empty', in a different sense, and, indeed, in more than one. For there can be two different derivatives from the same stem, one of which has developed into a word with a full meaning and the other into a watered-down final syllable or suffix, both of which, however, are pronounced exactly the same. The identity of sound between a full word and a watered-down syllable may also be a chance one. In both cases the joke-technique can take advantage of the conditions thus prevailing in the linguistic material.

A joke, for instance, which is attributed to Schleiermacher, is of importance to us as being an almost pure example of these technical methods:[2] '*Eifersucht* [jealousy] is a *Leidenschaft* [passion] which *mit Eifer sucht* [with eagerness seeks] what *Leiden schafft* [causes pain].'

This is undeniably in the nature of a joke, though not particularly effective as one. A quantity of factors are absent

1. ['*Wie geht's?*' Literally, 'how do you walk?']
2. [Jokes of this type are necessarily more than usually untranslatable.]

here which might mislead us in analysing other jokes so long as we examined each of those factors separately. The thought expressed in the wording is worthless; the definition it gives of jealousy is in any case thoroughly unsatisfactory. There is not a trace of 'sense in nonsense', of 'hidden meaning' or of 'bewilderment and illumination'. No efforts will reveal a 'contrast of ideas': a contrast between the words and what they mean can be found only with great difficulty. There is no sign of abbreviation; on the contrary, the wording gives an impression of prolixity. And yet it is a joke, and even a very perfect one. At the same time, its only striking characteristic is the one in the absence of which the joke disappears: the fact that here the same words are put to multiple uses. We can then choose whether to include this joke in the sub-class of those in which words are used first as a whole and then divided up (e.g. Rousseau or Antigone) or in the other sub-class in which the multiplicity is produced by the full or the watered-down meaning of the verbal constituents. Apart from this, only one other factor deserves notice from the point of view of the technique of jokes. We find here an unusual state of things established: a kind of 'unification' has taken place, since 'Eifersucht [jealousy]' is defined by means of its own name – by means of itself, as it were. This, as we shall see [p. 104 ff.], is also a technique of jokes. These two factors, therefore, must in themselves be sufficient to give a remark the character of a joke.

If now we enter still further into the variety of forms of the 'multiple use' of the same word, we suddenly notice that we have before us examples of 'double meaning' or 'play upon words' – forms which have long been generally known and recognized as a technique of jokes. Why have we taken the trouble to discover afresh what we might have gathered from the most superficial essay on jokes? To begin with, we can only plead in our own justification that we have nevertheless brought out another aspect of the same phenomenon of linguistic expression. What is supposed by the authorities to show the character of jokes as a kind of 'play' has been classified by us under the heading of 'multiple use'.

The further cases of multiple use, which can also be brought together under the title of 'double meaning' as a new, third group, can easily be divided into sub-classes, which, it is true, cannot be separated from one another by essential distinctions any more than can the third group as a whole from the second. We find:

(a) Cases of the double meaning of a *name* and of a *thing* denoted by it. For instance: 'Discharge thyself of our company, Pistol!' (Shakespeare [*II Henry IV*, Act II, Scene 4].)

'More *Hof* [courting] than *Freiung* [marriage]' said a witty Viennese about a number of pretty girls who had been admired for many years but had never found a husband. 'Hof' and 'Freiung' are the names of two neighbouring squares in the centre of Vienna.

'Vile Macbeth does not rule here in Hamburg: the ruler here is *Banko* [bank-money]' (Heine [*Schnabelewopski*, Chapter III]).

Where the name cannot be used (we should perhaps say 'mis-used') unaltered, a double meaning can be got out of it by one of the slight modifications we are familiar with:

'Why,' it was asked, in times that are now past, 'have the French rejected *Lohengrin*?' 'On Elsa's (Elsass [Alsace]) account.'

(b) Double meaning arising from the *literal* and *metaphorical* meanings of a word. This is one of the most fertile sources for the technique of jokes. I will quote only one example:

A medical friend well known for his jokes once said to Arthur Schnitzler the dramatist:[1] 'I'm not surprised that you've become a great writer. After all your father held a mirror up to his contemporaries.' The mirror which was handled by the dramatist's father, the famous Dr Schnitzler, was the laryngo-

1. [Who was himself a doctor of medicine.]

scope.[1] A well-known remark of Hamlet's tells us that the purpose of a play, and so also of the dramatist who creates it, is 'to hold, as 'twere, the mirror up to nature; to show virtue her own feature, scorn her own image, and the very age and body of the time his form and pressure' (Act III, Scene 2).

(c) Double meaning proper, or *play upon words*. This may be described as the ideal case of 'multiple use'. Here no violence is done to the word; it is not cut up into its separate syllables, it does not need to be subjected to any modification, it does not have to be transferred from the sphere it belongs to (the sphere of proper names, for instance) to another one. Exactly as it is and as it stands in the sentence, it is able, thanks to certain favourable circumstances, to express two different meanings.

Examples of this are at our disposal in plenty:

One of Napoleon III's first acts when he assumed power was to seize the property of the House of Orleans. This excellent play upon words was current at the time: 'C'est le premier vol de l'aigle.' ['It is the eagle's first *vol.*'] '*Vol*' means 'flight' but also 'theft' (quoted by Fischer, 1889 [80]).

Louis XV wanted to test the wit of one of his courtiers, of whose talent he had been told. At the first opportunity he commanded the gentleman to make a joke of which he, the king, should be the '*sujet* [subject]'. The courtier at once made the clever reply: 'Le roi n'est pas sujet.' ['The King is not a subject.' Also in Fischer, loc. cit.]

A doctor, as he came away from a lady's bedside, said to her husband with a shake of his head: 'I don't like her looks.' 'I've not liked her looks for a long time,' the husband hastened to agree.

The doctor was of course referring to the lady's condition; but he expressed his anxiety about the patient in words which

1. [The German word is '*Kehlkopfspiegel*', literally, 'larynx mirror'. Johann Schnitzler (1835–93), was world-famous for his pioneering work in laryngology.]

the husband could interpret as a confirmation of his own marital aversion.

Heine said of a satirical comedy: 'This satire would not have been so biting if its author had had more to bite.' This joke is more an example of metaphorical and literal double meaning than of a play upon words proper. But what is to be gained by drawing a sharp distinction here?

Another good example of play upon words is told by the authorities (Heymans and Lipps) in a form which makes it unintelligible.[1] Not long ago I came upon the correct version and setting of the anecdote in a collection of jokes which has not proved of much use apart from this.[2]

'One day Saphir and Rothschild met each other. After they had chatted for a little while, Saphir said: "Listen, Rothschild, my funds have got low, you might lend me a hundred ducats." "Oh well!" said Rothschild, "that'll suit me all right – but only on condition that you make a joke." "That'll suit me all right too," replied Saphir. "Good. Then come to my office to-morrow." Saphir appeared punctually. "Ah!" said Rothschild, when he saw him come in, "*Sie kommen um Ihre 100 Dukaten* [You've come about your hundred ducats]." "No," answered Saphir, "*Sie kommen um Ihre 100 Dukaten* [You're going to lose your hundred ducats] because I shan't dream of paying you back before the Day of Judgement."'[3]

1. [In the original this unsatisfactory form of the anecdotes is inserted by Freud as a footnote at this point. It will, we believe, be easier for English readers if this footnote is transferred to the *end* of the correct version of the story as told by Freud in the text.]

2. Hermann (1904).

3. ['*Sie kommen um . . .*' may mean equally 'You are coming about' or 'You are losing'.] – "'Saphir," so Heymans tells us, "was asked by a rich creditor whom he had come to visit: '*Sie kommen wohl um die 300 Gulden*? [No doubt you've come about the 300 florins?]' and he replied: '*Nein, Sie kommen um die 300 Gulden* [No, you're going to lose the 300 florins].' In giving this answer he was expressing his meaning in a perfectly correct and by no means unusual form." That is in fact the

'What do these statues *vorstellen* [represent or put forward]?' asked a stranger to Berlin of a native Berliner, looking at a row of monuments in a public square. 'Oh, well,' was the reply, 'either their right leg or their left leg.'[1]

'At this moment I cannot recall all the students' names, and of the professors there are some who still have no name at all' (Heine, *Harzreise*).

We shall be giving ourselves practice, perhaps, in diagnostic differentiation if at this point we insert another well-known joke about professors. 'The distinction between Professors Ordinary [*ordentlich*] and Professors Extraordinary [*ausserordentlich*][2] is that the ordinary ones do nothing extraordinary and the extraordinary ones do nothing properly [*ordentlich*].' This, of course, is a play on the two meanings of the words '*ordentlich*' and '*ausserordentlich*': viz. on the one hand 'inside' and 'outside' the '*ordo* (the Establishment)' and on the other hand 'efficient' and 'outstanding'. But the conformity between this

---

case. Saphir's answer, *considered in itself*, is in perfect order. We understand, too, what he means to say – namely that he has no intention of paying his debt. But Saphir makes use of the same words that had previously been used by his creditor. We therefore cannot avoid also taking them in the sense in which they had been used by the latter. And in that case Saphir's answer no longer has any meaning whatever. The creditor is not "coming" at all. Nor can he be coming "about the 300 florins" – that is, he cannot be coming to bring 300 florins. Moreover, as a creditor, it is not his business to bring but to demand. Since Saphir's words are in this way recognized as being at once sense and nonsense, a comic situation arises' (Lipps, 1898, 97).

The version which I have given in full in the text above for the sake of clarity shows that the technique of the joke is far simpler than Lipps supposes. Saphir does not come to *bring* the 300 florins but to *fetch* them from the rich man. Accordingly the discussions of 'sense and nonsense' in this joke become irrelevant.

1. This play upon words is further discussed below. [There is no trace of any such further discussion, and it seems probable that this footnote should be attached at the end of the preceding paragraph, as the Saphir-Rothschild joke is in fact discussed again, on p. 79 below.]

2. [I.e. full professors and assistant professors.]

joke and some others we have already met reminds us that here 'multiple use' is far more noticeable than the 'double meaning'. All through the sentence we hear nothing but a constantly recurring '*ordentlich*', sometimes in that form and sometimes modified in a negative sense (cf. p. 67). Moreover, the feat is again achieved here of defining a concept by means of its own wording (cf. the example of '*Eifersucht* [jealousy]', p. 68), or, more precisely, of defining (even if only negatively) two correlative concepts by means of one another, which produces an ingenious interlacement. Finally, the aspect of 'unification' can also be stressed here – the eliciting of a more intimate connection between the elements of the statement than one would have had a right to expect from their nature.

'The beadle[1] Sch[äfer] greeted me quite as a colleague, for he too is a writer, and has often mentioned me in his half-yearly writings; and apart from that, he has often *cited*[2] me, and if he did not find me at home he was always kind enough to write the *citation* in chalk on my study door' (Heine, *Harzreise*).

Daniel Spitzer [cf. p. 66, *n*. 1], in his *Wiener Spaziergänge*, produced a laconic biographical description, which is certainly also a good joke, of a social type which flourished at the time of the outbreak of speculation [following the Franco-Prussian War]: 'Iron front[3] – iron cash-box – Iron Crown.' (This last was an order which carried noble rank with it.) A striking example of 'unification' – everything, as it were, made of iron! The various, but not very markedly contrasting, meanings of the epithet 'iron' make these 'multiple uses' possible.

Another example of a play upon words may make the transition to a fresh sub-species of the technique of double meaning easier. The joking medical colleague already men-

1. [A university officer (at Göttingen) in charge of undergraduate discipline.]

2. [For breaches of discipline.]

3. [I.e. of a 'hard-faced' business man.]

tioned above (on p. 70) was responsible for this joke at the time of the Dreyfus case: 'This girl reminds me of Dreyfus. The army doesn't believe in her innocence.'

The word 'innocence', on the double meaning of which the joke is constructed, has in the one context its usual meaning, with 'fault' or 'crime' as its opposite; but in the other context it has a *sexual* meaning, of which the opposite is 'sexual experience'. Now there are a very large number of similar examples of double meaning, in all of which the effect of the joke depends quite specially on the sexual meaning. For this group we may reserve the name of '*double entendre* [*Zweideutigkeit*]'.

An excellent example of a *double entendre* of this kind is Spitzer's joke which has already been recorded on p. 66: 'Some people think that the husband has earned a lot and so has been able to lay by a bit [*sich etwas zurückgelegt*]; others again think that the wife has lain back a bit [*sich etwas zurückgelegt*] and so has been able to earn a lot.'

But if we compare this example of double meaning accompanied by *double entendre* with other examples, a distinction becomes evident which is not without its interest from the point of view of technique. In the 'innocence' joke, the one meaning of the word was just as obvious as the other; it would really be hard to decide whether its sexual or non-sexual meaning was the more usual and familiar. But it is otherwise with Spitzer's example. In this the commonplace meaning of the words '*sich etwas zurückgelegt*' is by far the more prominent, whereas their sexual meaning is, as it were, covered and hidden and might even escape the notice of an unsuspecting person altogether. By way of a sharp contrast let us take another example of double meaning, in which no attempt is made at thus concealing the sexual meaning: for instance, Heine's description of the character of a complaisant lady: 'She could *abschlagen*[1] nothing except her own water.' This sounds like a piece of obscenity and hardly

1. ['To refuse'; vulgarly 'to urinate'.]

gives the impression of a joke.[1] This peculiarity, however, where in a case of double meaning the two meanings are not equally obvious, can also occur in jokes with no sexual reference – whether because one meaning is more usual than the other or because it is brought to the front by a connection with the other parts of the sentence. (Cf., for instance, 'C'est le premier vol de l'aigle' [p. 71].) I propose to describe all these as 'double meaning with an allusion'.

[4]

We have already made the acquaintance of such a large number of different joke-techniques that I fear there is some danger of losing our grasp of them. Let us therefore try to summarize them:

I. Condensation:

>   (a) with formation of composite word,
>   (b) with modification.

II. Multiple use of the same material:

>   (c) as a whole and in parts,
>   (d) in a different order,
>   (e) with slight modification,
>   (f) of the same words full and empty.

III. Double meaning:

>   (g) meaning as a name and as a thing,
>   (h) metaphorical and literal meanings,
>   (i) double meaning proper (play upon words),

1. Cf. on this Fischer (1889, 86). He gives the name of '*Zweideutigkeit*', which I have applied differently in the text, to jokes with a double meaning in which the two meanings are not equally prominent but in which one lies behind the other. Nomenclature of this kind is a matter of convention; linguistic usage has arrived at no firm decision.

(j) *double entendre,*
(k) double meaning with an allusion.

This variety and number of techniques has a confusing effect. It might make us feel annoyed at having devoted ourselves to a consideration of the technical methods of jokes, and might make us suspect that after all we have exaggerated their importance as a means for discovering the essential nature of jokes. If only this convenient suspicion were not contradicted by the one incontestable fact that the joke invariably disappears as soon as we eliminate the operation of these techniques from its form of expression! So, in spite of everything, we are led to look for the unity in this multiplicity. It ought to be possible to bring all these techniques under a single heading. As we have already said [p. 70], it is not difficult to unite the second and third groups. Double meaning (play upon words) is indeed only the ideal case of the multiple use of the same material. Of these the latter is evidently the more inclusive concept. The examples of dividing up, of rearrangement of the same material and of multiple use with slight modification (c, d and e) might – though only with some difficulty – be brought under the concept of double meaning. But what is there in common between the technique of the first group (condensation with substitute-formation) and that of the two others (multiple use of the same material)?

Well, something very simple and obvious, I should have thought. The multiple use of the same material is, after all, only a special case of condensation; play upon words is nothing other than a condensation *without* substitute-formation; condensation remains the wider category. All these techniques are dominated by a tendency to compression, or rather to saving. It all seems to be a question of economy. In Hamlet's words: 'Thrift, thrift, Horatio!'

Let us test this economy on the different examples. 'C'est le premier vol de l'aigle [p. 71].' It is the eagle's first flight. Yes, but it is a thieving flight. Luckily for the existence of this joke, '*vol*' means not only 'flight' but 'theft' as well. Has no condensation and economy been made? Most certainly. There has been a saving of the whole of the second thought and it has been dropped without leaving a substitute. The double meaning of the word '*vol*' has made such a substitute unnecessary; or it would be equally true to say that the word '*vol*' contains the substitute for the suppressed thought without any addition or change having to be made to the first one. That is the advantage of a double meaning.

Another example: 'Iron front – iron cash-box – Iron Crown' [p. 74]. What an extraordinary saving compared with an expression of the same thought in which 'iron' finds no place: 'With the help of the necessary boldness and lack of conscience it is not difficult to amass a large fortune, and for such services a title will of course be a suitable reward.'

Condensation, and therefore economy, is indeed quite unmistakably present in these examples. But it should be present in *every* example. Where is the economy hidden in such jokes as Rousseau – *roux et sot*' [pp. 62–3] or 'Antigone – *Antik? oh, nee*' [p. 63], in which we first noticed the absence of condensation and which were our principal motive for putting forward the technique of the repeated use of the same material? It is true that here we should not find that condensation would meet the case; but if instead of it we take the more inclusive concept of economy, we can manage without difficulty. It is easy to point out what we save in the case of Rousseau, Antigone, etc. We save having to express a criticism or give shape to a judgement; both are already there in the name itself. In the example of '*Leidenschaft – Eifersucht* [passion – jealousy]' [p. 68] we save ourselves the trouble of laboriously constructing a definition: '*Eifersucht, Leidenschaft*' – '*Eifer sucht*' ['eagerness seeks'], '*Leiden schafft*' ['causes pain']. We have only to add the linking words and there we have our definition ready made. The case is similar in all the other examples that have so far been analysed.

Where there is least saving, as in Saphir's play upon words 'Sie kommen um Ihre 100 Dukaten' [p. 72], there is at any rate a saving of the necessity for framing a new wording for the reply; the wording of the question is sufficient for the answer. The saving is not much, but in it the joke lies. The multiple use of the same words for question and answer is certainly an 'economy'. Like Hamlet's view of the rapid sequence of his father's death and his mother's marriage:

> The funeral baked-meats
> Did coldly furnish forth the marriage tables. [Act I, Scene 2.]

But before we accept the 'tendency to economy' as the most general characteristic of the technique of jokes and ask such questions as where it comes from, what it signifies and how the joke's yield of pleasure arises from it, we must find space for a doubt which has a right to be heard. It may be that every joke-technique shows the tendency to save something in expression; but the relation is not reversible. Not every economy of expression, not every abbreviation, is on that account a joke as well. We reached this point once before, when we were still hoping to find the process of condensation in every joke, and raised the justifiable objection that a laconic remark is not enough to constitute a joke [p. 60]. There must therefore be some peculiar kind of abbreviation and economy on which the characteristic of being a joke depends; and until we know the nature of that peculiarity our discovery of the common element in the techniques of jokes brings us no nearer to a solution of our problem. And let us, further, have the courage to admit that the economies made by the joke-technique do not greatly impress us. They may remind us, perhaps, of the way in which some housewives economize when they spend time and money on a journey to a distant market because vegetables are to be had there a few farthings cheaper. What does a joke save by its technique? The putting together of a few new words, which would mostly have emerged without any trouble. Instead of that, it has to take the trouble to search out the one word which covers the two thoughts. Indeed, it must often first transform one of the thoughts into an unusual form which will provide a basis for its combination with the second thought. Would it not have been simpler, easier, and, in fact, more economical to have expressed the two thoughts as they happened to come, even if this involved no common form of expression? Is not the economy in words uttered more than balanced by the expenditure on intellectual effort? And who saves by that? Who gains by it?

We can evade these doubts provisionally if we transpose them to another place. Have we really already discovered all the kinds of joke-technique? It will certainly be more prudent to collect fresh examples and subject them to analysis.

[5]

We have in fact not yet considered a large – perhaps the most numerous – group of jokes, influenced, perhaps, by the contempt with which they are regarded. They are the kind which are generally known as '*Kalauer*' ('*calembourgs*') ['puns']¹ and which pass as the lowest form of verbal joke, probably because they are the 'cheapest' – can be made with the least trouble. And they do in fact make the least demand on the technique of expression, just as the play upon words proper makes the highest. While in the latter the two meanings should find their expression in identically the same word, which on that account is usually said only once, it is enough for a pun if the two words expressing the two meanings recall each other by some vague similarity, whether they have a general similarity of structure or a rhyming assonance, or whether they share the same first few letters, and so on. A quantity of examples like

1. [The German '*Kalauer*' is here throughout translated by 'pun' though as will be seen Freud uses the word in a much wider sense than the English word will bear.]

his lady as an 'Indian prince', he throws off the mask and confesses: 'Madame, I have deceived you . . . I have no more ever been in *Kalkutta* [Calcutta] than the *Kalkuttenbraten* [roast Calcutta fowl] that I ate for luncheon yesterday.' The mistake in this joke clearly lies in the fact that the two similar words in it are not merely similar but actually identical. The bird which he had eaten roast is so called, because it comes, or is supposed to come, from the same Calcutta.

Fischer (1889, 78) has devoted much attention to these forms of joke, and tries to distinguish them sharply from 'play upon words'. 'A pun is a bad play upon words, since it plays upon the word not as a word but as a sound.' The play upon words, however, 'passes from the sound of the word to the word itself' [ibid., 79]. On the other hand, he classes such jokes as *famillionär*, Antigone (*Antik? oh, nee*), etc., among the 'sound jokes'. I see no necessity for following him in this. In a play upon words, in our view, the word is also only a sound-image, to which one meaning or another is attached. But here, too, linguistic usage makes no sharp distinctions; and if it treats 'puns' with contempt and 'play upon words' with a certain respect, these judgements of value seem to be determined by considerations other than technical ones. It is worth while paying attention to the kind of jokes that are told one as 'puns'. There are some people who, when they are in high spirits, can, for considerable periods of time, answer every remark addressed to them with a pun. One of my friends, who is a model of discretion where his serious achievements in science are concerned, is apt to boast of this ability. When on one occasion he was holding the company breathless in this way and admiration was expressed for his staying power: 'Yes,' he said, 'I am lying here *auf der Ka-Lauer*.'[1] And when he was finally begged to stop, he agreed to on condition that he was appointed '*Poeta Ka-laureatus*'. Both of these, however, are excellent jokes of condensation with formation of composite words. ('I am

1. ['*Kalauer*' = 'pun.' '*Auf der Lauer*' = 'on the look-out.']

lying here *auf der Lauer* [on the look-out] for making *Kalauer* [puns].')

In any case we can already gather from the disputes about the delimitation of puns and play upon words that the former will not be able to help us to discover a completely new joke-technique. If, in the case of puns, we give up the claim for the use of the *same* material in more than one sense, nevertheless the accent falls on rediscovering what is familiar, on the correspondence between the two words that make up the pun; and consequently puns merely form a sub-species of the group which reaches its peak in the play upon words proper.

[6]

But there really are jokes whose technique resists almost any attempt to connect it with the groups that have so far been considered.

'The story is told of Heine that he was in a Paris *salon* one evening conversing with the dramatist Soulié,[1] when there came into the room one of those financial kings of Paris whom people compare with Midas – and not merely on account of their wealth. He was soon surrounded by a crowd who treated him with the greatest deference. "Look there!" Soulié remarked to Heine, "Look at the way the nineteenth century is worshipping the Golden Calf!" With a glance at the object of so much admiration, Heine replied, as though by way of correction: "Oh, he must be older than that by now!"' (Fischer, 1889, 82–3.)

Where shall we look for the technique of this excellent joke? In a play upon words, thinks Fischer: 'Thus, for instance, the words "Golden Calf" can mean both Mammon and idolatry. In the one case the gold is the main thing and in the other the statue of the animal; it may also serve to characterize, in not precisely flattering terms, someone who has a great deal of

1. [Frédéric Soulié (1800–1847), French dramatist and novelist.]

money and very little sense' (loc. cit.). If we make the experiment of removing the expression 'Golden Calf', we certainly get rid of the joke at the same time. We make Soulié say: 'Look there! Look at the way the people are crowding round the stupid fellow simply because he's rich!' This is no longer a joke and Heine's reply is also made impossible.

But we must recall that what we are concerned with is not Soulié's simile – which is a possible joke – but Heine's reply, which is certainly a much better one. That being so, we have no right to touch the phrase about the Golden Calf: it remains as the precondition of Heine's *mot* and our reduction must be directed only to the latter. If we expand the words 'Oh, he must be older than that by now!' we can only replace them by something like: 'Oh, he's not a calf any longer; he's a full-grown ox!'[1] Thus what was necessary for Heine's joke was that he should no longer take the 'Golden Calf' in a metaphorical but in a personal sense and should apply it to the rich man himself. It may even be that this double meaning was already present in Soulié's remark.

But just a moment! It looks now as though this reduction has not done away with Heine's joke completely, but on the contrary has left its essence untouched. The position now is that Soulié says: 'Look there! Look at the way the nineteenth century is worshipping the Golden Calf!' and Heine replies: 'Oh, he's not a calf any longer; he's an ox already!' And in this reduced version it is still a joke. But no other reduction of Heine's *mot* is possible.

It is a pity that this fine example involves such complicated technical conditions. We can arrive at no clarification of it. So we will leave it and look for another one in which we seem to detect an internal kinship with its predecessor.

It is one of the 'bath jokes' which treat of the Galician Jews' aversion to baths. For we do not insist upon a patent of nobility from our examples. We make no inquiries about their origin

1. [See footnote 3, p. 59.]

but only about their efficiency – whether they are capable of making us laugh and whether they deserve our theoretical interest. And both these two requirements are best fulfilled precisely by Jewish jokes.

'Two Jews met in the neighbourhood of the bath-house. "Have you taken a bath?" asked one of them. "What?" asked the other in return, "is there one missing?"'

If one laughs at a joke really heartily, one is not in precisely the best mood for investigating its technique. Hence some difficulties arise over making one's way into these analyses. 'It was a comical misunderstanding,' we are inclined to say. Yes but what is the technique of the joke? Clearly the use of the word 'take' in two meanings. For one of the speakers 'take' was the colourless auxiliary; for the other it was the verb with its sense unwatered down. Thus it is a case of the same word used 'full' and 'empty' (Group II (f) [p. 76]). If we replace the expression 'taken a bath' by the equivalent and simpler 'bathed', the joke vanishes. The reply no longer fits. Thus the joke is once again attached to the form of expression 'taken a bath'.

That is so. But nevertheless it seems as though in this case too the reduction has been applied at the wrong point. The joke lies not in the question but in the answer – the second question: 'What? is there one missing?' And this answer cannot be robbed of being a joke by an extension or modification, so long as its sense is not interfered with. We have an impression, too, that in the second Jew's reply the disregarding of the bath is more important than the misunderstanding of the word 'take'. But here once more we cannot see our way clearly, and we will look for a third example.

It is again a Jewish joke; but this time it is only the setting that is Jewish, the core belongs to humanity in general. No doubt this example too had its unwanted complications, but fortunately they are not the same ones that have so far prevented us from seeing clearly.

'An impoverished individual borrowed 25 florins from a prosperous acquaintance, with many asseverations of his necessitous circumstances. The very same day his benefactor met him again in a restaurant with a plate of salmon mayonnaise in front of him. The benefactor reproached him: "What? You borrow money from me and then order yourself salmon mayonnaise? Is *that* what you've used my money for?" "I don't understand you," replied the object of the attack: "if I haven't any money I *can't* eat salmon mayonnaise, and if I have some money I *mustn't* eat salmon mayonnaise. Well, then, when *am* I to eat salmon mayonnaise?"'

Here at last no more trace of a double meaning is to be found. Nor can the repetition of 'salmon mayonnaise' contain the joke's technique, for it is not 'multiple use' of the same material but a real repetition of identical material called for by the subject-matter of the anecdote. We may for a time be quite baffled by this analysis and may even think of taking refuge in denying that the anecdote – though it made us laugh – possesses the character of a joke.

What more is there deserving of comment in the impoverished person's reply? That it has been very markedly given the form of a logical argument. But quite unjustifiably, for the reply is in fact illogical. The man defends himself for having spent the money lent to him on a delicacy and asks, with an appearance of reason, *when* he is to eat salmon. But that is not the correct answer. His benefactor is not reproaching him with treating himself to salmon precisely on the day on which he borrowed the money; he is reminding him that in his circumstances he has no right to think of such delicacies *at all*. The impoverished *bon vivant* disregards this only possible meaning of the reproach, and answers another question as though he had misunderstood the reproach.

Can it be that the technique of this joke lies precisely in this *diverting* of the reply from the meaning of the reproach? If so, a similar change of standpoint, a similar shifting of the psychical emphasis, may perhaps be traceable in the two earlier examples, which we felt were akin to his one.

And, lo and behold! this suggestion is an easy success and in fact reveals the technique of those examples. Soulié pointed out to Heine that society in the nineteenth century worshipped the 'Golden Calf' just as did the Jews in the Wilderness. An appropriate answer by Heine might have been 'Yes, such is human nature; thousands of years have made no change in it', or something similar by way of assent. But Heine diverted his answer from the thought suggested to him and made no reply to it at all. He made use of the double meaning of which the phrase 'Golden Calf' is capable to branch off along a side-track. He caught hold of one component of the phrase, 'Calf', and replied, as though the emphasis in Soulié's remark had been upon it: 'Oh, he's not a calf any longer' . . . etc.[1]

The diversion in the bath-joke is even plainer. This example calls for a graphic presentation:

The first Jew asks: 'Have you taken a *bath*?' The emphasis is on the element 'bath'.

The second replies as though the question had been: 'Have you *taken* a bath?'

This shifting of the emphasis is only made possible by the wording 'taken a bath'. If it had run 'have you bathed?' no displacement would have been possible. The non-joking answer would then have been: 'Bathed? What d'you mean? I don't know what that is.' But the technique of the joke lies in the displacement of the accent from 'bath' to 'taken'.[2]

1. Heine's answer combines two joke-techniques: a diversion combined with an allusion. He did not say straight out: 'He's an ox.'

2. The word 'take [*nehmen*]' is very well adapted to form a basis for play upon words owing to the variety of ways in which it can be used. I will give a plain example, as a contrast to the displacement jokes reported above: 'A well-known stock-exchange speculator and bank-director was walking with a friend along the Ringstrasse [the main Vienna boulevard]. As they went past a café he remarked: "Let's go inside and take something!" His friend held him back: "But, Herr

Let us go back to the 'salmon mayonnaise', since it is the most straightforward example. What is new in it deserves our attention in various directions. First we must give a name to the technique brought to light in it. I propose to describe it as 'displacement', since its essence lies in the division of the train of thought, the displacement of the psychical emphasis on to a topic other than the opening one. Our next task is to inquire into the relation between the technique of displacement and the form of expression of the joke. Our example ('salmon mayonnaise') shows us that a displacement joke is to a high degree independent of verbal expression. It depends not on words but on the train of thought. No replacement of the words will enable us to get rid of it so long as the sense of the answer is retained. Reduction is only possible if we change the train of thought and make the gourmet reply directly to the reproach which he had evaded in the version represented in the joke. The reduced version would then run: 'I can't deny myself what tastes good to me, and it's a matter of indifference to me where I get the money from to pay for it. There you have the explanation of why I'm eating salmon mayonnaise on the very day you've lent me the money.' But that would not be a joke; it would be a piece of cynicism.

It is instructive to compare this joke with another that is very close to it in meaning:

'A man who had taken to drink supported himself by tutoring in a small town. His vice gradually became known, however, and as a result he lost most of his pupils. A friend was commissioned to urge him to mend his ways. "Look, you could get the best tutoring in the town if you would give up drinking. So do give it up!" "Who do you think you are?" was the

Hofrat, the place is full of people!"' [It may be pointed out that both this joke and the bath-joke above lose their effectiveness in translation because in both cases the natural 'empty' word would not be 'take' in English but 'have': 'Have you had a bath?' and 'Let's have something.']

indignant reply. "I do tutoring so that I can drink. Am I to give up drinking so that I can get tutoring?"'

This joke gives the same appearance of being logical that we saw in the 'salmon mayonnaise'; but it is not a displacement joke. The reply was a direct one. The cynicism which was concealed in the former joke is openly admitted in this one: 'Drinking is the most important thing for me.' Actually the technique of this joke is extremely scanty and cannot explain its effectiveness. It consists simply in the rearrangement of the same material or, more precisely, in the reversal of the relation of means and ends between drinking and doing or getting tutoring. As soon as my reduction ceases to emphasize this factor in its form of expression, the joke fades; for instance: 'What a senseless suggestion! The important thing for me is the drinking, not the tutoring. After all, tutoring is only a means to enable me to go on drinking.' So the joke did in fact depend on its form of expression.

In the bath-joke the dependence of the joke on its wording ('Have you taken a bath?') is unmistakable, and a change in it involves the disappearance of the joke. For in this case the technique is a more complicated one – a combination of double meaning (sub-species f)[1] and displacement. The wording of the question admits a double meaning, and the joke is produced by the answer disregarding the meaning intended by the questioner and catching on to the subsidiary meaning. We are accordingly in a position to find a reduction which allows the double meaning of the wording to persist and yet destroys the joke; we can do this merely by undoing the displacement:

'Have you taken a bath?' – 'What do you think I've taken? A bath? What's that?' But this is no longer a joke, but a malicious or facetious exaggeration.

1. [I.e. 'use of the same word "full" and "empty"'. In the table on pp. 76–7, sub-species f is included in Group II (multiple use of the same material), not in Group III (double meaning). But, as is pointed out on p. 70, Groups II and III merge into each other.]

A precisely similar part is played by the double meaning in Heine's joke about the 'Golden Calf'. It enables the answer to make a diversion from the suggested train of thought (which is effected in the 'salmon mayonnaise' joke without any such assistance from the wording). In the reduction Soulié's remark and Heine's reply would perhaps run: 'The way in which the people here are crowding round the man simply because he's rich reminds one vividly of the worship of the Golden Calf.' And Heine: 'That he should be honoured in this way because of his wealth doesn't strike me as the worst of it. In what you say you're not putting enough stress on the fact that because of his wealth people forgive him his stupidity.' In this way the double meaning would be retained but the displacement joke would be destroyed.

But at this point we must be prepared to meet an objection which will assert that these fine distinctions are seeking to tear apart what belongs together. Does not every double meaning give occasion for a displacement – for a diversion of the train of thought from one meaning to the other? And are we prepared, then, to allow 'double meaning' and 'displacement' to be set up as representatives of two quite different types of joke-technique? Well, it is true that this relation between double meaning and displacement does exist, but it has nothing to do with our distinguishing the different joke–techniques. In the case of double meaning a joke contains nothing other than a word capable of multiple interpretation, which allows the hearer to find the transition from one thought to another – a transition which, stretching a point, might be equated with a displacement. In the case of a displacement joke, however, the joke it-self contains a train of thought in which a displacement of this kind has been accomplished. Here the displacement is part of the work which has created the joke; it is not part of the work necessary for understanding it. If this distinction is not clear to us, we have an unfailing means of bringing it tangibly before our eyes in our attempts at reduction. But there is one merit which we will not deny to this objection. It draws our attention to the necessity of not confusing the psychical processes involved in the *construction* of the joke (the 'joke-work'[1]) with the psychical processes involved in *taking in* the joke (the work of understanding). Our present inquiry is only concerned with the former.[2]

Are there other examples of the displacement technique? They are not easy to find. A straightforward instance is afforded by the following joke, which moreover is not characterized by the appearance of logic which was so much overstressed in our model case:

'A horse-dealer was recommending a saddle-horse to a customer. "If you take this horse and get on it at four in the morning you'll be at Pressburg by half-past six." – "What should I be doing in Pressburg at half-past six in the morning?"'

Here the displacement leaps to the eye. The dealer obviously mentions the early hour of arriving at the provincial town simply in order to demonstrate the horse's capacity by an example. The customer disregards the animal's capacity, which he does not question, and merely enters into the data of the example that has been chosen. The reduction of this joke is accordingly easy to give.

Greater difficulties are presented by another example the

1. [The term here introduced serves to emphasize the resemblance between the processes concerned in producing jokes and dreams which has already been hinted at above (p. 61.). The whole question is fully discussed in Chapter VI below.]

2. For the latter, see later chapters of this book. – A few further words of explanation are perhaps not unnecessary here. Displacement habitually takes place between a remark and a reply which pursues the train of thought in a direction other than that in which it was started by the original remark. The justification for distinguishing displacement from double meaning is most convincingly shown by the examples in which the two are combined – where, that is, the wording of the remark admits of a double meaning which is not intended by the speaker, but which points the way for the reply to make a displacement. (See the examples [pp. 88–9].)

technique of which is most obscure, but which can nevertheless be solved as double meaning combined with displacement. The joke describes the prevarication of a 'Schadchen' (a Jewish marriage-broker), and is thus one of a group with which we shall often be concerned.

'The Schadchen had assured the suitor that the girl's father was no longer living. After the betrothal it emerged that the father was still alive and was serving a prison sentence. The suitor protested to the Schadchen, who replied: "Well, what did I tell you? You surely don't call that living?"'

The double meaning lies in the word 'living', and the displacement consists in the Schadchen shifting the meaning of the word from its ordinary sense, as a contrast to 'dead', to the sense which it has in the phrase 'that's not living'. In doing so he explains his former pronouncement retrospectively as having had a double meaning, though any such multiple meaning was decidedly remote in this particular case. So far the technique would seem similar to that in the 'Golden Calf' joke and the bath-joke. But here there is another factor to be considered which by its prominence interferes with our understanding of the technique. It might be described as a 'characterizing' joke: it seeks by an example to illustrate a marriage-broker's characteristic mixture of mendacious impudence and readiness of repartee. We shall find that this is only the outer shell, the façade, of the joke; its meaning – that is to say, its purpose – is something different. And we must postpone the attempt at a reduction of it.[1]

After these complicated examples, which have been so hard to analyse, it will be with satisfaction that we are able to turn once more to an example which can be recognized as a perfectly straightforward and transparent sample of a displacement joke:

'A Schnorrer [Jewish beggar] approached a wealthy baron with a request for the grant of some assistance for his journey to

1. See Chapter III below [p. 149 ff.].

Ostend. The doctors, he said, had recommended him sea-bathing to restore his health. "Very well," said the rich man, "I'll give you something towards it. But must you go precisely to Ostend, which is the most expensive of all sea-bathing resorts?" – "Herr Baron," was the reproachful reply, "I consider nothing too expensive for my health."' This is no doubt a correct point of view, but not correct for a petitioner. The answer is given from the point of view of a rich man. The *Schnorrer* behaves as though it was his own money that he was to sacrifice for his health, as though the money and the health were the concern of the same person.[1]

[7]

Let us start once more from that highly instructive example 'salmon mayonnaise'. It, too, presented us with a façade, in which a striking parade of logical thinking was exhibited; and we learnt from analysing it that this logic was used to conceal a piece of faulty reasoning – namely, a displacement of the train of thought. This may serve to remind us, if only by means of a contrasting connection, of other jokes which, quite the other way, undisguisedly exhibit a piece of nonsense or stupidity. We shall be curious to learn what may be the technique of such jokes.

I will begin with the most forcible and at the same time the plainest example of the whole group. Once again it is a Jewish joke:

'Itzig had been declared fit for service in the artillery. He was clearly an intelligent lad, but intractable and without any interest in the service. One of his superior officers, who was friendlily disposed to him, took him on one side and said to him: "Itzig, you're no use to us. I'll give you a piece of advice: buy yourself a cannon and make yourself independent!"'

This advice, which may raise a hearty laugh, is obvious non-

1. [This joke reappears on p. 158 below.]

sense. Cannons are not to be bought and an individual cannot make himself independent as a military unit – set himself up in business, as it were. But it is impossible to doubt for a moment that the advice is not mere nonsense but joking nonsense – an excellent joke. How then is the nonsense turned into a joke?

Not much reflection is needed. We can infer from the authorities' comments indicated above in the introduction [p. 42] that there is sense behind joking nonsense such as this, and that it is this sense that makes the nonsense into a joke. The sense in our example is easy to find. The officer who gives Artilleryman Itzig this nonsensical advice is only making himself out stupid to show Itzig how stupidly he himself is behaving. He is copying Itzig: 'I'll give you some advice that's as stupid as you are.' He enters into Itzig's stupidity and makes it clear to him by taking it as the basis of a suggestion which would fit in with Itzig's wishes: if Itzig possessed a cannon of his own and carried out military duties on his own account, how useful his intelligence and ambition would be to him! In what good order he would keep his cannon and how familiar he would make himself with its mechanism so as to meet the competition of the other possessors of cannons!

I will interrupt the analysis of this example, to point out the same sense in nonsense in a shorter and simpler, though less glaring, case of a nonsensical joke:

'Never to be born would be the best thing for mortal men.'[1] 'But,' adds the philosophical comment in *Fliegende Blätter*,[2] 'this happens to scarcely one person in a hundred thousand.'

This modern addition to an ancient saw is an evident piece of nonsense, made sillier by the ostensibly cautious 'scarcely'. But the addition is attached to the original statement as an indisputably correct limitation, and is thus able to open our eyes to the fact that this solemnly accepted piece of wisdom is itself not much better than a piece of nonsense. Anyone who is not

1. [*Contest of Homer and Hesiod*, Section 316.]
2. [A well-known comic weekly.]

born is not a mortal man at all, and there is no good and no best for him. Thus the nonsense in the joke serves to uncover and demonstrate another piece of nonsense, just as in the example of Artilleryman Itzig.

And here I can add a third instance, which, from its content, would scarcely deserve the lengthy description that it requires, but which once again exemplifies with special clarity the use of nonsense in a joke to demonstrate another piece of nonsense.

'A man who was obliged to go on a journey confided his daughter to a friend with the request that he should watch over her virtue during his absence. Some months later he returned, and found that she was pregnant. As was natural, he reproached his friend, who, however, seemed unable to explain the misfortune. "Well," asked the father at last, "where did she sleep?" – "In the room with my son." – "But how could you let her sleep in the same room as your son after I'd begged you so to look after her?" – "After all there was a screen between them. Your daughter's bed was on one side and my son's bed on the other, with the screen between them." – "And suppose he walked round the screen?" – "Yes, there is that," replied the other thoughtfully; "it might have happened like that."'

We can arrive with the greatest ease at the reduction of this joke, whose qualities have otherwise little to recommend it. It would obviously run: 'You have no right to reproach me. How could you be so stupid as to leave your daughter in a house where she is bound to live in the constant company of a young man? How would it be possible for an outsider to answer for a girl's virtue in such circumstances?' Here, then, the friend's apparent stupidity is only a reflection of the father's stupidity. The reduction has disposed of the stupidity in the joke and at the same time of the joke itself. The element 'stupidity' itself has not been got rid of: it is to be found at another point in the context of the sentence after it has been reduced to its original meaning.

We can now attempt a reduction of the joke about the cannon. The officer should have said: 'Itzig, I know you're an intelligent man of business. But I assure you it is very stupid of you if you can't see that it is impossible to behave in the army in the same way as in business life, where each person acts for himself and against the others. In military life subordination and co-operation are the rule.'

The technique of the nonsensical jokes which we have so far considered really consists, therefore, in presenting something that is stupid and nonsensical, the sense of which lies in the revelation and demonstration of something else that is stupid and nonsensical.

Has this use of absurdity in joke-technique always the same significance? Here is one more example which gives an affirmative reply:

'When on one occasion Phocion[1] was applauded after making a speech, he turned to his friends and asked: "What have I said that's stupid, then?"'

The question sounds absurd. But we see its meaning at once: 'What have I said, then, that can have pleased these stupid people so much? I ought to feel ashamed of the applause. If what I said has pleased stupid people, it cannot itself have been very sensible.'

Other examples, however, can teach us that absurdity is very often used in joke-technique without serving the purpose of demonstrating another piece of nonsense:

'A well-known University teacher, who was in the habit of peppering his unattractive special subject with numerous jokes, was congratulated on the birth of his youngest child, who was granted to him when he had already reached an advanced age. "Yes," he replied to his well-wishers, "it is remarkable what human hands can accomplish."' – This answer seems quite specially nonsensical and out of place. Children, after all, are regarded as a blessing of God, quite in contrast to human

1. [The Athenian statesman.]

handiwork. But it soon occurs to us that after all the answer has a meaning and, at that, an obscene one. There is no question here of the happy father making himself out stupid in order to show that something or someone else is stupid. The apparently senseless answer makes a surprising, a bewildering impression on us, as the authorities would say. As we have seen [p. 42 f.] they attribute the whole effect of jokes like this to an alternation between 'bewilderment and illumination'. We shall try later [p. 181] to form a judgement on this; for the moment we must be content to stress the fact that the technique of this joke lies in its presentation of something bewildering and nonsensical.

A joke of Lichtenberg's takes a quite special place among these 'stupid' jokes:

'He wondered how it is that cats have two holes cut in their skin precisely at the place where their eyes are.' To wonder about something that is in fact only the statement of an identity is undoubtedly a piece of stupidity [see below, p. 136.]. It reminds one of Michelet's exclamation[1] which was meant to be taken seriously, and which to the best of my recollection runs: 'How beautifully Nature has arranged it that as soon as a child comes into the world it finds a mother ready to take care of it!' Michelet's pronouncement is a real piece of stupidity, but Lichtenberg's is a joke which makes use of stupidity for some purpose and behind which something lies. But what? For the moment, we must admit, no answer can be given.

[8]

We have now already found from two groups of examples that the joke-work makes use of deviations from normal thinking – of displacement and absurdity – as technical methods for producing a joking form of expression. It is no doubt justifiable to expect that other kinds of faulty reasoning may find a

1. *La femme* [1860].

similar use. And it is in fact possible to produce a few examples of the sort:

'A gentleman entered a pastry-cook's shop and ordered a cake; but he soon brought it back and asked for a glass of liqueur instead. He drank it and began to leave without having paid. The proprietor detained him. "What do you want?" asked the customer. – "You've not paid for the liqueur." – "But I gave you the cake in exchange for it." – "You didn't pay for that either." – 'But I hadn't eaten it.'''

This anecdote too has an appearance of logic about it, which, as we already know, is a suitable façade for a piece of faulty reasoning. The mistake evidently lies in the crafty customer's constructing a connection which did not exist between the giving back of the cake and the taking of the liqueur in its place. The episode in fact fell into two processes, which were independent of each other so far as the vendor was concerned and were substitutes for each other only from the point of view of the purchaser's intention. First he took the cake and gave it back, and therefore owed nothing for it; then he took the liqueur, and for it he owed payment. We might say that the customer used the relation 'in exchange for' with a double meaning. But it would be more correct to say that by means of a double meaning he constructed a connection which was not in reality valid.[1]

This is an opportunity for making a not unimportant admission. We are engaged in investigating the technique of jokes as shown in examples; and we should therefore be certain that

1. [*Footnote added* 1912:] A similar nonsensical technique appears if a joke seeks to maintain a connection which seems to be excluded by the special conditions implied in its content. Such, for instance, is Lichtenberg's knife without a blade which has no handle. [This is further explained in a passage near the end of the 'History of the Psycho-Analytic Movement' (1914*d*).] So, too, the joke repeated by Von Falke [1897]: 'Is this the place where the Duke of Wellington spoke those words?' – 'Yes, it is the place; but he never spoke the words.' [Cf. Von Falke's *Memoirs*, p. 271.]

the examples we have chosen are really genuine jokes. It is the case, however, that in a number of instances we are in doubt whether the particular example ought to be called a joke or not. We have no criterion at our disposal before our investigation has given us one. Linguistic usage is untrustworthy and itself needs to have its justification examined. In coming to our decision we can base ourselves on nothing but a certain 'feeling', which we may interpret as meaning that the decision is made in our judgement in accordance with particular criteria that are not yet accessible to our knowledge. In the case of our last example we must feel a doubt whether it should be represented as a joke, or perhaps as a 'sophistical' joke, or simply as a piece of sophistry. For the fact is that we do not yet know in what the characteristic of being a joke resides.

On the other hand, the next example, which exhibits a type of faulty reasoning that may be said to be complementary to the former instance, is an undoubted joke. It is once again a story of a marriage-broker:

'The *Schadchen* was defending the girl he had proposed against the young man's protests. "I don't care for the mother-in-law," said the latter. "She's a disagreeable, stupid person." – "But after all you're not marrying the mother-in-law. What you want is her daughter." – "Yes, but she's not young any longer, and she's not precisely a beauty." – "No matter. If she's neither young nor beautiful she'll be all the more faithful to you." – "And she hasn't much money." – "Who's talking about money? Are you marrying money then? After all it's a wife that you want." – "But she's got a hunchback too." – "Well, what *do* you want? Isn't she to have a single fault?"'

What was really in question, then, was an unbeautiful girl, no longer young, with a scanty dowry and an unpleasant mother, who was moreover the victim of a serious deformity – not very inviting conditions for contracting a marriage. The marriage broker was able, in the case of each one of these defects, to point out how it would be possible to come to terms with it. He was then able to claim that the inexcusable hunch-back was the single defect that every individual must be allowed to possess. Once more there is the appearance of logic which is characteristic of a piece of sophistry and which is intended to conceal the faulty reasoning. Clearly the girl had a number of defects – several that might be overlooked and one that it was impossible to disregard; she was unmarriageable. The broker behaved as though each separate defect was got rid of by his evasions, whereas in fact each one of them left a certain amount of depreciation behind which had to be added to the next one. He insisted on treating each defect in isolation and refused to add them up into a total.

The same omission is the core of another piece of sophistry which has been much laughed over, but whose right to be called a joke might be doubted:

'A. borrowed a copper kettle from B. and after he had re-turned it was sued by B. because the kettle now had a big hole in it which made it unusable. His defence was: "First, I never borrowed a kettle from B. at all; secondly, the kettle had a hole in it already when I got it from him; and thirdly, I gave him back the kettle undamaged."' Each one of these defences is valid in itself, but taken together they exclude one another. A. was treating in isolation what had to be regarded as a con-nected whole, just as the marriage-broker treated the girl's defects. We might also say: 'A. has put an "and" where only an "either – or" is possible.'[1]

We find another piece of sophistry in the following mar-riage-broker story:

'The would-be bridegroom complained that the bride had one leg shorter than the other and limped. The *Schadchen* con-tradicted him: "You're wrong. Suppose you marry a woman with healthy, straight limbs! What do you gain from it? You never have a day's security that she won't fall down, break a leg and afterwards be lame all her life. And think of the suffer-

1. [This anecdote is further discussed below on p. 266.]

ing then, the agitation, and the doctor's bill! But if you take *this* one, that can't happen to you. Here you have a *fait accompli*.'"

The appearance of logic is very thin in this case, and no one will be ready to prefer an already 'accomplished misfortune' to one that is merely a possibility. The fault in this train of thought can be more easily shown in another example – a story which I cannot entirely divest of its dialect:

'In the temple at Cracow the Great Rabbi N. was sitting and praying with his disciples. Suddenly he uttered a cry, and, in reply to his disciples' anxious inquiries, exclaimed: "At this very moment the Great Rabbi L. has died in Lemberg." The community put on mourning for the dead man. In the course of the next few days people arriving from Lemberg were asked how the Rabbi had died and what had been wrong with him; but they knew nothing about it, and had left him in the best of health. At last it was established with certainty that the Rabbi L. in Lemberg had not died at the moment at which the Rabbi N. had observed his death by telepathy, since he was still alive. A stranger took the opportunity of jeering at one of the Cracow Rabbi's disciples about this occurrence: "Your Rabbi made a great fool of himself that time, when he saw the Rabbi L. die in Lemberg. The man's alive to this day." "That makes no difference," replied the disciple. "Whatever you may say, the *Kück*[1] from Cracow to Lemberg was a magnificent one."'

The faulty reasoning common to the last two examples is here undisguisedly admitted. The value of phantasy is exalted unduly in comparison with reality; a possibility is almost equated with an actual event. The distant look across the stretch of country separating Cracow and Lemberg would have been an impressive telepathic achievement if it had produced something that was true. But the disciple was not concerned with that. It might after all have possibly happened that the

1. [A Yiddish word] from the German '*gucken* [to look or peep]': 'look', 'distant look'.

Rabbi in Lemberg had died at the moment at which the
Cracow Rabbi announced his death; and the disciple displaced the emphasis from the condition subject to which the
teacher's achievement deserved admiration on to an uncon-
ditional admiration of the achievement. '*In magnis rebus voluisse
sat est*'[1] expresses a similar point of view. Just as in this example
reality is disregarded in favour of possibility, so in the former
one the marriage-broker suggests to the would-be bridegroom
that the possibility of a woman being made lame by an accident
should be regarded as something far more important than the
question of whether she is really lame or not.

This group of 'sophistical' pieces of faulty reasoning is
resembled by another interesting group in which the faulty
reasoning can be described as 'automatic'. It may be due to no
more than a whim of chance that all the examples that I shall
bring forward of this new group are once more *Schadchen*
stories:

'A *Schadchen* had brought an assistant with him to the discussion about the proposed bride, to bear out what he had to
say. "She is straight as a pine-tree," said the *Schadchen*. – "As a
pine-tree," repeated the echo. – "And she has eyes that ought
to be seen!" – "What eyes she has!" confirmed the echo. –
"And she is better educated than anyone!" – "What an education!" – "It's true there's one thing," admitted the broker,
"she has a small hump." – "And *what* a hump!" the echo confirmed once more.' The other stories are analogous, but have
more sense.

'The bridegroom was most disagreeably surprised when the
bride was introduced to him, and drew the broker on one side
and whispered his remonstrances: "Why have you brought me
here?" he asked reproachfully. "She's ugly and old, she squints
and has bad teeth and bleary eyes ..." – "You needn't

1. ['In great things it is enough to have wished.' The quotation, in a
slightly different form – '*in magnis et voluisse sat est*' – is from Proper-
tius, *Elegies*, x, 6.]

lower your voice," interrupted the broker, "she's deaf as well."'

'The bridegroom was paying his first visit to the bride's house in the company of the broker, and while they were waiting in the *salon* for the family to appear, the broker drew attention to a cupboard with glass doors in which the finest set of silver plate was exhibited. "There! Look at that! You can see from these things how rich these people are." – "But," asked the suspicious young man, "mightn't it be possible that these fine things were only collected for the occasion – that they were borrowed to give an impression of wealth?" – "What an idea!" answered the broker protestingly. "Who do you think would lend these people anything?"'

The same thing happens in all three cases. A person who has reacted in the same way several times in succession repeats this mode of expression on the next occasion, when it is unsuitable and defeats his own intentions. He neglects to adapt himself to the needs of the situation, by giving way to the automatic action of habit. Thus, in the first story the assistant forgets that he was brought along in order to prejudice the would-be bridegroom in favour of the proposed bride. And since to begin with he has performed his task and underlined the bride's advantages by repeating each one as it is brought forward, he goes on to underline her timidly admitted hump, which he should have minimized. The broker in the second story is so much fascinated by the enumeration of the bride's defects and infirmities that he completes the list out of his own knowledge, though that was certainly not his business or purpose. In the third story, finally, he allows himself to be so much carried away by his eagerness to convince the young man of the family's wealth that, in order to establish one confirmatory point, he brings up something that is bound to upset all his efforts. In every case automatic action triumphs over the expedient modification of thought and expression.

This is easy to see; but it is bound to have a confusing effect when we notice that these three stories have as much right to be called 'comic' as we had to produce them as 'jokes'. The uncovering of psychical automatism is one of the techniques of the comic, just as is any kind of revelation or self-betrayal. We suddenly find ourselves faced at this point with the problem of the relation of jokes to the comic which we intended to evade (see the introduction [p. 39]). Are these stories perhaps only 'comic' and not 'jokes'? Is the comic operating here by the same methods as jokes do? And, once again, what constitutes the peculiar characteristics of jokes?

We must keep to our view that the technique of this last group of jokes that we have examined lies in nothing else than in bringing forward 'faulty reasoning'. But we are obliged to admit that their examination has so far led us more into obscurity than understanding. Nevertheless we do not abandon our expectation that a more complete knowledge of the techniques of jokes will lead us to a result which can serve as a starting point for further discoveries.

[9]

The next examples of jokes, with which we shall pursue our inquiry, offer an easier task. Their technique, in particular, reminds us of what we already know.

First, here is a joke of Lichtenberg's:

'January is the month in which we offer our dear friends wishes, and the rest are the months in which they are not fulfilled.'

Since these jokes are to be described as refined rather than strong, and work by methods that are unobtrusive, we will begin by presenting a number of them in order to intensify their effect:

'Human life falls into two halves. In the first half we wish the second one would come; and in the second we wish the first one were back.'

'Experience consists in experiencing what we do not wish to experience.'

(Both these last two are from Fischer, 1889 [59–60].)

These examples cannot fail to remind us of a group with which we have already dealt and which is distinguished by the 'multiple use of the same material' [p. 65 ff.]. The last example in particular will raise the question of why we did not include it in that group instead of introducing it here in a fresh connection. 'Experience' is once again described in its own terms, just as 'jealousy' was earlier (p. 68). I should not be inclined to dispute this classification very seriously. But as regards the other two examples (which are of a similar nature), I think another factor is more striking and more important than the multiple use of the same words, in which in this case there is nothing that fringes on double meaning. I should like in particular to stress the fact that here new and unexpected unities are set up, relations of ideas to one another, definitions made mutually or by reference to a common third element. I should like to name this process 'unification'. It is clearly analogous to condensation by compression into the same words. Thus the two halves of human life are described by a mutual relation discovered to exist between them: in the first we wish the second would come and in the second we wish the first were back. Speaking more precisely, two very similar mutual relations have been chosen for representation. To the similarity of the relations there corresponds a similarity of the words, which may indeed remind us of the multiple use of the same material: 'wish ... would come' – 'wish ... back'. In Lichtenberg's joke, January and the months contrasted with it are characterized by a (once again, modified) relation to a third element; these are the good wishes, which are received in the first month and not fulfilled in the remaining ones. Here the distinction from the multiple use of the same material (which approximates to double meaning) is very clear.[1]

1. In order to give a better description of 'unification' than the examples

Here is a neat example of a unification joke which needs no explanation:

'The French poet J. B. Rousseau wrote an Ode to Posterity. Voltaire was not of opinion that the poem merited survival, and jokingly remarked: "This poem will not reach its destination"' (Fischer, 1889 [123]).

---

above allow of, I will make use of something I have already mentioned [p. 65n.] – namely the peculiar negative relation that holds between jokes and riddles, according to which the one conceals what the other exhibits. Many of the riddles with the production of which G. T. Fechner, the philosopher, passed his time when he was blind, are characterized by a high degree of unification, which lends them a special charm. Take, for instance, as a neat example, Riddle No. 203 (Dr Mises' [pseudonym of Fechner] *Rätselbüchlein*, 4th edition, enlarged, n.d.):

> Die beiden ersten finden ihre Ruhestätte
> Im Paar der andern, und das Ganze macht ihr Bette.

[My two first (*Toten*, the dead) find their resting-place in my two last (*Gräber*, graves), and my whole (*Totengräber*, grave-digger) makes their bed.]

We are told nothing about the two pairs of syllables that have to be guessed except a relation that holds between them, and about the whole we are only told its relation to the first pair.

The following are two examples of description by relation to the same or a slightly modified third element:

> Die erste Silb' hat Zähn' und Haare,
> Die zweite Zähne in den Haaren.
> Wer auf den Zähnen nicht hat Haare,
> Vom Ganzen kaufe keine Waren.   No. 170.

[The first syllable has teeth and hair (*Ross*, horse), the second had teeth in the hair (*Kamm*, comb). No one who has not hair on his teeth i.e. who is not able to look after his interests) should buy goods from the whole (*Rosskamm*, horse-dealer).]

> Die erste Silbe frisst,
> Die andere Silbe isst,
> Die dritte wird gefressen,
> Das Ganze wird gegessen.   No. 168.

This last example draws attention to the fact that it is essentially unification that lies at the bottom of jokes that can be described as 'ready repartees'. [Cf. p. 68.] For repartee consists in the defence going to meet the aggression, in 'turning the tables on someone' or 'paying someone back in his own coin' – that is, in establishing an unexpected unity between attack and counter-attack. For instance:

'An innkeeper had a whitlow on his finger and the baker said to him: "You must have got that by putting your finger in your beer." "It wasn't that," replied the innkeeper, "I got a piece of your bread under my nail"' (from Überhorst [1900, 2]).

'Serenissimus[1] was making a tour through his provinces and noticed a man in the crowd who bore a striking resemblance to his own exalted person. He beckoned to him and asked: "Was your mother at one time in service in the Palace?" – "No, your Highness," was the reply, "but my father was."'

'Duke Charles of Württemberg happened on one of his

[The first syllable gobbles (*Sau*, sow), the second syllable eats (*Er*, he), the third is gobbled (*Kraut*, weeds), the whole is eaten (*Sauerkraut*). N.B. In German two different but similar verbs are used for 'to eat' according to whether the process is performed by animals or human beings.]

The most perfect instance of unification is to be found in a riddle of Schleiermacher's, which cannot be denied the character of a joke:

> Von der letzten umschlungen
> Schwebt das vollendete Ganze
> Zu den zwei ersten empor.

[Entwined by my last (*Strick*, rope), my completed whole (*Galgenstrick*, rogue) swings to the top of my two first (*Galgen*, gallows).]

The great majority of all such riddles lack unification. That is to say, the clue by which one syllable is to be guessed is quite independent of those that point to the second or third, as well as of the indication which is to lead to the separate discovery of the whole.

1. [The name conventionally given to Royal Personages by comic periodicals under the German Empire.]

rides to come upon a dyer who was engaged on his job. Pointing to the grey horse he was riding, the Duke called out: "Can you dye him blue?" "Yes, of course, your Highness," came the answer, "if he can stand boiling."' [Fischer, 1889, 107.]

In this excellent *tu quoque*, in which a nonsensical question is met by an equally impossible condition, there is another technical factor at work which would have been absent if the dyer had answered: 'No, your Highness. I'm afraid the horse wouldn't stand boiling.'

Unification has another, quite specially interesting technical instrument at its disposal: stringing things together with the conjunction 'and'. If things are strung together in this way it implies that they are connected: we cannot help understanding it so. For instance, when Heine, speaking of the city of Göttingen in the *Harzreise*, remarks: 'Speaking generally, the inhabitants of Göttingen are divided into students, professors, philistines and donkeys', we take this grouping in precisely the sense which Heine emphasizes in an addition to the sentence: 'and these four classes are anything but sharply divided.' Or, again, when [ibid.] he speaks of the school in which he had to put up with 'so much Latin, caning and Geography', this series, which is made even more transparent by the position of the 'caning' between the two educational subjects, tells us that the unmistakable view taken by the schoolboys of the caning certainly extended to Latin and Geography as well.

Among the examples given by Lipps [1898, 177] of 'joking enumeration' ('co-ordination'), we find the following lines quoted as being closely akin to Heine's 'students, professors, philistines and donkeys':

> Mit einer Gabel und mit Müh'
> Zog ihn die Mutter aus der Brüh.

> [With a fork and much to-do
> His mother dragged him from the stew.]

It is as though (Lipps comments), the *Müh* [trouble, to-do] were an instrument like the fork. We have a feeling, however, that these lines, though they are very comic, are far from being a joke, while Heine's list undoubtedly is one. We may perhaps recall these examples later, when we need no longer evade the problem of the relation between the comic and jokes. [See below, p. 274.]

[10]

We observed in the example of the Duke and the dyer that it would remain a joke by unification if the dyer had replied: '*No*, I'm afraid the horse wouldn't stand boiling.' But his actual reply was: '*Yes*, your Highness, if he can stand boiling.' The replacement of the really appropriate 'no' by a 'yes' constitutes a new technical method of joking, the employment of which we will pursue in some other examples.

A joke similar to the one we have just mentioned (also quoted by Fischer [1889, 107–8]) is simpler:

'Frederick the Great heard of a preacher in Silesia who had the reputation of being in contact with spirits. He sent for the man and received him with the question "You can conjure up spirits?" The reply was: "At your Majesty's command. But they don't come."' It is quite obvious here that the method used in the joke lay in nothing else than the replacing of the only possible answer 'no' by its opposite. In order to carry out the replacement, it was necessary to add a 'but' to the 'yes'; so that 'yes' and 'but' are equivalent in sense to 'no'.

This 'representation by the opposite', as we shall call it, serves the joke-work in various forms. In the next two examples it appears almost pure:

'This lady resembles the Venus of Milo in many respects: she, too, is extraordinarily old, like her she has no teeth, and there are white patches on the yellowish surface of her body' (Heine).

Here we have a representation of ugliness through resemblances to what is most beautiful. It is true that these resemblances can only exist in qualities that are expressed in terms with a double meaning or in unimportant details. This latter feature applies to our second example – 'The Great Spirit', by Lichtenberg:

'He united in himself the characteristics of the greatest men. He carried his head askew like Alexander; he always had to wear a *toupet* like Caesar; he could drink coffee like Leibnitz; and once he was properly settled in his armchair, he forgot eating and drinking like Newton, and had to be woken up like him; he wore his wig like Dr Johnson, and he always left a breeches-button undone like Cervantes.'

Von Falke (1897, 271) brought home a particularly good example of representation by the opposite from a journey to Ireland, an example in which no use whatever is made of words with a double meaning. The scene was a wax-work show (as it might be, Madame Tussaud's). A guide was conducting a company of old and young visitors from figure to figure and commenting on them: 'This is the Duke of Wellington and his horse,' he explained. Whereupon a young lady asked: 'Which is the Duke of Wellington and which is his horse?' 'Just as you like, my pretty child,' was the reply. 'You pays your money and you takes your choice.'

The reduction of this Irish joke would be: 'Shameless the things these wax-work people dare to offer the public! One can't distinguish between the horse and its rider! (Facetious exaggeration.) And that's what one pays one's money for!' This indignant exclamation is then dramatized, based on a small occurrence. In place of the public in general an individual lady appears and the figure of the rider is particularized: he must be the Duke of Wellington, who is so extremely popular in Ireland. But the shamelessness of the proprietor or guide, who takes money out of people's pockets and offers them nothing in return, is represented by the opposite – by a speech

THE TECHNIQUE OF JOKES

in which he boasts himself a conscientious man of business, who has nothing more closely at heart than regard for the rights which the public has acquired by its payment. And now we can see that the technique of this joke is not quite a simple one. In so far as it enables the swindler to insist on his conscientiousness it is a case of representation by the opposite; but in so far as it effects this on an occasion on which something quite different is demanded of him – so that he replies with business-like respectability where what we expect of him is the identification of the figures – it is an instance of displacement. The technique of the joke lies in a combination of the two methods.

No great distance separates this example from a small group which might be described as 'overstatement' jokes. In these the 'yes' which would be in place in the reduction is replaced by a 'no', which, however, on account of its content, has the force of an intensified 'yes', and *vice versa*. A denial is a substitute for an overstated confirmation. Thus, for instance, in Lessing's epigram:[1]

> Die gute Galathee! Man sagt, sie schwärz' ihr Haar;
> Da doch ihr Haar schon schwarz, als sie es kaufte, war.

> [Good Galathea blacks her hair, 'tis thought;
> And yet her hair was black when it was bought.]

Or Lichtenberg's malicious defence of philosophy:
'There are more things in heaven and earth than are dreamt of in your philosophy,' said Prince Hamlet contemptuously. Lichtenberg knew that this condemnation is not nearly severe enough, for it does not take into account all the objections that can be made to philosophy. He therefore added what was missing: 'But there is much, too, in philosophy that is not to be found in heaven or earth.' His addition, it is true, emphasizes the way in which philosophy compensates us for the insuffici-

1. ['Auf die Galathee', *Sinngedichte*.] Modelled on one in the Greek Anthology.

ency for which Hamlet censures it. But this compensation implies another and still greater reproach.

Two Jewish jokes, though they are of a coarse type, are even clearer, since they are free from any trace of displacement:

'Two Jews were discussing baths. "I have a bath every year," said one of them, "whether I need one or not."'

It is obvious that this boastful insistence on his cleanliness only serves to convict him of uncleanliness.

'A Jew noticed the remains of some food in another one's beard. "I can tell you what you had to eat yesterday." – "Well, tell me." – "Lentils, then." – "Wrong: the day before yesterday!"'

The following example is an excellent 'overstatement' joke, which can easily be traced back to representation by the opposite:

'The King condescended to visit a surgical clinic and came on the professor as he was carrying out the amputation of a leg. He accompanied all its stages with loud expressions of his royal satisfaction: "Bravo! bravo! my dear Professor!" When the operation was finished, the professor approached him and asked him with a deep bow: "Is it your Majesty's command that I should remove the other leg too?"'

The professor's thoughts during the royal applause could certainly not have been expressed unaltered: 'This makes it look as though I were taking off the poor fellow's bad leg by royal command and only for the royal satisfaction. After all I really have other reasons for the operation.' But he then goes to the King and says: 'I have no reasons for carrying out an operation other than your Majesty's command. The applause you honoured me with has made me so happy that I only await your Majesty's orders to amputate the sound limb too.' In this way he succeeds in making himself understood by saying the opposite of what he thinks but must keep to himself. This opposite is an overstatement that cannot be believed.

As these examples show, representation by the opposite is an instrument of joke-technique that is used frequently and works powerfully. But there is something else that we should not overlook: namely that this technique is by no means peculiar to jokes. When Mark Antony, after he has made a long speech in the Forum and has reversed the emotional attitude of his audience round Caesar's corpse, finally exclaims once more:

> 'For Brutus is an honourable man ...'

he knows that the people will now shout back to him the true sense of his words:

> 'They were traitors: honourable men!'

Or when *Simplicissimus*[1] describes a collection of incredible pieces of brutality and cynicism as the expressions of 'men of feeling', this too is a representation by the opposite. But we call this 'irony' and no longer a joke. The only technique that characterizes irony is representation by the opposite. Moreover we read and hear of 'ironical jokes'. So it can no longer be doubted that technique alone is insufficient to characterize the nature of jokes. Something further is needed which we have not yet discovered. But on the other hand it remains an uncontradicted fact that if we undo the technique of a joke it disappears. For the time being we may find difficulty in thinking how these two fixed points that we have arrived at in explaining jokes can be reconciled.

[11]

If representation by the opposite is one of the technical methods of jokes, we can expect that jokes may also make use of its contrary – representation by something *similar* or akin. A further pursuit of our inquiry will in fact show us that this is the technique of a fresh and particularly comprehensive group of conceptual jokes.[2] We shall describe the peculiarity of this

1. [The famous Munich comic weekly.]
2. [As contrasted with verbal jokes. See below, p. 132.]

technique far more appropriately if, instead of representation by something 'akin', we say by something 'correlated' or 'connected'. We will take our start, in fact, with this latter characteristic and illustrate it at once by an example.

Here is an American anecdote: 'Two not particularly scrupulous business men had succeeded, by dint of a series of highly risky enterprises, in amassing a large fortune, and they were now making efforts to push their way into good society. One method, which struck them as a likely one, was to have their portraits painted by the most celebrated and highly-paid artist in the city, whose pictures had an immense reputation. The precious canvases were shown for the first time at a large evening party, and the two hosts themselves led the most influential connoisseur and art critic up to the wall upon which the portraits were hanging side by side, to extract his admiring judgement on them. He studied the works for a long time, and then, shaking his head, as though there was something he had missed, pointed to the gap between the pictures and asked quietly: "But where's the Saviour?"' (i.e. 'I don't see the picture of the Saviour').

The meaning of this remark is clear. It is once again a question of the representation of something that cannot be expressed directly. How does this 'indirect representation' come about? Starting from the representation in the joke, we trace the path backwards through a series of easily established associations and inferences.

We can guess from the question 'Where's the Saviour? Where's the picture of the Saviour?' that the sight of the two pictures had reminded the speaker of a similar sight, familiar to him, as to us, which however, included an element that was missing here – the picture of the Saviour between two other pictures. There is only one such situation: Christ hanging between the two thieves. The missing element is brought into prominence by the joke. The similarity lies in the pictures, hanging to the right and left of the Saviour, which the joke passes over; it can only consist in the fact that the pictures hanging on the walls are pictures of thieves. What the critic wanted to say but could not say was: 'You are a couple of rascals' or, in greater detail: 'What do I care about your pictures? You are a couple of rascals – I know that!' And he did in fact end by saying it by means of a few associations and inferences, using the method which we speak of as an 'allusion'.

We at once recall where we have already come across allusion – in connection, namely, with double meaning. When two meanings are expressed in one word and one of them is so much more frequent and usual that it occurs to us at once, while the second is more out of the way and therefore less prominent, we proposed to speak of this as 'double meaning with an allusion' [p. 76]. In a whole number of the examples we have already examined we remarked that the technique was not a simple one, and we now perceive that the 'allusion' was the complicating factor in them. (See, for instance, the inversion joke about the wife who has lain back a bit and so has been able to earn a lot [p. 66] or the nonsensical joke about the man who replied to congratulations on the birth of his youngest child by saying that it was remarkable what human hands could accomplish (p. 96).

In the American anecdote we now have before us an allusion without any double meaning, and we see that its characteristic is replacement by something linked to it in a conceptual connection. It may easily be guessed that the utilizable connection can be of more than one kind. In order not to lose ourselves in a maze of detail, we will discuss only the most marked variants and these only in a few examples.

The connection used for the replacement may be merely a resemblance in sound, so that this sub-species becomes analogous to puns among verbal jokes. Here, however, it is not the resemblance in sound between two *words*, but between whole sentences, characteristic phrases, and so on.

For instance, Lichtenberg coined the saying: 'New spas

cure well', which at once reminds us of the proverb: 'New brooms sweep clean.' The two phrases share the first one and a half words and the last word, as well as the whole structure of the sentence.[1] And there is no doubt that the sentence came into the witty philosopher's head as an imitation of the familiar proverb. Thus Lichtenberg's saying becomes an allusion to the proverb. By means of this allusion something is suggested that is not said straight out – namely that something else is responsible for the effects produced by spas besides the unvarying characteristics of thermal springs.

A similar technical solution applies to another jest [*Scherz*] or joke [*Witz*][2] of Lichtenberg's: 'A girl scarcely twelve *Moden* [modes] old.' This sounds like 'twelve *Monden* [moons]', i.e. months, and may originally have been a slip of the pen for the latter, which is a permissible expression in poetry. But it also makes good sense to use the changing fashion instead of the changing moon as a method of determining a woman's age.

The connection may also consist in similarity except for a 'slight modification'. So that this technique, too, is parallel to a verbal technique [p. 66]. Both species of joke make almost the same impression, but they can be better distinguished from each other if we consider the processes of the joke-work.

Here is an example of a verbal joke or pun of this kind: Marie Wilt was a great singer, famous, however, for the compass not only of her voice. She suffered the humiliation of having the title of a play based on Jules Verne's well-known novel used as an allusion to her misshapen figure: 'Round the Wilt in 80 Days'.[3]

1. [In the German the first syllables of 'spas (*Bäder*)' and 'brooms (*Besen*)' sound alike; and in the German proverb the last word is 'well (*gut*)'.]

2. [The distinction between the two is discussed at length in a later chapter (p. 178 ff.).]

3. [The German for 'world' is '*Welt*'.]

Or: 'Every fathom a queen', a modification of Shakespeare's familiar 'Every inch a king'. The allusion to this quotation was made with reference to an aristocratic and over-life-size lady. No very serious objection could really be made if anyone were to prefer to include this joke among the 'condensations accompanied by modifications as substitute'. (See 'tête-à-bête', p. 57.)

A friend said of someone who had lofty views but was obstinate in the pursuit of his aims: 'Er hat ein Ideal vor dem Kopf [He had an ideal in front of his head].' The current phrase is: 'Ein Brett vor dem Kopf haben' [literally, 'to have a board in front of one's head' – 'to be dense']. The modification alludes to this phrase and makes use of its meaning for its own purposes. Here, once more, the technique might be described as 'condensation with modification'.

It is almost impossible to distinguish between 'allusion by means of modification' and 'condensation with substitution', if the modification is limited to a change of letters. For instance: 'Dichteritis'.[1] This allusion to the scourge of 'Diphteritis [diphtheria]' represents authorship by unqualified persons as another public danger.

Negative particles make very neat allusions possible at the cost of slight alterations:

'My fellow-unbeliever Spinoza', says Heine. 'We, by the ungrace of God, day-labourers, serfs, negroes, villeins ...' is how Lichtenberg begins a manifesto (which he carries no further) made by these unfortunates – who certainly have more right to this title than kings and princes have to its unmodified form.

Finally, another kind of allusion consists in 'omission', which may be compared to condensation without the formation of a substitute. Actually, in every allusion something is omitted, viz. the train of thought leading to the allusion. It only depends on whether the more obvious thing is the gap in the wording of

1. [A non-existent word, which might be translated 'authoritis' – from 'Dichter (an author)'.]

the allusion or the substitute which partly fills the gap. Thus a series of examples would lead us back from blatant omission to allusion proper.

Omission without a substitute is shown in the following example:[1] There is a witty and pugnacious journalist in Vienna, whose biting invective has repeatedly led to his being physically maltreated by the subjects of his attacks. On one occasion, when a fresh misdeed on the part of one of his habitual opponents was being discussed, somebody exclaimed: 'If X hears of this, he'll get his ears boxed again.'[2] The technique of this joke includes, in the first place, bewilderment at its apparent nonsense, since we cannot see how getting one's ears boxed can be an immediate consequence of having heard something. The absurdity of the remark disappears if we insert in the gap: 'he'll write such a scathing article upon the man that . . . etc.' Allusion by means of omission, combined with nonsense, are accordingly the technical methods used in this joke.

'He praises himself so much that the price of fumigating candles is going up.' (Heine.) This gap is easy to fill. What is omitted has been replaced by an inference, which then leads back to what has been omitted, in the form of an allusion: 'self-praise stinks'.

And now once again two Jews outside the bath-house:

One of them sighed: 'Another year gone by already!'

These examples leave us in no doubt that here the omission forms part of the allusion.

There is still quite a marked gap to be seen in our next example, though it is a genuine and correct allusive joke. After an artists' carnival in Vienna a jest-book was circulated, in

1. [Freud quoted this example in a footnote to his analysis of the 'Rat Man' (1909*d*), Section II (A), to illustrate the use of a similar technique in obsessional symptoms.]

2. [The 'X' in question was Karl Kraus, who has already been referred to above (p. 59).]

which, among others, the following highly remarkable epigram appeared:

'A wife is like an umbrella. Sooner or later one takes a cab.'

An umbrella is not enough protection against rain. The 'sooner or later' can only mean 'if it rains hard', and a cab is a public vehicle. But since we are only concerned here with the *form* of the analogy, we will postpone the closer examination of this joke to a later moment. [See p. 156 f.]

Heine's 'Bäder von Lucca' contains a regular wasp's nest of the most stinging allusions and makes the most ingenious use of this form of joke for polemical purposes (against Count Platen).[1] Long before the reader can suspect what is afoot, there are foreshadowings of a particular theme, peculiarly ill-adapted for direct representation, by allusions to material of the most varied kind – for instance, in Hirsch-Hyacinth's verbal contortions: 'You are too stout and I am too thin; you have a good deal of imagination and I have all the more business sense; I am a *practicus* and you are a *diarrheticus*; in short you are my complete anti*podex*.' – 'Venus *Urinia*' – 'the stout Gudel von *Dreck*wall' of Hamburg, and so on.[2] In what follows, the events described by the author take a turn which seems at first merely to display his mischievous spirit but soon reveals its symbolic relation to his polemical purpose and at the same time shows itself as allusive. Eventually[3] the attack on

1. [August, Count von Platen (1796–1835), the lyric poet, had aroused Heine's enmity by a satirical work on the romantic movement. He was a sublimated homosexual.]

2. [These instances all touch on anal material. Venus 'Urinia', though on the surface suggesting urine, is a malapropism for 'Urania', the heavenly, homosexual, love of Plato's *Symposium*. 'Gudel' was a real, aristocratic and wealthy Hamburg lady, to whom Hyacinth here gives the anal-sounding pseudonym of 'Dreckwall' (*Dreck* = excrement). All these examples will be found in Chapter IX of 'Die Bäder von Lucca' (Part III of Heine's *Reisebilder*). The rest of that chapter is concerned with predominantly anal anecdotes.]

3. [In Chapter XI, the last in the book.]

Platen bursts out, and thenceforward allusions to the theme (with which we have already been made acquainted) of the Count's love for men gushes out and overflows in every sentence of Heine's attack on his opponent's talents and character. For instance:

'Even though the Muses do not favour him, he has the Genius of Speech in his power, or rather he knows how to do violence to him. For he does not possess the free love of that Genius, he must unceasingly pursue this young man, too, and he knows how to capture only the outer forms, which, despite their lovely curves never speak nobly.'

'He is like the ostrich, which believes he is well hidden if he sticks his head in the sand, so that only his behind can be seen. Our exalted bird would have done better to hide his behind in the sand and show us his head.'

Allusion is perhaps the commonest and most easily manageable method of joking and is at the bottom of the majority of short-lived jokes which we are accustomed to weaving into our conversations and which will not bear being uprooted from their original soil and kept in isolation. But it precisely reminds us once more of the fact that had begun to puzzle us in our consideration of the technique of jokes. An allusion in itself does not constitute a joke; there are correctly constructed allusions which have no claim to such a character. Only allusions that possess that character can be described as jokes. So that the criterion of jokes, which we have pursued into their technique, eludes us there once again.

I have occasionally described allusion as 'indirect representation'; and we may now observe that the various species of allusion, together with representation by the opposite and other techniques that have still to be mentioned, may be united into a single large group, for which 'indirect representation' would be the most comprehensive name. 'Faulty reasoning', 'unification', 'indirect representation' – these, then, are the headings under which we can classify those techniques of conceptual jokes which we have come to know.

If we examine our material further, we seem to recognize a fresh sub-species of indirect representation which can be precisely characterized but of which few examples can be adduced. This is representation by something small or very small[1] – which performs the task of giving full expression to a whole characteristic by means of a tiny detail. This group can be brought under the classification of 'allusion', if we bear in mind that this smallness is related to what has to be represented, and can be seen to proceed from it. For instance:

'A Galician Jew was travelling in a train. He had made himself really comfortable, had unbuttoned his coat and put his feet up on the seat. Just then a gentleman in modern dress entered the compartment. The Jew promptly pulled himself together and took up a proper pose. The stranger fingered through the pages of a notebook, made some calculations, reflected for a moment and then suddenly asked the Jew: "Excuse me, when is Yom Kippur (the Day of Atonement)?" "Oho!" said the Jew, and put his feet up on the seat again before answering.'

It cannot be denied that this representation by something small is related to the 'tendency to economy' which we were left with as the last common element after our investigation of verbal technique [p. 77 ff.].

Here is a very similar example:

'The doctor, who had been asked to look after the Baroness at her confinement, pronounced that the moment had not come, and suggested to the Baron that in the meantime they should have a game of cards in the next room. After a while a cry of pain from the Baroness struck the ears of the two men:

1. [Displacement **on** to something very small was later recognized by Freud as a characteristic mechanism in obsessional neurosis. See the 'Rat Man' case history (1909*d*), Section II (C).]

"Ah, mon Dieu, que je souffre!" Her husband sprang up, but the doctor signed to him to sit down: "It's nothing. Let's go on with the game!" A little later there were again sounds from the pregnant woman: "Mein Gott, mein Gott, what terrible pains!" – "Aren't you going in, Professor?" asked the Baron. – "No, no. It's not time yet." – At last there came from next door an unmistakable cry of "Aa-ee, aa-ee, aa-ee!" The doctor threw down his cards and exclaimed: "*Now* it's time."'

This successful joke demonstrates two things from the ex-ample of the way in which the cries of pain uttered by an aristo-cratic lady in child-birth changed their character little by little. It shows how pain causes primitive nature to break through all the layers of education, and how an important decision can be properly made to depend on an apparently trivial pheno-menon.

[12]

There is another kind of indirect representation used by jokes, namely the 'analogy'. We have kept it back so long because the consideration of it comes up against new difficulties, or makes particularly evident difficulties that we have already come up against in other connections. We have already admitted that in some of the examples we have examined we have not been able to banish a doubt as to whether they ought to be regarded as jokes at all [e.g. pp. 86 and 98]; and in this uncertainty we have recognized that the foundations of our inquiry have been seriously shaken. But I am aware of this uncertainty in no other material more strongly or more frequently than in jokes of analogy. There is a feeling – and this is probably true of a large number of other people under the same conditions – which tells me 'this is a joke, I can pronounce this to be a joke' even before the hidden essential nature of jokes has been discovered. This feeling leaves me in the lurch most often in the case of joking analogies. If to begin with I unhesitatingly pronounce an analogy to be a joke, a moment later I seem to notice that the enjoyment it gives me is of a quality different from what I am accustomed to derive from a joke. And the circumstance that joking analogies are very seldom able to provoke the explosive laugh which signalizes a good joke makes it impossible for me to resolve the doubt in my usual way – by limiting myself to the best and most effective examples of a species.

It is easy to demonstrate that there are remarkably fine and effective examples of analogies that do not in the least strike us as being jokes. The fine analogy between the tenderness in Ottilie's diary and the scarlet thread of the English navy (p. 55n.) is one such. And I cannot refrain from quoting in the same sense another one, which I am never tired of admiring and the effect of which I have not grown out of. It is the analogy with which Ferdinand Lassalle ended one of his celebrated speeches for the defence ('Science and the Workers'): 'Upon a man such as I have shown you this one to be, who has devoted his life to the watchword "Science and the Workers", being convicted, if it were his lot, would make no more impression than would the bursting of a retort upon a chemist deep in his scientific experiments. As soon as the interruption is past, with a slight frown over the rebelliousness of his material, he will quietly pursue his researches and his labours.'

A rich selection of apt and joking analogies are to be found among Lichtenberg's writings (the second volume of the Göttingen edition of 1853), and it is from there that I shall take the material for our investigation.

'It is almost impossible to carry the torch of truth through a crowd without singeing someone's beard.'

No doubt that seems to be a joke; but on closer examination we notice that the joking effect does not arise from the analogy itself but from a subsidiary characteristic. 'The torch of truth' is not a new analogy but one that has been common for a very long time and has become reduced to a *cliché* – as always happens when an analogy is lucky and accepted into linguistic usage.

Though we scarcely notice the analogy any longer in the phrase 'the torch of truth', it is suddenly given back its full original force by Lichtenberg, since an addition is now made to the analogy and a consequence is drawn from it. But we are already familiar with a process like this of giving its full meaning to a watered-down expression as a technique of joking. It finds a place in the multiple use of the same material (p. 67 f.). It might quite well be that the joking impression produced by Lichtenberg's remark arises only from its dependence on this joke-technique.

The same judgement may certainly apply as well to another joking analogy by the same author:

'To be sure, the man was not a great light [*Licht*], but a great candlestick [*Leuchter*] ... He was a Professor of Philosophy.'

To describe a man of learning as a great light, a *lumen mundi*, has long ceased to be an effective analogy, whether or not it originally had an effect as a joke. But the analogy is refreshed, it is given back its full force, if a modification is derived from it and a second, new, analogy is thus obtained from it. The way in which this second analogy comes about seems to be what determines the joke, not the two analogies themselves. This would be an instance of the same joke-technique as in the example of the torch.

The following example seems to have the character of a joke for another reason, but one that must be judged similarly:

'Reviews seem to me to be a kind of childish illness to which new-born books are more or less liable. There are examples of the healthiest dying of it; and the weakest often get through it. Some escape it altogether. Attempts have often been made to guard against it by the amulets of preface and dedication, or even to inoculate against it by judgements of one's own. But this does not always help.'

The comparison of reviews to a childish illness is founded in the first instance on the fact of being exposed to them shortly after first seeing the light of day. I cannot venture to decide whether up to this point the comparison has the character of a joke. But it is then carried further: it turns out that the subsequent fate of new books can be represented within the framework of the same analogy or through related analogies. A prolongation like this of an analogy is undoubtedly in the nature of a joke, but we already know what technique it has to thank for this – it is a case of unification, the making of an unsuspected connection. The character of the unification is not altered by the fact that here it consists in making an addition to a previous analogy.

In another group of analogies one is tempted to shift what is undoubtedly an impression that has the character of a joke on to another factor, which once again has in itself nothing to do with the nature of the analogy. These are analogies which contain a striking juxtaposition, often a combination that sounds absurd, or which are replaced by something of the sort as the outcome of the analogy. The majority of the Lichtenberg examples belong to this group.

'It is a pity that one cannot see the learned entrails of authors so as to discover what they have eaten.' The 'learned' entrails is a bewildering and indeed absurd epithet, which is only explained by the analogy. What if the impression of its being a joke were due entirely to the bewildering character of the juxtaposition? If so, it would correspond to a method of joking with which we are quite familiar – 'representation by absurdity' [p. 93 ff.].

Lichtenberg has used the same analogy between the ingestion of reading and instructive matter and the ingestion of physical nourishment for another joke:

'He thought very highly of learning at home, and was therefore entirely in favour of learned stall-feeding.'

Other analogies by the same author exhibit the same absurd, or at least remarkable, assignment of epithets, which, as we now begin to see, are the true vehicles of the joke:

'That is the weather side of my moral constitution; I can stand things there quite well.'

'Everyone has his moral backside,[1] which he does not show except in case of need and which he covers as long as possible with the breeches of respectability.'

'Moral backside' – the assignment of this remarkable epithet is the outcome of an analogy. But in addition, the analogy is continued further with an actual play upon words – 'need' – and a second even more unusual juxtaposition ('the breeches of respectability'), which is perhaps a joke in itself; for the breeches, since they are the breeches of respectability, themselves, as it were, become a joke. We need not be surprised, then, if the whole gives us the impression of being an analogy that is a very good joke. We begin to notice that we are inclined, quite generally, where a characteristic attaches only to a part of a whole, to extend it in our estimation to the whole itself. The 'breeches of respectability', incidentally, recall some similarly bewildering lines of Heine's:

> . . . Bis mir endlich,
> endlich alle Knöpfe rissen
> an der Hose der Geduld.

> [. . . Till at last,
> at last every button bursts
> on my breeches of patience.][2]

There can be no doubt that these last two analogies have a characteristic that we do not find in every good (that is to say, in every apt) analogy. They are to a great degree 'debasing', as we might put it. They juxtapose something of a high category, something abstract (in these instances, 'respectability' and 'patience'), with something of a very concrete and even low kind ('breeches'). We shall have to consider in another connection whether this peculiarity has anything to do with the

1. [In English in the original.]
2. [*Romanzero*, Book III (*Hebräische Melodien*), Jehuda ben Halevy IV.]

joke. Here we will try to analyse another example in which this disparaging characteristic is quite specially plain. Weinberl, the clerk in Nestroy's farce *Einen Jux will er sich machen* [*He wants to have a spree*], pictures to himself how one day, when he is a respectable old business man, he will remember the days of his youth: 'When the ice in front of the warehouse of memory has been hacked up like this in a friendly talk,' he says, 'when the arched doorway of old times has been unlocked again and the showcase of the imagination is fully stocked with goods from the past ...' These are, to be sure, analogies between abstract and very commonplace concrete things; but the joke depends – whether entirely or in part – on the fact that a clerk is making use of analogies taken from the domain of his everyday activities. But the bringing of these abstractions into connection with the ordinary things with which his life is normally filled is an act of *unification*.

Let us return to the Lichtenberg analogies:

'The motives that lead us to do anything might be arranged like the thirty-two winds [= points of the compass] and might be given names in a similar way: for instance, "bread-bread-fame" or "fame-fame-bread".'[1] As is so often the case with Lichtenberg's jokes, the impression of something apt, witty and shrewd is so prominent that our judgement upon the nature of what constitutes the joke is misled by it. If some amount of joke is admixed with the admirable meaning in a remark of this kind, we are probably led into declaring that the whole thing is an excellent joke. I should like, rather, to hazard the statement that everything in it that is really in the nature of a joke arises from our surprise at the strange combination 'bread-bread-fame'. As a joke, therefore, it would be a 'representation by absurdity'.

A strange juxtaposition or the attribution of an absurd epithet can stand by itself as the outcome of an analogy:

1. [Freud returned to this analogy nearly thirty years later in his open letter to Einstein *Why War?* (1933*b*).]

'A *zweischläfrige* woman.' 'An *einschläfriger* church-pew.'[1] (Both by Lichtenberg.) Behind both these there is an analogy with a bed; in both of them, besides the 'bewilderment' the technical factor of 'allusion' is in operation – an allusion in one case to the sleepy effects of sermons and in the other to the inexhaustible topic of sexual relations.

So far we have found that whenever an analogy strikes us as being in the nature of a joke it owes this impression to the admixture of one of the joke-techniques that are familiar to us. But a few other examples seem at last to provide evidence that an analogy can in itself be a joke.

This is how Lichtenberg describes certain odes:

'They are in poetry what Jakob Böhme's[2] immortal works are in prose – a kind of picnic, in which the author provides the words and the reader the sense.'

'When he philosophizes, he throws as a rule an agreeable moonlight over things, which pleases in general but shows no single thing clearly.'

Or here is Heine:

'Her face resembled a palimpsest, on which, beneath the fresh black monastic manuscript of the text of a Church Father, there lurk the half-obliterated lines of an ancient Greek love-poem.' [*Harzreise*.]

Or let us take the lengthy analogy, with a highly degrading[3] purpose, in the 'Bäder von Lucca' [*Reisebilder* III]:

'A catholic cleric behaves rather like a clerk with a post in a large business house. The Church, the big firm, of which the Pope is head, gives him a fixed job and, in return, a fixed salary. He works lazily, as everyone does who is not working for his own profit, who has numerous colleagues and can easily

1. [These two German words – meaning literally 'that can sleep two' and 'that can sleep one' – are ordinarily applied to beds, i.e. 'double' and 'single'. *Einschläfrig*, however, can also mean 'soporific'.]

2. [Jakob Böhme (1575–1624), the German protestant mystic.]

3. [See below, p. 261*n*.]

escape notice in the bustle of a large concern. All he has at heart is the credit of the house and still more its maintenance, since if it should go bankrupt he would lose his livelihood. A protestant cleric, on the other hand, is in every case his own principal and carries on the business of religion for his own profit. He does not, like his catholic fellow-traders, carry on a wholesale business but only retail. And since he must himself manage it alone, he cannot be lazy. He must advertise his articles of faith, he must depreciate his competitors' articles, and, genuine retailer that he is, he stands in his retail shop, full of business envy of all the great houses, and particularly of the great house in Rome, which pays the wages of so many thousands of book-keepers and packers and has its factories in all four quarters of the globe.'

In the face of this and many other examples, we can no longer dispute the fact that an analogy can in itself possess the characteristic of being a joke, without this impression being accounted for by a complication with one of the familiar joke-techniques. But, that being so, we are completely at a loss to see what it is that determines the joking characteristic of analogies, since that characteristic certainly does not reside in analogy as a form of expression of thought or in the operation of making a comparison. All we can do is to include analogy among the species of 'indirect representation' used by the joke-technique and we must leave unresolved the problem which we have met with much more clearly in the case of analogies than in the methods of joking that we came across earlier. No doubt, moreover, there must be some special reason why the decision whether something is a joke or not offers greater difficulties in analogies than in other forms of expression.

This gap in our understanding gives us no grounds, however, for complaining that this first investigation has been without results. In view of the intimate connection which we must be prepared to attribute to the different characteristics of jokes, it would be imprudent to expect that we could completely explain one side of the problem before we have so much as cast a glance at the others. We shall no doubt have now to attack the problem from another direction.

Can we feel sure that none of the possible techniques of jokes has escaped our investigation? Of course not. But a continued examination of fresh material can convince us that we have got to know the commonest and most important technical methods of the joke-work – at all events as much as is required for forming a judgement on the nature of that psychical process. So far we have not arrived at any such judgement; but on the other hand we are now in possession of an important indication of the direction from which we may expect to receive further light upon the problem. The interesting processes of condensation accompanied by the formation of a substitute, which we have recognized as the core of the technique of verbal jokes, point towards the formation of dreams, in the mechanism of which the same psychical processes have been discovered. This is equally true, however, of the techniques of conceptual jokes – displacement, faulty reasoning, absurdity, indirect representation, representation by the opposite – which reappear one and all in the technique of the dream-work. Displacement is responsible for the puzzling appearance of dreams, which prevents our recognizing that they are a continuation of our waking life. The use of absurdity and nonsense in dreams has cost them the dignity of being regarded as psychical products and has led the authorities to suppose that a disintegration of the mental activities and a cessation of criticism, morality and logic are necessary conditions of the formation of dreams. Representation by the opposite is so common in dreams that even the popular books of dream-interpretation, which are on a completely wrong tack, are in the habit of taking it into account. Indirect representation – the replacement of a dream-thought by an allusion, by something small, a symbolism akin to analogy – is precisely what distinguishes the mode of expression of dreams from that of our waking life.[1] So far-reaching an agreement between the methods of the joke-work and those of the dream-work can scarcely be a matter of chance. To demonstrate this agreement in detail and to examine its basis will be one of our later tasks. [See Chapter VI below.]

1. Cf. Chapter VI ('The Dream-Work') of my *Interpretation of Dreams* (1900a).

III

THE PURPOSES OF JOKES

[1]

WHEN at the end of my last chapter I wrote down Heine's comparison of a catholic priest to an employee in a wholesale business and of a protestant one to a retail merchant, I was aware of an inhibition which was trying to induce me not to make use of the analogy. I told myself that among my readers there would probably be a few who felt respect not only for religion but for its governors and assistants. Such readers would merely be indignant about the analogy and would get into an emotional state which would deprive them of all interest in deciding whether the analogy had the appearance of being a joke on its own account or as a result of something extra added to it. With other analogies – for instance, the neighbouring one of the agreeable moonlight which a particular philosophy throws over things – there seemed to be no need for worry about the disturbing effect they might have on a section of my readers. The most pious man would remain in a state of mind in which he could form a judgement on our problem.

It is easy to divine the characteristic of jokes on which the difference in their hearers' reaction to them depends. In the one case the joke is an end in itself and serves no particular aim, in the other case it does serve such an aim – it becomes *tendentious*. Only jokes that have a purpose[1] run the risk of meeting with people who do not want to listen to them.

1. [The German substantive '*Tendenz*' is throughout this book translated 'purpose' (cf. 'a play with a purpose'). The German adjective derived from it, however, (*tendenziös*) has become a naturalized English word and is accordingly translated here 'tendentious'.]

Non-tendentious jokes were described by Vischer as 'abstract' jokes. I prefer to call them 'innocent' jokes.

Since we have already divided jokes into 'verbal' and 'conceptual' jokes according to the material handled by their technique, it devolves on us now to examine the relation between that classification and the new one that we are introducing. The relation between verbal and conceptual jokes on the one hand and abstract and tendentious jokes on the other is not one of mutual influence; they are two wholly independent classifications of joking products. Some people may perhaps have gained an impression that innocent jokes are predominantly verbal jokes, but that the more complex technique of conceptual jokes is mostly employed for definite purposes. But there are innocent jokes that work with play upon words and similarity of sound, and equally innocent ones that employ all the methods of conceptual jokes. And it is just as easy to show that a tendentious joke need be nothing other than a verbal joke as regards its technique. For instance, jokes that 'play about' with proper names often have an insulting and wounding purpose, though, needless to say, they are verbal jokes. But the most innocent of all jokes are once more verbal jokes; for instance, the *Schüttelreime*,[1] which have recently become so popular and in which the multiple use of the same material with a modification entirely peculiar to it constitutes the technique:

> Und weil er Geld in *M*enge *h*atte
> lag stets er in der *H*änge*m*atte

> [And because he had money in quantities
> He always lay in a hammock.]

It may be hoped that no one will question that the enjoyment derived from these otherwise unpretentious rhymes is the same as that by which we recognize jokes.

1. [Literally, 'shaking-up rhymes'. It will be seen that these are a rhyming form of what we know as 'Spoonerisms'.]

Good examples of abstract or innocent conceptual jokes are to be found in plenty among the Lichtenberg analogies, with some of which we have already become acquainted. I add a few more:

'They had sent a small octavo volume to Göttingen, and had got back something that was a quarto in body and soul.'

'In order to erect this building properly, it is above all necessary that good foundations shall be laid; and I know of none firmer than if, upon every course of masonry *pro*, one promptly lays a course *contra*.'

'One person procreates a thought, a second carries it to be baptized, a third begets children by it, a fourth visits it on its deathbed and a fifth buries it.' (Analogy with unification.)

'Not only did he disbelieve in ghosts; he was not even frightened of them.' Here the joke lies entirely in the nonsensical form of representation, which puts what is commonly thought less of into the comparative and uses the positive for what is regarded as more important. If this joking envelope is removed, we have: 'it is much easier to get rid of a fear of ghosts intellectually than to escape it when the occasion arises'. This is no longer in the least a joke, though it is a correct and still too little appreciated psychological discovery – the same one which Lessing expressed in a well-known sentence:

'Not all are free who mock their chains.'[1]

I may take the opportunity that this affords of getting rid of what is nevertheless a possible misunderstanding. For 'innocent' or 'abstract' jokes are far from having the same meaning as jokes that are 'trivial' or 'lacking in substance'; they merely connote the opposite of the 'tendentious' jokes that will be discussed presently. As our last example shows, an innocent – that is, a non-tendentious – joke may also be of great substance, it may assert something of value. But the substance of a joke is independent of the joke and is the substance of the thought,

1. [*Nathan der Weise*, Act IV, Scene 4.]

which is here, by means of a special arrangement, expressed as a joke. No doubt, just as watch-makers usually provide a particularly good movement with a similarly valuable case, so it may happen with jokes that the best achievements in the way of jokes are used as an envelope for thoughts of the greatest substance.

If now we draw a sharp distinction in the case of conceptual jokes between the substance of the thought and the joking envelope, we shall reach a discovery which may throw light on much of our uncertainty in judging jokes. For it turns out – and this is a surprising thing – that our enjoyment of a joke is based on a combined impression of its substance and of its effectiveness as a joke and that we let ourselves be deceived by the one factor over the amount of the other. Only after the joke has been reduced do we become aware of this false judgement.

Moreover, the same thing is true of verbal jokes. When we are told that 'experience consists in experiencing what one does not wish to experience' [p. 105], we are bewildered and think we have learnt a new truth. It is a little time before we recognize under this disguise the platitude of 'Injury makes one wise'. [Adversity is the best teacher.] (Fischer [1889, 59].) The apt way in which the joke succeeds in defining 'experience' almost purely by the use of the word 'to experience' deceives us into overvaluing the substance of the sentence. Just the same thing is true of Lichtenberg's 'January' joke of unification (p. 104), which has nothing more to tell us than something we have already long known – that New Year's wishes come true as seldom as other wishes. So too in many similar cases.

And we find just the contrary with other jokes, in which the aptness and truth of the thought tricks us into calling the whole sentence a brilliant joke – whereas only the thought is brilliant and the joke's achievement is often feeble. Precisely in Lichtenberg's jokes the kernel of thought is frequently far more valuable than the joking envelope to which we unjustifiably extend our appreciation. Thus, for instance, the remark about the 'torch of truth' (p. 123) is an analogy that scarcely amounts to a joke, but it is so apt that we are inclined to insist that the sentence is a particularly good joke.

Lichtenberg's jokes are outstanding above all on account of their intellectual content and the certainty with which they hit their mark. Goethe was quite right in saying of that author that in fact his joking and jesting ideas concealed problems; it would have been even more correct to say that they touch on the solution of problems. When, for instance, he remarked as a joke: 'He had read Homer so much that he always read "*Agamemnon*" instead of "*angenommen* [supposed]"' – the technique used is 'stupidity' plus 'similarity of sound' – Lichtenberg had discovered nothing less than the secret of misreading.[1]

Similarly with a joke the technique of which struck us as most unsatisfactory (p. 97): 'He wondered how it is that cats have two holes cut in their skin precisely at the place where their eyes are.' The stupidity that is paraded here is only apparent. In fact, behind this simple remark lies the great problem of teleology in the structure of animals. It was by no means so completely a matter of course that the palpebral fissure should open at the point at which the cornea is exposed, until the theory of evolution had thrown light on the coincidence.

We shall bear in mind the fact that we receive from joking remarks a total impression in which we are unable to separate the share taken by the thought content from the share taken by the joke-work. It may be that later on we shall find a still more significant parallel to this. [Cf. p. 186.]

1. See my *Psychopathology of Everyday Life* (1901*b*) [Chapter X, *P.F.L.*, 5, 277. See also Chapter VI (A), Example 8 (added in 1910), ibid., 160. The joke is also discussed at the end of the second of Freud's *Introductory Lectures* (1916–17), *P.F.L.*, 1, 65.]

[2]

From the point of view of throwing theoretical light on the nature of jokes, innocent jokes are bound to be of more value to us than tendentious ones, and trivial jokes of more value than profound ones. Innocent and trivial jokes are likely to put the problem of jokes before us in its purest form, since with them we avoid the danger of being confused by their purpose or having our judgement misled by their good sense. On the basis of such material our discoveries can make fresh advances.

I will select the most innocent possible example of a verbal joke:

'A girl to whom a visitor was announced while she was at her toilet complained: "Oh, what a shame that one mayn't let oneself be seen just when one's at one's most *anziehend*" '1 (Kleinpaul, 1890).

Since, however, doubts arise in me after all as to whether I have a right to describe this joke as being non-tendentious, I will replace it by another one which is extremely simple and should really not be open to that objection.

At the end of a meal in a house to which I had been invited as a guest, a pudding of the kind known as a '*Roulard*'2 was served. It requires some skill on the part of the cook to make it; so one of the guests asked: 'Made in the house?' To which the host replied: 'Yes, indeed. A home-*roulard*.'3

This time we will not examine the technique of the joke; we propose to turn our attention to another factor, which is actually the most important one. When those of us present heard this improvised joke it gave us pleasure – which I can clearly recall – and made us laugh. In this instance, as in countless others, the hearers' feeling of pleasure cannot have arisen from the purpose of the joke or from its intellectual content; there is nothing left

1. ['*Anziehend*' means both 'dressing' and 'attractive'.]
2. [This should perhaps be spelt '*Roulade*'.]
3. [In the original the words 'Home Rule' are added in English.]

open to us but to bring that feeling of pleasure into connection with the technique of the joke. The technical methods of joking which we have earlier described – condensation, displacement, indirect representation and so on – thus possess the power of evoking a feeling of pleasure in the hearer, though we cannot in the least see how they may have acquired this power. In this simple way we arrive at the second thesis in our clarification of jokes; the first (p. 49) asserted that the characteristic of jokes lay in their form of expression. Let us further reflect that this second thesis has in fact taught us nothing new. It merely isolates what was already included in an observation we had made earlier. It will be recalled that when we had succeeded in reducing a joke (that is, in replacing its form of expression by another one, while carefully preserving its sense) it had lost not only its character as a joke but also its power to make us laugh – our enjoyment of the joke.

We cannot proceed further at this point without a discussion with our philosophical authorities.

The philosophers, who count jokes a part of the comic and who treat of the comic itself under the heading of aesthetics, define an aesthetic idea by the condition that in it we are not trying to get anything from things or do anything with them, that we are not needing things in order to satisfy one of our major vital needs, but that we are content with contemplating them and with the enjoyment of the idea. 'This enjoyment, this kind of ideation, is the purely aesthetic one, which lies only in itself, which has its aim only in itself and which fulfils none of the other aims of life' (Fischer, 1889, 20). [Cf. p. 40 f., above.]

We shall scarcely be contradicting this statement of Fischer's – we shall perhaps be doing no more than translating his thoughts into our mode of expression – if we insist that the joking activity should not, after all, be described as pointless or aimless, since it has the unmistakable aim of evoking pleasure in its hearers. I doubt if we are in a position to undertake *anything* without having an intention in view. If we do not require our mental apparatus at the moment for supplying one of our indispensable satisfactions, we allow it itself to work in the direction of pleasure and we seek to derive pleasure from its own activity. I suspect that this is in general the condition that governs all aesthetic ideation, but I understand too little of aesthetics to try to enlarge on this statement. As regards joking, however, I can assert, on the basis of the two discoveries we have already made, that it is an activity which aims at deriving pleasure from mental processes, whether intellectual or otherwise. No doubt there are other activities which have the same aim. They are perhaps differentiated according to the fields of mental activity from which they seek to derive pleasure or perhaps according to the methods of which they make use. We cannot for the moment decide about this; but we hold firmly to the view that the joke-technique and the tendency towards economy by which it is partly governed (p. 77 ff.) have been brought into connection with the production of pleasure.

But before we set about solving the riddle of how the technical methods of the joke-work are able to excite pleasure in the hearer, we have to recall the fact that, with a view to simplification and greater perspicuity, we have left tendentious jokes entirely on one side. We must, after all, try to throw light on the question of what the purposes of jokes are, and how they serve those purposes.

There is, first and foremost, one observation which warns us not to leave tendentious jokes on one side in our investigation of the origin of the pleasure we take in jokes. The pleasurable effect of innocent jokes is as a rule a moderate one; a clear sense of satisfaction, a slight smile, is as a rule all it can achieve in its hearer. And it may be that a part even of this effect is to be attributed to the joke's intellectual content, as we have seen from suitable examples (p. 136). A non-tendentious joke scarcely ever achieves the sudden burst of laughter which makes tendentious ones so irresistible.[1] Since the technique of both can be

1. [So in the German.]

the same, a suspicion may be aroused in us that tendentious jokes, by virtue of their purpose, must have sources of pleasure at their disposal to which innocent jokes have no access.

The purposes of jokes can easily be reviewed. Where a joke is not an aim in itself – that is, where it is not an innocent one – there are only two purposes that it may serve, and these two can themselves be subsumed under a single heading. It is either a *hostile* joke (serving the purpose of aggressiveness, satire, or defence) or an *obscene* joke (serving the purpose of exposure). It must be repeated in advance that the technical species of the joke – whether it is a verbal or a conceptual joke – bears no relation to these two purposes.

It is a much lengthier business to show the way in which jokes serve these two purposes. In this investigation I should prefer to deal first not with the hostile jokes but with the exposing jokes. It is true that these have been far more rarely deemed worthy of investigation, as though aversion to the thing itself had here been transferred to the discussion of it. But we will not allow ourselves to be disconcerted by this, for we shall immediately come upon a marginal case of joking which promises to bring us enlightenment on more than one obscurity.

We know what is meant by 'smut': the intentional bringing into prominence of sexual facts and relations by speech. This definition, however, is no more valid than other definitions. In spite of this definition, a lecture on the anatomy of the sexual organs or the physiology of procreation need not have a single point of contact with smut. It is a further relevant fact that smut is directed to a particular person, by whom one is sexually excited and who, on hearing it, is expected to become aware of the speaker's excitement and as a result to become sexually excited in turn. Instead of this excitement the other person may be led to feel shame or embarrassment, which is only a reaction against the excitement and, in a roundabout way, is an admission of it. Smut is thus originally directed towards women and may be equated with attempts at seduction. If a man in a company of men enjoys telling or listening to smut, the original situation, which owing to social inhibitions cannot be realized, is at the same time imagined. A person who laughs at smut that he hears is laughing as though he were the spectator of an act of sexual aggression.

The sexual material which forms the content of smut includes more than what is *peculiar* to each sex; it also includes what is *common* to both sexes and to which the feeling of shame extends – that is to say, what is excremental in the most comprehensive sense. This is, however, the sense covered by sexuality in childhood, an age at which there is, as it were, a cloaca within which what is sexual and what is excremental are barely or not at all distinguished.[1] Throughout the whole range of the psychology of the neuroses, what is sexual includes what is excremental, and is understood in the old, infantile, sense.

Smut is like an exposure of the sexually different person to whom it is directed. By the utterance of the obscene words it compels the person who is assailed to imagine the part of the body or the procedure in question and shows her that the assailant is himself imagining it. It cannot be doubted that the desire to see what is sexual exposed is the original motive of smut.

It can only help to clarify things if at this point we go back to fundamental facts. A desire to see the organs peculiar to each sex exposed is one of the original components of our libido. It may itself be a substitute for something earlier and go back to a hypothetical primary desire to touch the sexual parts. As so often, looking has replaced touching.[2] The libido for looking and touching is present in everyone in two forms, active and passive, male and female; and, according to the pre-

---

1. See my *Three Essays on the Theory of Sexuality* (1905d), which is appearing at the same time as the present work.

2. Cf. Moll's instinct of 'contrectation' (Moll, 1898). [Moll, who introduced the term, described the 'instinct of contrectation' as the impulse to come into contact with another person.]

ponderance of the sexual character, one form or the other predominates. It is easy to observe the inclination to self-exposure in young children. In cases in which the germ of this inclination escapes its usual fate of being buried and suppressed, it develops in men into the familiar perversion known as exhibitionism. In women the inclination to passive exhibitionism is almost invariably buried under the imposing reactive function of sexual modesty, but not without a loophole being left for it in relation to clothes. I need only hint at the elasticity and variability in the amount of exhibitionism that women are permitted to retain in accordance with differing convention and circumstances.

In men a high degree of this trend persists as a portion of their libido, and it serves to introduce the sexual act. When this urge makes itself felt at the first approach to a woman, it must make use of words, for two reasons; firstly, to announce itself to her, and secondly, because if the idea is aroused by speech it may induce a corresponding excitement in the woman herself and may awaken an inclination in her to passive exhibitionism. A wooing speech like this is not yet smut, but it passes over into it. If the woman's readiness emerges quickly the obscene speech has a short life; it yields at once to a sexual action. It is otherwise if quick readiness on the woman's part is not to be counted on, and if in place of it defensive reactions appear. In that case the sexually exciting speech becomes an aim in itself in the shape of smut. Since the sexual aggressiveness is held up in its advance towards the act, it pauses at the evocation of the excitement and derives pleasure from the signs of it in the woman. In so doing, the aggressiveness is no doubt altering its character as well, just as any libidinal impulse will if it is met by an obstacle. It becomes positively hostile and cruel, and it thus summons to its help against the obstacle the sadistic components of the sexual instinct.

The woman's inflexibility is therefore the first condition for the development of smut, although, to be sure, it seems merely to imply a postponement and does not indicate that further efforts will be in vain. The ideal case of a resistance of this kind on the woman's part occurs if another man is present at the same time – a third person – for in that case an immediate surrender by the woman is as good as out of the question. This third person soon acquires the greatest importance in the development of the smut; to begin with, however, the presence of the woman is not to be overlooked. Among country people or in inns of the humbler sort it will be noticed that it is not until the entrance of the barmaid or the innkeeper's wife that smuttiness starts up. Only at higher social levels is the opposite found, and the presence of a woman brings the smut to an end. The men save up this kind of entertainment, which originally presupposed the presence of a woman who was feeling ashamed, till they are 'alone together'. So that gradually, in place of the woman, the onlooker, now the listener, becomes the person to whom the smut is addressed, and owing to this transformation it is already near to assuming the character of a joke.

From this point onwards our attention will be drawn to two factors: the part played by the third person, the listener, and the conditions governing the subject-matter of the smut itself.

Generally speaking, a tendentious joke calls for three people: in addition to the one who makes the joke, there must be a second who is taken as the object of the hostile or sexual aggressiveness, and a third in whom the joke's aim of producing pleasure is fulfilled. We shall have later to examine the deeper reasons for this state of things; for the moment let us keep to the fact to which this testifies – namely that it is not the person who makes the joke who laughs at it and who therefore enjoys its pleasurable effect, but the inactive listener. In the case of smut the three people are in the same relation. The course of events may be thus described. When the first person finds his libidinal impulse inhibited by the woman, he develops a hostile trend against that second person and calls on the originally interfering third person as his ally. Through the first person's smutty speech the woman is exposed before the third, who, as listener, has not been bribed by the effortless satisfaction of his own libido.

It is remarkable how universally popular a smutty interchange of this kind is among the common people and how it unfailingly produces a cheerful mood. But it also deserves to be noticed that in this complicated procedure, which involves so many of the characteristics of tendentious jokes, none of the formal requirements which characterize jokes are made of the smut itself. The uttering of an undisguised indecency gives the first person enjoyment and makes the third person laugh.

Only when we rise to a society of a more refined education do the formal conditions for jokes play a part. The smut becomes a joke and is only tolerated when it has the character of a joke. The technical method which it usually employs is the allusion – that is, replacement by something small, something remotely connected, which the hearer reconstructs in his imagination into a complete and straightforward obscenity. The greater the discrepancy between what is given directly in the form of smut and what it necessarily calls up in the hearer, the more refined becomes the joke and the higher, too, it may venture to climb into good society. As can easily be shown from examples, smut which has the characteristics of a joke has at its disposal, apart from allusion, whether coarse or refined, all the other methods of verbal and conceptual jokes.

And here at last we can understand what it is that jokes achieve in the service of their purpose. They make possible the satisfaction of an instinct (whether lustful or hostile) in the face of an obstacle that stands in its way. They circumvent this obstacle and in that way draw pleasure from a source which the obstacle had made inaccessible. The obstacle standing in the way is in reality nothing other than women's incapacity to tolerate undisguised sexuality, an incapacity correspondingly increased with a rise in the educational and social level. The woman who is thought of as having been present in the initial situation is afterwards retained as though she were still present, or in her absence her influence still has an intimidating effect on the men. We can observe how men of a higher class are at once induced, when they are in the company of girls of an inferior class, to reduce their smutty jokes to the level of simple smut.

The power which makes it difficult or impossible for women, and to a lesser degree for men as well, to enjoy undisguised obscenity is termed by us 'repression'; and we recognize in it the same psychical process which, in cases of serious illness, keeps whole complexes of impulses, together with their derivatives, away from consciousness, and which has turned out to be the main factor in the causation of what are known as psychoneuroses. It is our belief that civilization and higher education have a large influence in the development of repression, and we suppose that, under such conditions, the psychical organization undergoes an alteration (that can also emerge as an inherited disposition) as a result of which what was formerly felt as agreeable now seems unacceptable and is rejected with all possible psychical force. The repressive activity of civilization brings it about that primary possibilities of enjoyment, which have now, however, been repudiated by the censorship in us, are lost to us. But to the human psyche all renunciation is exceedingly difficult, and so we find that tendentious jokes provide a means of undoing the renunciation and retrieving what was lost. When we laugh at a refined obscene joke, we are laughing at the same thing that makes a peasant laugh at a coarse piece of smut. In both cases the pleasure springs from the same source. We, however, could never bring ourselves to laugh at the coarse smut; we should feel ashamed or it would seem to us disgusting. We can only laugh when a joke has come to our help.

Thus what we suspected to begin with [p. 139] seems to be confirmed: namely that tendentious jokes have sources of pleasure at their disposal besides those open to innocent jokes, in which all the pleasure is in some way linked to their technique. And we may also once more repeat that with tendentious jokes we are not in a position to distinguish by our feeling what part of the pleasure arises from the sources of their technique and what part from those of their purpose. Thus, strictly speaking, we do not know what we are laughing at. With all obscene jokes we are subject to glaring errors of judgement about the 'goodness' of jokes so far as this depends on formal determinants; the technique of such jokes is often quite wretched, but they have immense success in provoking laughter.

[3]

We will now examine the question of whether jokes play the same part in the service of a *hostile* purpose.

Here, from the outset, we come upon the same situation. Since our individual childhood, and, similarly, since the childhood of human civilization, hostile impulses against our fellow men have been subject to the same restrictions, the same progressive repression, as our sexual urges. We have not yet got so far as to be able to love our enemies or to offer our left cheek after being struck on the right. Furthermore, all moral rules for the restriction of active hatred give the clearest evidence to this day that they were originally framed for a small society of fellow clansmen. In so far as we are all able to feel that we are members of one people, we allow ourselves to disregard most of these restrictions in relation to a foreign people. Nevertheless, within our own circle we have made some advances in the control of hostile impulses. As Lichtenberg puts it in drastic terms: 'Where we now say "Excuse me!" we used to give a box on the ears.' Brutal hostility, forbidden by law, has been replaced by verbal invective; and a better knowledge of the interlinking of human impulses is more and more robbing us – by its consistent 'tout comprendre c'est tout pardonner' – of the capacity for feeling angry with a fellow man who gets in our way. Though as children we are still endowed with a powerful inherited disposition to hostility, we are later taught by a higher personal civilization that it is an unworthy thing to use abusive language; and even where fighting has in itself remained permissible, the number of things which may not be employed as methods of fighting has extraordinarily increased. Since we have been obliged to renounce the expression of hostility by deeds – held back by the passionless third person, in whose interest it is that personal security shall be preserved – we have, just as in the case of sexual aggressiveness, developed a new technique of invective, which aims at enlisting this third person against our enemy. By making our enemy small, inferior, despicable or comic, we achieve in a roundabout way the enjoyment of overcoming him – to which the third person, who has made no efforts, bears witness by his laughter.

We are now prepared to realize the part played by jokes in hostile aggressiveness. A joke will allow us to exploit something ridiculous in our enemy which we could not, on account of obstacles in the way, bring forward openly or consciously; once again, then, the joke *will evade restrictions and open sources of pleasure that have become inaccessible*. It will further bribe the hearer with its yield of pleasure into taking sides with us without any very close investigation, just as on other occasions we ourselves have often been bribed by an innocent joke into overestimating the substance of a statement expressed jokingly. This is brought out with perfect aptitude in the common phrase '*die Lacher auf seine Seite ziehen* [to bring the laughers over to our side]'.

Let us, for instance, consider Herr N.'s jokes, which were scattered over the last chapter. They are all of them pieces of invective. It is as though Herr N. wanted to exclaim aloud: 'The Minister for Agriculture is himself an ox! [p. 59.]' 'Don't talk to me about * * *! He's bursting with vanity! [P. 57.]' 'I've never in my life read anything more boring than this historian's essays on Napoleon in Austria! [P. 54.]' But the high position he occupies makes it impossible for him to give out his judgements in that form. And so they make use of a joke to help them, and this guarantees them a reception with the hearer which they would never have found in a non-joking form, in spite of the truth they might contain. One of these jokes is particularly instructive – the one about the 'red *Fadian*' [p. 54], perhaps the most impressive of all of them. What is there about it that makes us laugh and diverts our interest so completely from the question of whether or not an injustice has been done to the poor author? The joking form, of course – that is to say, the joke; but what is there about it that we are laughing at? No doubt at the person himself, who is introduced to us as the 'red *Fadian*', and in particular at his having red hair. Educated people have broken themselves of the habit of laughing at physical defects, and moreover they do not include having red hair among the laughable physical failings. But there is no doubt that it is so regarded by schoolboys and the common people – and this is still true even at the level of education of certain municipal and parliamentary representatives. And now Herr N. has made it possible in the most ingenious manner for us, grown-up and sensitive people, to laugh like the schoolboys at the historian X's red hair. This was certainly not Herr N.'s intention; but it is most doubtful whether a person who gives free play to a joke must necessarily know its precise intention.

If in these cases the obstacle to the aggressiveness which the joke helped to evade was an internal one – an aesthetic objection to the invective – elsewhere it can be of a purely external sort. This was so in the case in which Serenissimus asked a stranger by whose similarity to his own person he had been struck: 'Was your mother in the Palace at one time?' and the repartee was: 'No, but my father was' [p. 107]. The person to whom the question was put would no doubt have liked to knock down the impertinent individual who dared by such an allusion to cast a slur on his beloved mother's memory. But the impertinent individual was Serenissimus, whom one may not knock down or even insult unless one is prepared to purchase that revenge at the price of one's whole existence. The insult must therefore, it would seem, be swallowed in silence. But fortunately a joke shows the way in which the insult may be safely avenged – by making use of the technical method of unification in order to take up the allusion and turn it back against the aggressor. Here the impression of a joke is so much determined by its purpose that, in face of the joking character of the rejoinder, we are inclined to forget that the question asked by the aggressor had itself the character of a joke with the technique of allusion.

The prevention of invective or of insulting rejoinders by external circumstances is such a common case that tendentious jokes are especially favoured in order to make aggressiveness or criticism possible against persons in exalted positions who claim to exercise authority. The joke then represents a rebellion against that authority, a liberation from its pressure. The charm of caricatures lies in this simple factor: we laugh at them even if they are unsuccessful simply because we count rebellion against authority as a merit.

If we bear in mind the fact that tendentious jokes are so highly suitable for attacks on the great, the dignified and the mighty, who are protected by internal inhibitions and external circumstances from direct disparagement, we shall be obliged to take a special view of certain groups of jokes which seem to be concerned with inferior and powerless people. I am thinking of the anecdotes about marriage-brokers, some of which we became acquainted with in the course of our investigation of the various techniques of conceptual jokes. In a few of them, for instance in the examples 'She's deaf as well' [p. 103] and 'Who would lend these people anything?' [loc. cit.], the broker is laughed at for his improvidence and thoughtlessness and he becomes comic because the truth escapes him as it were automatically. But does what we have learnt of the nature of tendentious jokes on the one hand and on the other hand our great enjoyment of these stories fit in with the paltriness of the people whom these jokes seem to laugh at? Are they worthy opponents of the jokes? Is it not rather the case that the jokes only put forward the marriage-brokers in order to strike at something more important? Is it not a case of saying one thing and meaning another? It is really not possible to reject this view.

This interpretation of the broker anecdotes may be carried further. It is true that there is no *necessity* for my entering into them, that I can content myself with regarding these anecdotes as '*Schwänke* [funny stories]' and deny that they have the character of a joke. Thus jokes can also have a subjective determinant of this kind. Our attention has now been drawn to that possibility and we shall have to examine it later [Chapter V]. It declares that only what I allow to be a joke *is* a joke. What is a joke to me may be merely a comic story to other people. But if a joke admits of this doubt, the reason can only be that it has a façade – in these instances a comic one – in the contemplation of which one person is satiated while another may try to peer behind it. A suspicion may arise, moreover, that this façade is intended to dazzle the examining eye and that these stories have therefore something to conceal.

In any case, if our marriage-broker anecdotes are jokes, they are all the better jokes because, thanks to their façade, they are in a position to conceal not only what they have to say but also the fact that they have something – forbidden – to say. The continuation of this interpretation – and this uncovers the hidden meaning and reveals these anecdotes with a comic façade as tendentious jokes – would be as follows. Anyone who has allowed the truth to slip out in an unguarded moment is in fact glad to be free of pretence. This is a correct and profound piece of psychological insight. Without this internal agreement no one lets himself be mastered by the automatism which in these cases brings the truth to light.[1] But this converts the laugh-

1. This is the same mechanism that governs slips of the tongue and other phenomena of self-betrayal. See *The Psychopathology of Everyday Life* (1901*b*) [e.g. Chapter V].

able figure of the *Schadchen* into a sympathetic one, deserving of pity. How happy the man must be to be able at last to throw off the burden of pretence, since he makes use of the first chance of shouting out the very last scrap of truth! As soon as he sees that the case is lost, that the bride does not please the young man, he gladly betrays yet another concealed defect which has escaped notice, or he takes the opportunity of producing an argument that settles a detail in order to express his contempt for the people he is working for: 'I ask you – who would lend these people anything?' The whole of the ridicule in the anecdote now falls upon the parents, barely touched on in it, who think this swindle justified in order to get their daughter a husband, upon the pitiable position of girls who let themselves be married on such terms, and upon the disgracefulness of marriage contracted on such a basis. The marriage-broker is the right man to express such criticisms, for he knows most about these abuses; but he must not say them aloud, for he is a poor man whose existence depends on exploiting them. The popular mind, which created these stories, and others like them, is torn by a similar conflict; for it knows that the sacredness of marriages after they have been contracted is grievously affected by the thought of what happened at the time when they were arranged.

Let us recall, too, what we observed while we were investigating the technique of jokes: that in jokes nonsense often replaces ridicule and criticism in the thoughts lying behind the joke [p. 96]. (In this respect, incidentally, the joke-work is doing the same thing as the dream-work.) Here we find the fact confirmed once again. That the ridicule and criticism are not directed against the figure of the broker, who only appears in the examples we have quoted as a whipping-boy, is shown by another class of jokes in which the marriage-broker is represented, on the contrary, as a superior person, whose dialectical powers prove sufficient to meet any difficulty. They are anecdotes with a logical instead of a comic façade – sophisti-

cal conceptual jokes. In one of them (p. 100f.) the broker succeeds in arguing away the bride's defect of being lame. It is at
least a '*fait accompli*'; another wife, with straight limbs, would
on the contrary be in constant danger of falling down and
breaking her leg, and this would be followed by illness, pains,
and the expenses of treatment, all of which would be spared in
the case of the woman who is lame already. Or there is another
anecdote [p. 99], in which he succeeds in repelling a whole
series of complaints made by the suitor against the bride,
meeting each one with good arguments till he replies to the last,
which cannot be countered: 'What *do* you want? Isn't she to
have a single fault?', as though there were not necessarily something left over from the earlier objections. There is no difficulty
in showing the weak spot in the argument in these two examples, and we did so in examining their technique. But what
interests us now is something different. If the broker's speech is
given such a marked appearance of logic which, on careful
examination, is recognizable as being only an appearance, the
truth behind it is that the joke declares the broker to be in the
right; the thought does not venture to do so seriously but replaces the seriousness by the appearance which the joke presents.
But here, as so often, a jest betrays something serious. We shall
not be mistaken if we assume of all these anecdotes with a
logical façade that they really mean what they assert for reasons
that are intentionally faulty. It is only this employment of
sophistry for the disguised representation of the truth that gives
it the character of a joke, which is thus essentially dependent on
its purpose. For what is hinted at in the two anecdotes is that it is
really the suitor who is making himself ridiculous when he
collects the bride's different advantages together with so much
care, though all of them are weak, and when, in doing so, he
forgets that he must be prepared to take as his wife a human
being with her inevitable defects; while, on the other hand, the
one characteristic that would make marriage with the woman's
more or less imperfect personality tolerable – mutual attraction

and readiness for affectionate adaptation – is quite left out of account in the whole transaction.

The mockery directed at the suitor in these examples, in which the broker quite appropriately plays the part of a superior, is expressed much more plainly in other anecdotes. The plainer these stories are, the less joke-technique do they contain; they are, as it were, only marginal cases of jokes, with the technique of which they no longer have anything in common but the construction of a façade. But owing to their having the same purpose and to its being concealed behind the façade, they produce the complete effect of a joke. Moreover, the poverty of their technical methods explains how it is that many of these jokes cannot, without suffering damage, dispense with the element of dialect, which has an effect similar to the joke technique.

A story of this sort, which, while possessing all the force of a tendentious joke, exhibits nothing of its technique, is the following: 'The marriage-broker asked: "What do you require of your bride?" – Answer: "She must be beautiful, she must be rich, and educated." – "Very good," said the broker, "but I count that as making three matches."' Here the rebuke to the man is delivered openly, and is no longer clothed as a joke.

In the examples we have considered hitherto, the disguised aggressiveness has been directed against *people* – in the broker jokes against everyone involved in the business of arranging a marriage: the bride and bridegroom and their parents. But the object of the joke's attack may equally well be institutions, people in their capacity as vehicles of institutions, dogmas of morality or religion, views of life which enjoy so much respect that objections to them can only be made under the mask of a joke and indeed of a joke concealed by its façade. Though the themes at which these tendentious jokes are aimed may be few, their forms and envelopes are very many and various. I think we shall do well to distinguish this class of tendentious joke by a special name. The appropriate name will emerge after we have interpreted a few examples of the class.

I may recall the two stories – one of the impoverished *gourmet* who was caught eating 'salmon mayonnaise' [p. 85 f.] and the other of the dipsomaniac tutor [p. 88 f.] – which we learnt to know as sophistical displacement jokes. I will now continue their interpretation. We have since heard that if an appearance of logic is tacked on to the façade of a story the thought would like to say seriously 'the man is right', but, owing to an opposing contradiction, does not venture to declare the man right except on a single point, on which it can easily be shown that he is *wrong*. The 'point' chosen is the correct compromise between his rightness and his wrongness; this, indeed, is no decision, but corresponds to the conflict within ourselves. The two anecdotes are simply epicurean. They say: 'Yes. The man is right. There is nothing higher than enjoyment and it is more or less a matter of indifference how one obtains it.' This sounds shockingly immoral and is no doubt not much better. But at bottom it is nothing other than the poet's *'Carpe diem'*,[1] which appeals to the uncertainty of life and the unfruitfulness of virtuous renunciation. If the idea that the man in the 'salmon mayonnaise' joke was right has such a repellent effect on us, this is only because the truth is illustrated by an enjoyment of the lowest kind, which it seems to us we could easily do without. In reality each of us has had hours and times at which he has admitted the rightness of this philosophy of life and has reproached moral doctrine with only understanding how to demand without offering any compensation. Since we have ceased any longer to believe in the promise of a next world in which every renunciation will be rewarded by a satisfaction – there are, incidentally, very few pious people if we take renunciation as the sign of faith – *'Carpe diem'* has become a serious warning. I will gladly put off satisfaction: but do I know whether I shall still be here tomorrow? *'Di doman' non c'è certezza.'*[2]

1. [Horace, *Odes*, I, xi, 8.]
2. Lorenzo de' Medici [(1449–92): 'There is no certainty about tomorrow.' From *Il Trionfo di Bacco e di Arianna*].

I will gladly renounce all the methods of satisfaction proscribed by society, but am I certain that society will reward this renunciation by offering me one of the permitted methods – even after a certain amount of postponement? What these jokes whisper may be said aloud: that the wishes and desires of men have a right to make themselves acceptable alongside of exacting and ruthless morality. And in our days it has been said in forceful and stirring sentences that this morality is only a selfish regulation laid down by the few who are rich and powerful and who can satisfy their wishes at any time without any postponement. So long as the art of healing has not gone further in making our life safe and so long as social arrangements do no more to make it more enjoyable, so long will it be impossible to stifle the voice within us that rebels against the demands of morality. Every honest man will end by making this admission, at least to himself. The decision in this conflict can only be reached by the roundabout path of fresh insight. One must bind one's own life to that of others so closely and be able to identify oneself with others so intimately that the brevity of one's own life can be overcome; and one must not fulfil the demands of one's own needs illegitimately, but must leave them unfulfilled, because only the continuance of so many unfulfilled demands can develop the power to change the order of society. But not every personal need can be postponed in this way and transferred to other people, and there is no general and final solution of the conflict.

We now know the name that must be given to jokes like those that we have last interpreted. They are *cynical* jokes and what they disguise are cynicisms.

Among the institutions which cynical jokes are in the habit of attacking none is more important or more strictly guarded by moral regulations but at the same time more inviting to attack than the institution of marriage, at which, accordingly, the majority of cynical jokes are aimed. There is no more personal claim than that for sexual freedom and at no point has civilization tried to exercise severer suppression than in the sphere of sexuality. A single example will be enough for our purposes – the one mentioned on p. 119, 'An Entry in Prince Carnival's Album':

'A wife is like an umbrella – sooner or later one takes a cab.'

We have already discussed the complicated technique of this example: a bewildering and apparently impossible simile, which however, as we now see, is not in itself a joke; further, an allusion (a cab is a public vehicle); and, as its most powerful technical method, an omission which increases the unintelligibility. The simile may be worked out as follows. One marries in order to protect oneself against the temptations of sensuality, but it turns out nevertheless that marriage does not allow of the satisfaction of needs that are somewhat stronger than usual. In just the same way, one takes an umbrella with one to protect oneself from the rain and nevertheless gets wet in the rain. In both cases one must look around for a stronger protection: in the latter case one must take a public vehicle, and in the former a woman who is accessible in return for money. The joke has now been almost entirely replaced by a piece of cynicism. One does not venture to declare aloud and openly that marriage is not an arrangement calculated to satisfy a man's sexuality, unless one is driven to do so perhaps by the love of truth and eagerness for reform of a Christian von Ehrenfels.[1] The strength of this joke lies in the fact that nevertheless – in all kinds of roundabout ways – it *has* declared it.

A particularly favourable occasion for tendentious jokes is presented when the intended rebellious criticism is directed against the subject himself, or, to put it more cautiously, against someone in whom the subject has a share – a collective person,

---

1. See his essays (1903). [A later work of his was the starting-point of Freud's paper on '"Civilized" Sexual Morality and Modern Nervous Illness' (1908*d*). In that paper Freud himself embarked on some severe criticism of the institution of marriage.]

that is (the subject's own nation, for instance). The occurrence of self-criticism as a determinant may explain how it is that a number of the most apt jokes (of which we have given plenty of instances) have grown up on the soil of Jewish popular life. They are stories created by Jews and directed against Jewish characteristics. The jokes made about Jews by foreigners are for the most part brutal comic stories in which a joke is made unnecessary by the fact that Jews are regarded by foreigners as comic figures. The Jewish jokes which originate from Jews admit this too; but they know their real faults as well as the connection between them and their good qualities, and the share which the subject has in the person found fault with creates the subjective determinant (usually so hard to arrive at) of the joke-work. [Cf. p. 191 ff.] Incidentally, I do not know whether there are many other instances of a people making fun to such a degree of its own character.

As an example of this I may take the anecdote, quoted on p. 121., of a Jew in a railway train promptly abandoning all decent behaviour when he discovered that the newcomer into his compartment was a fellow-believer. We made the acquaintance of this anecdote as evidence of something being demonstrated by a detail, of representation by something very small. It is meant to portray the democratic mode of thinking of Jews, which recognizes no distinction between lords and serfs, but also, alas, upsets discipline and cooperation.

Another, especially interesting group of jokes portrays the relation of poor and rich Jews to one another. Their heroes are the '*Schnorrer* [beggar]' and the charitable householder or the Baron.

'A *Schnorrer*, who was allowed as a guest into the same house every Sunday, appeared one day in the company of an unknown young man who gave signs of being about to sit down to table. "Who is this?" asked the householder. "He's been my son-in-law," was the reply, "since last week. I've promised him his board for the first year."'

The purpose of these stories is always the same; it emerges most clearly in the next one:

'The *Schnorrer* begged the Baron for some money for a journey to Ostend; his doctor had recommended sea-bathing for his troubles. The Baron thought Ostend was a particularly expensive resort; a cheaper one would do equally well. The *Schnorrer*, however, rejected the proposal with the words: "Herr Baron, I consider nothing too expensive for my health."' This is an excellent displacement joke which we might have taken as a model for that class.[1] The Baron evidently wants to save his money, but the *Schnorrer* answers as though the Baron's money was his own, which he may then quite well value less than his health. Here we are expected to laugh at the impertinence of the demand; but it is rarely that these jokes are not equipped with a façade to mislead the understanding. The truth that lies behind is that the *Schnorrer*, who in his thoughts treats the rich man's money as his own, has actually, according to the sacred ordinances of the Jews, almost a right to make this confusion. The indignation raised by this joke is of course directed against a Law which is highly oppressive even to pious people.

Here is another anecdote:

'A *Schnorrer* on his way up a rich man's staircase met a fellow-member of his profession, who advised him to go no further. "Don't go up today," he said, "the Baron is in a bad mood today; he's giving nobody more than one florin." – "I'll go up all the same," said the first *Schnorrer*. "Why should I give him a florin? Does he give *me* anything?"'

This joke employs the technique of absurdity, since it makes the *Schnorrer* assert that the Baron gives him nothing at the very moment at which he is preparing to beg him for a gift.

1. [This joke has in fact already appeared as an example of a displacement joke (see p. 92 f.). Freud may perhaps, as an afterthought, have added it to the earlier chapter and then omitted to make the necessary change in the present passage.]

But the absurdity is only apparent. It is almost true that the rich man gives him nothing, since he is obliged by the Law to give him alms and should, strictly speaking, be grateful to him for giving him an opportunity for beneficence. The ordinary, middle-class view of charity is in conflict here with the religious one; it is in open rebellion against the religious one in the other story, of the Baron who, deeply moved by a *Schnorrer*'s tale of woe, rang for his servants: 'Throw him out! he's breaking my heart!' This open revelation of its purpose constitutes once more a marginal case of a joke. It is only in the fact that they present the matter as applied to individual cases that these last stories differ from a complaint which is no longer a joke: 'There is really no advantage in being a rich man if one is a Jew. Other people's misery makes it impossible to enjoy one's own happiness.'

Other stories, which are once again technically marginal cases of jokes, give evidence of a profoundly pessimistic cynicism. For instance:

'A man who was hard of hearing consulted the doctor, who correctly diagnosed that the patient probably drank too much brandy and was on that account deaf. He advised him against it and the deaf man promised to take his advice to heart. After a while the doctor met him in the street and asked him in a loud voice how he was. "Thank you," was the answer. "You needn't shout so loud, doctor. I've given up drinking and hear quite well again." A little while later they met once more. The doctor asked him how he was in his ordinary voice, but noticed that his question had not been understood. "Eh? What was that?" – "It seems to me you're drinking brandy again," shouted the doctor in his ear, "and that's why you're deaf again." "You may be right," replied the deaf man, "I *have* begun drinking brandy again and I'll tell you why. So long as I didn't drink I was able to hear. But nothing I heard was as good as the brandy."' Technically this joke is nothing other than an object-lesson: dialect or skill in narrative are necessary for raising a laugh, but in the background lies the sad question: may not the man have been right in his choice?

It is on account of the allusion made by these pessimistic stories to the manifold and hopeless miseries of the Jews that I must class them with tendentious jokes.

Other jokes, which are in the same sense cynical and which are not only Jewish anecdotes, attack religious dogmas and even the belief in God. The story of the Rabbi's '*Kück*' [p. 101], the technique of which lay in the faulty thinking which equated phantasy and reality (another possible view was to regard it as a displacement), is a cynical or critical joke of this kind, directed against miracle-workers and certainly against the belief in miracles as well. Heine is said to have made a definitely blasphemous joke on his death-bed. When a friendly priest reminded him of God's mercy and gave him hope that God would forgive him his sins, he is said to have replied: 'Bien sûr qu'il me pardonnera: c'est son métier.'[1] This is a disparaging comparison (technically perhaps only having the value of an allusion), since a '*métier*', a trade or profession, is what a workman or a doctor has – and he has only a single *métier*. But the force of the joke lies in its purpose. What it means to say is nothing else than: 'Of course he'll forgive me. That's what he's there for, and that's the only reason I've taken him on (as one engages one's doctor or one's lawyer).' So in the dying man, as he lay there powerless, a consciousness stirred that he had created God and equipped him with power so as to make use of him when the occasion arose. What was supposed to be the created being revealed itself just before its annihilation as the creator.

[4]

To the classes of tendentious jokes that we have considered so far –

1. ['Of course he'll forgive me: that's his job.']

exposing or obscene jokes,

aggressive (hostile) jokes,

cynical (critical, blasphemous) jokes –

I should like to add another, the fourth and rarest, the nature of which can be illustrated by a good example:

'Two Jews met in a railway carriage at a station in Galicia. "Where are you going?" asked one. "To Cracow," was the answer. "What a liar you are!" broke out the other. "If you say you're going to Cracow, you want me to believe you're going to Lemberg. But I know that in fact you're going to Cracow. So why are you lying to me?"'

This excellent story, which gives an impression of over-subtlety, evidently works by the technique of absurdity. The second Jew is reproached for lying because he says he is going to Cracow, which is in fact his destination! But the powerful technical method of absurdity is here linked with another technique, representation by the opposite, for, according to the uncontradicted assertion of the first Jew, the second is lying when he tells the truth and is telling the truth by means of a lie. But the more serious substance of the joke is the problem of what determines the truth. The joke, once again, is pointing to a problem and is making use of the uncertainty of one of our commonest concepts. Is it the truth if we describe things as they are without troubling to consider how our hearer will understand what we say? Or is this only jesuitical truth, and does not genuine truth consist in taking the hearer into account and giving him a faithful picture of our own knowledge? I think that jokes of this kind are sufficiently different from the rest to be given a special position. What they are attacking is not a person or an institution but the certainty of our knowledge itself, one of our speculative possessions. The appropriate name for them would therefore be 'sceptical' jokes.

[5]

In the course of our discussion of the purposes of jokes we have perhaps thrown light on a number of questions and have certainly come upon plenty of suggestions for further inquiries. But the findings of this chapter combine with those of the last one to present us with a difficult problem. If it is correct to say that the pleasure provided by jokes depends on the one hand on their technique and on the other hand on their purpose, from what common point of view can such different sources of the pleasure in jokes be brought together?

B. SYNTHETIC PART

IV

THE MECHANISM OF PLEASURE AND THE PSYCHOGENESIS OF JOKES

[I]

WE can now start out from an assured knowledge of the sources of the peculiar pleasure given us by jokes. We are aware that we may be deceived into confusing our enjoyment of the intellectual content of what is stated with the pleasure proper to jokes; but we know that that pleasure itself has at bottom two sources – the technique and the purposes of jokes. What we now want to discover is the way in which the pleasure arises from these sources, the mechanism of the pleasurable effect.

We shall, I think, find the explanation we are in search of far easier from tendentious jokes than from innocent ones. We will therefore begin with the former.

The pleasure in the case of a tendentious joke arises from a purpose being satisfied whose satisfaction would otherwise not have taken place. That a satisfaction such as this is a source of pleasure calls for no further remark. But the manner in which a joke leads to this satisfaction is linked with particular conditions, from which we may perhaps arrive at some further information. Two cases are to be distinguished here. The simpler one is where the satisfaction of the purpose is opposed by an external obstacle which is evaded by the joke. We found this, for instance, in the reply received by Serenissimus to his question of whether the mother of the man he was speaking to had ever lived in the Palace [p. 107] and in the critic's rejoinder to the two rich rascals who showed him their portraits: 'But where's the Saviour?' [p. 114.] In the former case the purpose was to answer one insult by another, and in the latter it was to hand across an insult instead of the assessment that had been asked for. What opposed the purpose were purely external factors – the powerful position of the people at whom the insults were directed. It may nevertheless strike us that, however much these and analogous jokes of a tendentious nature may satisfy us, they are not able to provoke much laughter.

It is otherwise when what stands in the way of the direct realization of the purpose is not an external factor but an internal obstacle, when an internal impulse opposes the purpose. This condition would seem, on our hypothesis, to be fulfilled in the jokes of Herr N., in whom a strong inclination to invective is held in check by a highly developed aesthetic culture. By the help of a joke, this internal resistance is overcome in the particular case and the inhibition lifted. By that means, as in the instance of the external obstacle, the satisfaction of the purpose is made possible and its suppression, together with the 'psychical damming-up'[1] that this would involve, is avoided. To that extent the mechanism of the generation of pleasure would be the same in the two cases.

Nevertheless, we are inclined here to go more deeply into the distinctions between the psychological situation in the cases of an external and an internal obstacle, for we have a suspicion that the removal of an internal obstacle may make an incomparably higher contribution to the pleasure. But I suggest that at this point we should exercise moderation and be satisfied for the moment with establishing what remains the essential point for us. The cases of an external and an internal obstacle differ only in the fact that in the latter an already existing inhibition is lifted and that in the former the erection of a new one is avoided. That being so, we shall not be relying too much on speculation if we assert that both for erecting and for maintaining a psychical inhibition some 'psychical expenditure'[2] is

1. [The phrase is from Lipps (1898, 72, etc.). See below, p. 208.]
2. [I.e. expenditure of psychical energy (p. 199 ff.).]

required. And, since we know that in both cases of the use of tendentious jokes pleasure is obtained, it is therefore plausible to suppose that *this yield of pleasure corresponds to the psychical expenditure that is saved.*

Here then we have once more come upon the principle of economy which we met first in discussing the technique of verbal jokes [p. 77 ff.]. But whereas in the earlier case we seemed to find the economy in the use of as few words as possible or of words as much alike as possible, we now have a suspicion of an economy in the far more comprehensive sense of psychical expenditure in general; and we must regard it as possible that a closer understanding of what is still the very obscure concept of 'psychical expenditure' may bring us nearer to the essential nature of jokes.

A certain lack of clarity which we have been unable to overcome in our handling of the mechanism of pleasure in tendentious jokes may be taken as an appropriate punishment for our having tried to clear up the more complex problem before the simpler one, tendentious jokes before innocent ones. We take note of the fact that *'economy in expenditure on inhibition or suppression'* appears to be the secret of the pleasurable effect of tendentious jokes, and pass on to the mechanism of pleasure in innocent jokes.

On the basis of suitable specimens of innocent jokes, in which there was no fear of our judgement being disturbed by their content or purpose, we were driven to conclude that the techniques of jokes are themselves sources of pleasure; and we shall now try to discover whether it may perhaps be possible to trace that pleasure back to economy in psychical expenditure. In one group of these jokes (play upon words) the technique consisted in focusing our psychical attitude upon the *sound* of the word instead of upon its *meaning* – in making the (acoustic) word-presentation itself take the place of its significance as given by its relations to thing-presentations.[1] It may really be suspected

1. [It was not until ten years later, in his metapsychological papers

that in doing so we are bringing about a great relief in psychical work and that when we make serious use of words we are obliged to hold ourselves back with a certain effort from this comfortable procedure. We can observe how pathological states of thought-activity, in which the possibility of concentrating psychical expenditure on a particular point is probably restricted, do in fact give this sort of sound-presentation of the word greater prominence than its meaning, and that sufferers in such states proceed in their speech on the lines (as the formula runs) of the 'external' instead of the 'internal' associations of the word-presentation. We notice, too, that children, who, as we know, are in the habit of still treating words as things,[1] tend to expect words that are the same or similar to have the same meaning behind them – which is a source of many mistakes that are laughed at by grown-up people. If, therefore, we derive unmistakable enjoyment in jokes from being transported by the use of the same or a similar word from one circle of ideas to another, remote one (in the 'Home-Roulard', for instance [p. 137], from the kitchen to politics), this enjoyment is no doubt correctly to be attributed to economy in psychical expenditure. The pleasure in a joke arising from a 'short-circuit' like this seems to be the greater the more alien the two circles of ideas that are brought together by the same word – the further apart they are, and thus the greater the economy which the joke's technical

that Freud dealt at greater length with the fact that 'the conscious presentation of the object can now be split up into the presentation of the *word* and the presentation of the *thing*', and enlarged on the importance of the distinction from the standpoint of psychopathology, as is indicated in the present passage. See in particular the closing pages of Section VII of the paper on 'The Unconscious' (1915e). His interest in the question, however, goes back much earlier – to the time of his monograph on aphasia (1891b).]

1. [Cf. a passage in Chapter VI, Section A, of *The Interpretation of Dreams* (1900a), P.F.L., **4**, 412. An example of this phenomenon is given in Section II of the 'Little Hans' case history (1909b).]

method provides in the train of thought. We may notice, too, that here jokes are making use of a method of linking things up which is rejected and studiously avoided by serious thought.[1]

In a second group of technical methods used in jokes – unification, similarity of sound, multiple use, modification of familiar phrases, allusions to quotations – we can single out as their common characteristic the fact that in each of them something familiar is rediscovered, where we might instead have expected something new. This rediscovery of what is familiar is pleasurable, and once more it is not difficult for us to recognize this pleasure as a pleasure in economy and to relate it to economy in psychical expenditure.

1. If I may be allowed to anticipate the exposition in the text, I can at this point throw light on the condition which seems to determine whether a joke is to be called a 'good' or a 'bad' one. If, by means of a word with two meanings or a word that is only slightly modified, I take a short cut from one circle of ideas to another, and if there is not at the same time a link between those circles of ideas which has a significant sense, then I shall have made a 'bad' joke. In a bad joke like this the only existing link between the two disparate ideas is the one word – the 'point' of the joke. The example of 'Home-Roulard' quoted above is a joke of this kind. A 'good' joke, on the other hand, comes about when what children expect [see above, p. 168] proves correct and the similarity between the words is shown to be really accompanied by another, important similarity in their sense. Such, for instance, is the example 'Traduttore – Traditore' [p. 67]. The two disparate ideas, which are here linked by an external association, are also united in a significant relation which indicates an essential kinship between them. The external association merely takes the place of the internal connection; it serves to point it out or make it clear. A 'translator' is not only called by a similar name to a 'traitor'; he actually *is* a kind of traitor and bears the name, as it were by right.

The distinction that is here developed coincides with the one which is to be introduced later [p. 178 ff.] between a 'jest' and a 'joke'. But it would be unjust to exclude examples like 'Home-Roulard' from the discussion of the nature of jokes. As soon as we take into consideration the peculiar pleasure derived from jokes, we find that the 'bad' jokes are by no means bad as jokes – that is, unsuitable for producing pleasure.

It seems to be generally agreed that the rediscovery of what is familiar, 'recognition', is pleasurable. Groos (1899, 153) writes: 'Recognition is always, unless it is too much mechanized (as, for instance, in dressing, . . .), linked with feelings of pleasure. The mere quality of familiarity is easily accompanied by the quiet sense of comfort which Faust felt when, after an uncanny encounter, he entered his study once again[1] . . . If the act of recognition thus gives rise to pleasure, we might expect that men would hit on the idea of exercising this capacity for its own sake – that is, would experiment with it in play. And in fact Aristotle regarded joy in recognition as the basis of the enjoyment of art, and it cannot be disputed that this principle should not be overlooked, even if it does not possess such far-reaching significance as Aristotle attributes to it.'

Groos goes on to discuss games whose characteristic lies in the fact that they intensify the joy in recognition by putting obstacles in its way – that is to say, by creating a 'psychical damming-up', which is got rid of by the act of recognition. His attempt at an explanation, however, abandons the hypothesis that recognition is pleasurable in itself, since, by referring to these games, he is tracing back the enjoyment of recognition to a joy in *power*, a joy in the overcoming of a difficulty. I regard the latter factor as secondary, and I see no reason to depart from the simpler view that recognition is pleasurable in itself – i.e., through relieving psychical expenditure – and that the games founded on this pleasure make use of the mechanism of damming-up only in order to increase the amount of such pleasure.

It is also generally acknowledged that rhymes, alliterations, refrains, and other forms of repeating similar verbal sounds which occur in verse, make use of the same source of pleasure – the rediscovery of something familiar. The 'sense of power' plays no perceptible part in these techniques, which show so much similarity to that of 'multiple use' in the case of jokes.

1. [Goethe, *Faust*, Part I, Scene 3.]

In view of the close connection between recognizing and remembering, it is not rash to suppose that there may also be a pleasure in remembering – that the act of remembering is in itself accompanied by a feeling of pleasure of similar origin. Groos seems not to be averse to such a hypothesis, but he derives it once again from the 'sense of power', to which he attributes (wrongly, in my view) the chief reason for enjoyment in almost all games.

The 'rediscovery of what is familiar' is the basis for the use of another technical resource in jokes, which we have not yet mentioned. I refer to the factor of 'topicality', which is a fertile source of pleasure in a great many jokes and which explains a few of the peculiarities in the life-history of jokes. There are jokes which are completely independent of this condition, and in a monograph on jokes we are obliged to make almost exclusive use of examples of that kind. But we cannot forget that, in comparison with these perennial jokes, we have perhaps laughed even more heartily at others which it is difficult for us to use now because they would call for long commentaries and even with such help would not produce their original effect. These latter jokes contained allusions to people and events which at the time were 'topical', which had aroused general interest and still kept it alive. When this interest had ceased and the business in question had been settled, these jokes too lost a part of their pleasurable effect and indeed a very considerable part. For instance, the joke made by my friendly host when he called a pudding that was being served a 'Home-Roulard' [p. 137] does not seem to me today nearly so good as it did at the time, when 'Home Rule' provided a standing head-line in the political columns of our daily papers. In attempting to estimate the merits of this joke I now attribute them to the fact that a single word has transported us, with the economy of a long détour in thought, from the circle of ideas of the kitchen to the remote one of politics. But at the time my account would have had to be different, and I should have said that this word

transported us from the circle of ideas of the kitchen to that of
politics, which was remote from it but was certain of our lively
interest because we were constantly concerned with it. Another
joke, 'This girl reminds me of Dreyfus; the army doesn't believe
in her innocence' [p. 75], has also faded today, though its
technical methods must have remained unaltered. The bewilderment caused by the comparison and the *double-entendre* in
the word 'innocence' cannot compensate for the fact that the
allusion, which at the time touched on an event cathected with
fresh excitement, today recalls a question that is settled. Here
is a joke which is still topical: 'The Crown Princess Louise
approached the crematorium in Gotha with the question of
how much a *Verbrennung* [cremation] costs. The management
replied: "Five thousand marks normally; but we will only
charge *you* three thousand as you have been *durchgebrannt*
[literally 'been burnt through' – slang for 'eloped'] once already."' A joke like this sounds irresistible today; in a short
time it will have sunk very considerably in our estimation; and
some time later still, in spite of its good play upon words, it will
lose its effect entirely, for it will be impossible to repeat it
without adding a commentary to explain who Princess Louise
was and the sense in which she was *durchgebrannt*.[1]

Thus a great number of the jokes in circulation have a certain
length of life: their life runs a course made up of a period of
flowering and a period of decay and it ends in complete
oblivion. The need which men feel for deriving pleasure from
their processes of thought is therefore constantly creating new
jokes based on the new interests of the day. The vital force of
topical jokes is not their own; it is borrowed, by the method of
allusion, from those other interests, the expiry of which determines the fate of the joke as well. The factor of topicality is a
source of pleasure, ephemeral it is true but particularly abun-

1. [It must accordingly be explained that Princess Louise was the
Crown Princess of Saxony who left her husband in 1903. For an account
of the strange circumstances, see her autobiography (1911).]

dant, which supplements the sources inherent in the joke itself. It cannot be simply equated with the rediscovery of what is familiar. It is concerned rather with a particular category of what is familiar, which must in addition possess the characteristic of being fresh, recent and untouched by forgetting. In the formation of dreams, too, we come across a special preference for what is recent[1] and we cannot escape a suspicion that association with what is recent is rewarded, and so facilitated, by a peculiar bonus of pleasure.

Unification, which is after all no more than repetition in the sphere of thought-connections instead of in that of subject-matter, was given special recognition by Fechner as a source of the pleasure in jokes. He writes (Fechner, 1897, 1, Chapter XVII): 'In my opinion the chief part in the field we are now considering is played by the principle of the unified linking of multiplicities; it requires support, however, from auxiliary determinants in order that the enjoyment which can be derived from these cases, with its peculiar character, may be carried over the threshold.'[2]

In all these cases of repeating the same connections or the same subject-matter in the words, or of rediscovering what is familiar or recent, it seems impossible to avoid deriving the pleasure felt in them from economy in psychical expenditure – provided that this line of approach turns out to be fruitful in throwing light on details and in arriving at new generalities. We are aware that we have still to make it clear how the economy comes about and what the meaning is of the expression 'psychical expenditure'.

The third group of techniques of jokes – for the most part of conceptual jokes – which comprises faulty thinking, displacements, absurdity, representation by the opposite, etc., may at a

1. [See *The Interpretation of Dreams*, e.g. *P.F.L.*, 4, 266–8 and 715–18.]
2. The title of Chapter XVII is 'On significant and joking similes, play upon words and other cases which bear the character of being amusing, funny or ridiculous'.

first glance seem to bear a special impress and to betray no kinship with the techniques of rediscovery of what is familiar or the replacement of object-associations by word-associations. Nevertheless it is particularly easy here to bring into play the theory of economy or relief in psychical expenditure.

It cannot be doubted that it is easier and more convenient to diverge from a line of thought we have embarked on than to keep to it, to jumble up things that are different rather than to contrast them – and, indeed, that it is *specially* convenient to admit as valid methods of inference that are rejected by logic and, lastly, to put words or thoughts together without regard to the condition that they ought also to make sense. This cannot be doubted; and these are precisely the things that are done by the joke-techniques which we are discussing. But the hypothesis that behaviour of this kind by the joke-work provides a source of pleasure will strike us as strange, since apart from jokes all such inefficient intellectual functioning produces in us nothing but unpleasurable defensive feelings.

'Pleasure in nonsense', as we may call it for short, is concealed in serious life to a vanishing point. In order to demonstrate it we must investigate two cases – one in which it is still visible and one in which it becomes visible again: the behaviour of a child in learning, and that of an adult in a toxically altered state of mind.

During the period in which a child is learning how to handle the vocabulary of his mother-tongue, it gives him obvious pleasure to 'experiment with it in play', to use Groos's words [p. 170]. And he puts words together without regard to the condition that they should make sense, in order to obtain from them the pleasurable effect of rhythm or rhyme. Little by little he is forbidden this enjoyment, till all that remains permitted to him are significant combinations of words. But when he is older attempts still emerge at disregarding the restrictions that have been learnt on the use of words. Words are disfigured by particular little additions being made to them, their forms are altered by certain manipulations (e.g. by reduplications or 'Zittersprache'[1]), or a private language may even be constructed for use among playmates. These attempts are found again among certain categories of mental patients.

Whatever the motive may have been which led the child to begin these games, I believe that in his later development he gives himself up to them with the consciousness that they are nonsensical, and that he finds enjoyment in the attraction of what is forbidden by reason. He now uses games in order to withdraw from the pressure of critical reason. But there is far more potency in the restrictions which must establish themselves in the course of a child's education in logical thinking and in distinguishing between what is true and false in reality; and for this reason the rebellion against the compulsion of logic and reality is deep-going and long-lasting. Even the phenomena of imaginative activity must be included in this [rebellious] category. The power of criticism has increased so greatly in the later part of childhood and in the period of learning which extends over puberty that the pleasure in 'liberated nonsense' only seldom dares to show itself directly. One does not venture to say anything absurd. But the characteristic tendency of boys to do absurd or silly things seems to me to be directly derived from the pleasure in nonsense. In pathological cases we often see this tendency so far intensified that once more it dominates the schoolboy's talk and answers. I have been able to convince myself in the case of a few boys of secondary school age who had developed neuroses that the unconscious workings of their pleasure in the nonsense they produced played no less a part in their inefficiency than did their real ignorance.

Nor, later on, does the University student cease these demon-

1. [This was a particular form of secret language in which the sound 'zitter' played a part. The topic had been touched on by Freud in the passage in *The Interpretation of Dreams* (1900a), P.F.L., 4, 412, already referred to (p. 168n.).]

strations against the compulsion of logic and reality, the dominance of which, however, he feels growing ever more
intolerant and unrestricted. A large amount of student 'rags'
are a part of this reaction. For man is a 'tireless pleasure-
seeker' – I forget where I came across this happy expression –
and any renunciation of a pleasure he has once enjoyed comes
hard to him. With the cheerful nonsense of his *Bierschwefel*,[1] for
instance, the student tries to rescue his pleasure in freedom of
thinking, of which he is being more and more deprived by the
schooling of academic instruction. Much later still, indeed,
when as a grown man he meets others in scientific congresses
and once more feels himself a learner, after the meeting is over
there comes the *Kneipzeitung*,[2] which distorts the new discoveries into nonsense, and offers him a compensation for the
fresh addition to his intellectual inhibition.

The *Bierschwefel* and the *Kneipzeitung* give evidence by their
names to the fact that the criticism which has repressed pleasure
in nonsense has already grown so powerful that it cannot be put
aside even temporarily without toxic assistance. A change in
mood is the most precious thing that alcohol achieves for
mankind, and on that account this 'poison' is not equally
indispensable for everyone. A cheerful mood, whether it is
produced endogenously or toxically, reduces the inhibiting
forces, criticism among them, and makes accessible once again
sources of pleasure which were under the weight of suppression. It is most instructive to observe how the standards of
joking sink as spirits rise. For high spirits replace jokes, just as
jokes must try to replace high spirits, in which possibilities of
enjoyment which are otherwise inhibited – among them the
pleasure in nonsense – can come into their own: 'Mit wenig
Witz und viel Behagen.'[3] Under the influence of alcohol the

1. ['*Bierschwefel*', a ludicrous speech delivered at a beer party.]
2. [A comic set of minutes. Literally, 'tavern newspaper'.]
3. ['With little wit and much enjoyment.' (Mephistopheles in Auer-
bach's Cellar, *Faust*, Part I, Scene 5.)]

grown man once more becomes a child, who finds pleasure in having the course of his thoughts freely at his disposal without paying regard to the compulsion of logic.

I hope I have now also shown that the absurdity-techniques of jokes are a source of pleasure. It need only be repeated that this pleasure arises from an economy in psychical expenditure or a relief from the compulsion of criticism.

If we look back once more at the three separate groups of joke-techniques, we see that the first and third of these groups – the replacement of thing-associations by word-associations and the use of absurdity – can be brought together as re-establishing old liberties and getting rid of the burden of intellectual upbringing; they are psychical reliefs, which can in a sense be contrasted with the economizing which constitutes the technique of the second group. Relief from psychical expenditure that is already there and economizing in psychical expenditure that is only about to be called for – from these two principles all the techniques of jokes, and accordingly all pleasure from these techniques, are derived. The two species of technique and of obtaining pleasure coincide – in the main at all events – with the distinction between verbal and conceptual jokes.

[2]

The preceding discussion has given us unawares an insight into the evolution or psychogenesis of jokes, which we will now examine more closely. We have made the acquaintance of preliminary stages of jokes, and their development into tendentious jokes will probably uncover fresh relations between the various characteristics of jokes. Before there is such a thing as a joke, there is something that we may describe as 'play' or as 'a jest'.

Play – let us keep to that name – appears in children while they are learning to make use of words and to put thoughts together. This play probably obeys one of the instincts which compel children to practise their capacities (Groos [1899]). In doing so they come across pleasurable effects, which arise from a repetition of what is similar, a rediscovery of what is familiar, similarity of sound, etc., and which are to be explained as unsuspected economies in physical expenditure.[1] It is not to be wondered at that these pleasurable effects encourage children in the pursuit of play and cause them to continue it without regard for the meaning of words or the coherence of sentences. *Play* with words and thoughts, motivated by certain pleasurable effects of economy, would thus be the first stage of jokes.

This play is brought to an end by the strengthening of a factor that deserves to be described as the critical faculty or reasonableness. The play is now rejected as being meaningless or actually absurd; as a result of criticism it becomes impossible. Now, too, there is no longer any question of deriving pleasure, except accidentally, from the sources of rediscovery of what is familiar, etc., unless it happens that the growing individual is overtaken by a pleasurable mood which, like the child's cheerfulness, lifts the critical inhibition. Only in such a case does the old game of getting pleasure become possible once more; but the individual does not want to wait for this to happen nor to renounce the pleasure that is familiar to him. He thus looks about for means of making himself independent of the pleasurable mood, and the further development towards jokes is governed by the two endeavours: to avoid criticism and to find a substitute for the mood.

And with this the second preliminary stage of jokes sets in – the *jest*. It is now a question of prolonging the yield of pleasure from play, but at the same time of silencing the objections

1. [The pleasure taken by children in repetition (to which there is a further reference below, p. 91), is a subject to which Freud recurred much later, in his discussion of his hypothesis of a 'compulsion to repeat' at the beginning of Chapter V of *Beyond the Pleasure Principle* (1920g).]

raised by criticism which would not allow the pleasurable feeling to emerge. There is only one way of reaching this end: the meaningless combination of words or the absurd putting together of thoughts must nevertheless have a meaning. The whole ingenuity of the joke-work is summoned up in order to find words and aggregations of thoughts in which this condition is fulfilled. All the technical methods of jokes are already employed here – in jests; moreover linguistic usage draws no consistent line between a jest and a joke. What distinguishes a jest from a joke is that the meaning of the sentence which escapes criticism need not be valuable or new or even good; it need merely be *permissible* to say the thing in this way, even though it is unusual, unnecessary or useless to say it in this way. In jests what stands in the foreground is the satisfaction of having made possible what was forbidden by criticism.

It is, for instance, simply a jest when Schleiermacher [see p. 68] defines *Eifersucht* [jealousy] as the *Leidenschaft* [passion] which *mit Eifer sucht* [with eagerness seeks] what *Leiden schafft* [causes pain]. It was a jest when Professor Kästner, who taught physics (and made jokes) at Göttingen in the eighteenth century, asked a student named Kriegk, when he was enrolling himself for his lectures, how old he was. 'Thirty years old' was the reply, whereupon Kästner remarked: 'Ah! so I have the honour of meeting the Thirty Years' War [*Krieg*]' (Kleinpaul, 1890). It was with a jest that the great Rokitansky[1] replied to the question of what were the professions of his four sons: 'Two *heilen* [heal] and two *heulen* [howl]' (two doctors and two singers). The information was correct and therefore not open to criticism; but it added nothing to what might have been expressed in the words in brackets. There can be no mistaking the fact that the answer was given the other form only on account of the pleasure which was produced by the unification and the similar sound of the two words.

1. [Carl Rokitansky (1804–78) was the founder of the Vienna school of pathological anatomy.]

I think now at length we see our way clearly. All through our consideration of the techniques of jokes we have been disturbed by the fact that they were not proper to jokes only; and yet the essence of jokes seemed to depend on them, since when they were got rid of by reduction the characteristics and the pleasure of the joke were lost. We now see that what we have described as the techniques of jokes – and we must in a certain sense continue to describe them so – are rather the sources from which jokes provide pleasure; and we feel that there is nothing strange in other procedures drawing from the same sources for the same end. The technique which is characteristic of jokes and peculiar to them, however, consists in their procedure for safeguarding the use of these methods of providing pleasure against the objections raised by criticism which would put an end to the pleasure. There is little that we can say in general about this procedure. The joke-work, as we have already remarked, shows itself in a choice of verbal material and conceptual situations which will allow the old play with words and thoughts to withstand the scrutiny of criticism; and with that end in view every peculiarity of vocabulary and every combination of thought-sequences must be exploited in the most ingenious possible way. We may be in a position later to characterize the joke-work by a particular property; for the moment it remains unexplained how the selection favourable for jokes can be made. The purpose and function of jokes, however – namely, the protection of sequences of words and thoughts from criticism – can already be seen in jests as their essential feature. Their function consists from the first in lifting internal inhibitions and in making sources of pleasure fertile which have been rendered inaccessible by those inhibitions; and we shall find that they remain loyal to this characteristic throughout their development.

We are also in a position now to assign its correct place to the factor of 'sense in nonsense' (cf. the introduction, p. 42), to which the authorities attribute such great importance as a distinguishing mark of jokes and as an explanation of their pleasurable effect. The two fixed points in what determines the nature of jokes – their purpose of continuing pleasurable play and their effort to protect it from the criticism of reason – immediately explain why an individual joke, though it may seem senseless from one point of view, must appear sensible, or at least allowable, from another. How it does so remains the affair of the joke-work; if it fails to do so, it is simply rejected as 'nonsense'. But there is no necessity for us to derive the pleasurable effect of jokes from the conflict between the feelings which arise (whether directly or along the path of 'bewilderment and enlightenment' [p. 43 f.]) from the simultaneous sense and nonsense of jokes. Nor have we any need to enter further into the question of how pleasure could arise from the alternation between 'thinking it senseless' and 'recognizing it as sensible'. The psychogenesis of jokes has taught us that the pleasure in a joke is derived from play with words or from the liberation of nonsense, and that the meaning of the joke is merely intended to protect that pleasure from being done away with by criticism.

In this way the problem of the essential character of jokes is already explained in jests. We may now turn to the further development of jests, to the point at which they reach their height in tendentious jokes. Jests still give the foremost place to the purpose of giving us enjoyment, and are content if what they say does not appear senseless or completely devoid of substance. If what a jest says possesses substance and value, it turns into a joke. A thought which would deserve our interest even if it were expressed in the most unpretentious form is now clothed in a form which must give us enjoyment on its own account.[1]

1. As an example which shows the difference between a jest and a joke proper we may take the excellent joking remark with which a member of the 'Bürger' Ministry in Austria answered a question about the cabinet's solidarity: 'How can we *einstehen* [stand up] for one another if we can't *ausstehen* [stand] one another?' Technique: use of the same

A combination like this can certainly not, we must suppose, have come about unintentionally; and we must try to discover the intention underlying the construction of the joke. An observation which we made earlier (in passing, as it seemed) will put us on the track. We said above (p. 136) that a good joke makes, as it were, a *total* impression of enjoyment on us, without our being able to decide at once what share of the pleasure arises from its joking form and what share from its apt thought-content. We are constantly making mistakes in this apportionment. Sometimes we over-estimate the goodness of the joke on account of our admiration of the thought it contains, another time, on the contrary, we over-estimate the value of the thought on account of the enjoyment given us by its joking envelope. We do not know what is giving us enjoyment and what we are laughing at. This uncertainty in our judgement, which must be assumed to be a fact, may have provided the motive for the construction of jokes in the proper sense of the word. The thought seeks to wrap itself in a joke because in that way it recommends itself to our attention and can seem more significant and more valuable, but above all because this wrapping bribes our powers of criticism and confuses them. We are inclined to give the *thought* the benefit of what has pleased us in the *form* of the joke; and we are no longer inclined to find anything wrong that has given us enjoyment and so to spoil the source of a pleasure. If the joke has made us laugh, moreover, a disposition most unfavourable for criticism will have been established in us; for in that case something will have

---

material with slight (contrary) modification. Logical and apposite thought: there can be no solidarity without mutual understanding. The contrary nature of the modification (*ein* [in] – *aus* [out]) corresponds to the incompatibility asserted in the thought and serves as a representation of it. – [The 'Bürger' Middle-Class) Ministry took office after the new Austrian constitution was established in 1867, but owing to internal disharmony only lasted for a couple of years. Cf. *The Interpretation of Dreams* (1900a), *P.F.L.*, 4, 281 f.]

forced us into the mood which play has previously sufficed to produce, and for which the joke has tried by every possible means to make itself a substitute. Even though we have earlier asserted that such jokes are to be described as innocent and not yet tendentious, we must not forget that strictly speaking only jests are non-tendentious – that is, serve solely the aim of producing pleasure. Jokes, even if the thought contained in them is non-tendentious and thus only serves theoretical intellectual interests, are in fact never non-tendentious. They pursue the second aim: to promote the thought by augmenting it and guarding it against criticism. Here they are once again expressing their original nature by setting themselves up against an inhibiting and restricting power – which is now the critical judgement.

This, the first use of jokes that goes beyond the production of pleasure, points the way to their further uses. A joke is now seen to be a psychical factor possessed of power: its weight, thrown into one scale or the other, can be decisive. The major purposes and instincts of mental life employ it for their own ends. The originally non-tendentious joke, which began as play, is *secondarily* brought into relation with purposes from which nothing that takes form in the mind can ultimately keep away. We know already what it is able to achieve in the service of the purpose of exposure, and of hostile, cynical and sceptical purposes. In the case of obscene jokes, which are derived from smut, it turns the third person who originally interfered with the sexual situation into an ally, before whom the woman must feel shame, by bribing him with the gift of its yield of pleasure. In the case of aggressive purposes it employs the same method in order to turn the hearer, who was indifferent to begin with, into a co-hater or co-despiser, and creates for the enemy a host of opponents where at first there was only one. In the first case it overcomes the inhibitions of shame and respectability by means of the bonus of pleasure which it offers; in the second it upsets the critical judgement which would otherwise have examined the dispute. In the third and fourth cases, in the service of cynical and sceptical purposes, it shatters respect for institutions and truths in which the hearer has believed, on the one hand by reinforcing the argument, but on the other by practising a new species of attack. Where argument tries to draw the hearer's criticism over on to its side, the joke endeavours to push the criticism out of sight. There is no doubt that the joke has chosen the method which is psychologically the more effective.

In this survey of the achievements of tendentious jokes, most prominence has been assumed by – what is more easily seen – the effect of jokes on the person who hears them. More important, however, from the point of view of our understanding, are the functions accomplished by jokes in the mind of the person who makes them or, to put it in the only correct way, the person to whom they occur. We have already proposed [p. 143] – and here we have occasion to repeat the notion – that we should try to study the psychical phenomena of jokes with reference to their distribution between two people. We will make a provisional suggestion that the psychical process provoked by the joke in the hearer is in most cases modelled on that which occurs in its creator. The external obstacle which is to be overcome in the hearer corresponds to an internal inhibition in the maker of the joke. At the least the *expectation* of an external obstacle is present in the latter as an inhibiting idea. In certain cases the internal obstacle which is overcome by the tendentious joke is obvious; in Herr N.'s jokes, for instance, we were able to assume (p. 147 f.) that not only did they make it possible for their hearers to enjoy aggressiveness in the form of insults, but that above all they made it possible for him to produce them. Among the various kinds of internal inhibition or suppression there is one which deserves our special interest, because it is the most far-reaching. It is given the name of 'repression', and is recognized by its function of preventing the impulses subjected to it, and their derivatives, from becoming conscious. Tendentious jokes, as we shall see, are able to release pleasure even from sources that have undergone repression. If, as has been suggested above, the overcoming of external obstacles can in this way be traced back to the overcoming of internal inhibitions and repressions, we may say that tendentious jokes exhibit the main characteristic of the joke-work – that of liberating pleasure by getting rid of inhibitions – more clearly than any other of the developmental stages of jokes. Either they strengthen the purposes which they serve, by bringing assistance to them from impulses that are kept suppressed, or they put themselves entirely at the service of suppressed purposes.

We may be ready to admit that this is what tendentious jokes achieve; yet we must bear in mind that we do not understand how they are able to put these achievements into effect. Their power lies in the yield of pleasure which they draw from the sources of play upon words and of liberated nonsense; but if we are to judge by the impressions gained from non-tendentious jests, we cannot possibly think the amount of this pleasure great enough to attribute to it the strength to lift deeply-rooted inhibitions and repressions. What we have before us here is in fact no simple effect of force but a more complex situation of release. Instead of setting out the long détour by which I reached an understanding of this situation, I will try to give a short synthetic exposition of it.

Fechner (1897, 1, Chapter V) has put forward a 'principle of aesthetic assistance or intensification', which he has expressed as follows: '*If determinants of pleasure that in themselves produce little effect converge without mutual contradiction, there results a greater, and often a much greater, outcome of pleasure than corresponds to the pleasure-value of the separate determinants – a greater pleasure than could be explained as the sum of the separate effects. Indeed, a convergence of this kind can even lead to a positive resultant of pleasure and the threshold of pleasure may be crossed, where the separate factors are too weak to do so: though they must, in comparison with others, show a perceptible advantage in enjoyableness.'* (Ibid., 51. The italics are Fechner's.)

The topic of jokes does not, I think, give us much opportunity of confirming the correctness of this principle, which can be shown to hold good in many other aesthetic structures. As regards jokes we have learnt something else, which at least fringes upon this principle: namely, that where several pleasure-giving factors operate together we are not able to attribute to each of them the share it has really taken in bringing about the result (see p. 136). We can, however, vary the situation that is assumed in the 'principle of assistance' and, as a result of these fresh conditions, arrive at a number of questions which would deserve reply. What happens in general if, in a combination, determinants of pleasure and determinants of unpleasure converge? On what does the outcome depend and what decides whether that outcome is in pleasure or unpleasure?

The case of tendentious jokes is a special one among these possibilities. An impulse or urge is present which seeks to release pleasure from a particular source and, if it were allowed free play, would release it. Besides this, another urge is present which works against this generation of pleasure – inhibits it, that is, or suppresses it. The suppressing current must, as the outcome shows, be a certain amount stronger than the suppressed one, which, however, is not on that account abolished. Now let us suppose that yet another urge makes its appearance which would release pleasure through the same process, though from other sources, and which thus operates in the same sense as the suppressed urge. What can the result be in such a case?

An example will give us our bearings better than this schematic discussion. Let us assume that there is an urge to insult a certain person; but this is so strongly opposed by feelings of propriety or of aesthetic culture that the insult cannot take place. If, for instance, it were able to break through as a result of some change of emotional condition or mood, this breakthrough by the insulting purpose would be felt subsequently with unpleasure. Thus the insult does not take place. Let us now suppose, however, that the possibility is presented of deriving a good joke from the material of the words and thoughts used for the insult – the possibility, that is, of releasing pleasure from other sources which are not obstructed by the same suppression. This second development of pleasure could, nevertheless, not occur unless the insult were permitted; but as soon as the latter *is* permitted the new release of pleasure is also joined to it. Experience with tendentious jokes shows that in such circumstances the suppressed purpose can, with the assistance of the pleasure from the joke, gain sufficient strength to overcome the inhibition, which would otherwise be stronger than it. The insult takes place, because the joke is thus made possible. But the enjoyment obtained is not only that produced by the joke: it is incomparably greater. It is so much greater than the pleasure from the joke that we must suppose that the hitherto suppressed purpose has succeeded in making its way through, perhaps without any diminution whatever. It is in such circumstances that the tendentious joke is received with the heartiest laughter.[1]

An examination of the determinants of laughing will perhaps lead us to a plainer idea of what happens when a joke affords assistance against suppression. [Cf. p. 197 ff. below.] Even now, however, we can see that the case of tendentious jokes is a special case of the 'principle of assistance'. A possibility of generating pleasure supervenes in a situation in which another possibility of pleasure is obstructed so that, as far as the latter alone is concerned, no pleasure would arise. The result is a generation of pleasure far greater than that offered by the supervening possibility. This has acted, as it were, as an

1. [Freud had already propounded a parallel theory, to explain the often exaggerated amount of affect experienced in dreams, in Chapter VI, Section H, of *The Interpretation of Dreams* (1900a), P.F.L., 4, 616 ff.]

incentive bonus; with the assistance of the offer of a small amount of pleasure, a much greater one, which would otherwise have been hard to achieve, has been gained. I have good reason to suspect that this principle corresponds with an arrangement that holds good in many widely separated departments of mental life and it will, I think, be expedient to describe the pleasure that serves to initiate the large release of pleasure as 'fore-pleasure', and the principle as the 'fore-pleasure principle'.[1]

We are now able to state the formula for the mode of operation of tendentious jokes. They put themselves at the service of purposes in order that, by means of using the pleasure from jokes as a fore-pleasure, they may produce new pleasure by lifting suppressions and repressions. If now we survey the course of development of the joke, we may say that from its beginning to its perfecting it remains true to its essential nature. It begins as play, in order to derive pleasure from the free use of words and thoughts. As soon as the strengthening of reasoning puts an end to this play with words as being senseless, and with thoughts as being nonsensical, it changes into a jest, in order that it may retain these sources of pleasure and be able to achieve fresh pleasure from the liberation of nonsense. Next, as a joke proper, but still a non-tendentious one, it gives its assistance to thoughts and strengthens them against the challenge of critical judgement, a process in which the 'principle of confusion of sources of pleasure' is of use to it. And finally it comes to the help of major purposes which are combating suppression, in order to lift their internal inhibitions by the

1. [Freud discussed the mechanism of fore-pleasure as it operates in the sexual act at considerable length in Section 1 of the third of his almost contemporary *Three Essays* (1905*d*). He also pointed out its use in aesthetic creations at the end of his paper on 'Creative Writers and Day-Dreaming' (1908*e*), as well as at the end of an earlier, posthumously published, paper on 'Psychopathic Characters on the Stage' (1942*a* [1905–6]), and again in Chapter VI of his *Autobiographical Study* (1925*d*).]

'principle of fore-pleasure'. Reason, critical judgement, suppression – these are the forces against which it fights in succession; it holds fast to the original sources of verbal pleasure and, from the stage of the jest onwards, opens new sources of pleasure for itself by lifting inhibitions. The pleasure that it produces, whether it is pleasure in play or pleasure in lifting inhibitions, can invariably be traced back to economy in psychical expenditure, provided that this view does not contradict the essential nature of pleasure and that it proves itself fruitful in other directions.[1]

1. Nonsense jokes, which have not had due attention paid to them in my account, deserve some supplementary consideration.

The importance which our views attach to the factor of 'sense in nonsense' might lead to a demand that every joke must be a nonsense joke. But this is not necessary, because it is only playing with *thoughts* that inevitably leads to nonsense; the other source of pleasure in jokes, playing with *words*, only gives that impression occasionally and does not invariably provoke the implied criticism. The twofold root of the pleasure in jokes – from playing with words and playing with thoughts, which corresponds to the very important distinction between verbal and conceptual jokes – makes it perceptibly more difficult to arrive at a concise formulation of general statements about jokes. Playing with words produces manifest pleasure as a result of the factors that have been enumerated above (recognition, and so on), and is consequently only to a small degree liable to suppression. Playing with thoughts cannot have its motive in this kind of pleasure; it meets with very energetic suppression, and the pleasure which it can yield is only pleasure in the lifting of an inhibition. It can accordingly be said that the pleasure in jokes exhibits a core of original pleasure in play and a casing of pleasure in lifting inhibitions. – We naturally do not perceive that our pleasure in a nonsense joke arises from our having succeeded in liberating a piece of nonsense in spite of its suppression; whereas we see directly that playing with words has given us pleasure. – The nonsense that still remains in a conceptual joke acquires secondarily the function of increasing our attention by bewildering us. It serves as a means of intensifying the effect of the joke, but only when it acts obtrusively, so that the bewilderment can hurry ahead of the understanding by a perceptible moment of time. The examples on p. 93 ff. have shown that in addition to this, nonsense in a joke can be used to represent a judgement contained in the thought. But this, too, is not the primary significance of nonsense in jokes.

[*Added* 1912:] A number of productions resembling jokes can be classed alongside of nonsense jokes. There is no appropriate name for them, but they might well be described as 'idiocy masquerading as a joke'. There are countless numbers of them, and I will only select two samples:

'A man at the dinner table who was being handed fish dipped his two hands twice in the mayonnaise and then ran them through his hair. When his neighbour looked at him in astonishment, he seemed to notice his mistake and apologized: "I'm so sorry, I thought it was spinach."'

Or: '"Life is a suspension bridge," said one man. – "Why is that?" asked the other. – "How should *I* know?" was the reply.'

These extreme examples have an effect because they rouse the expectation of a joke, so that one tries to find a concealed sense behind the nonsense. But one finds none: they really are nonsense. The pretence makes it possible for a moment to liberate the pleasure in nonsense. These jokes are not entirely without a purpose; they are a 'take-in', and give the person who tells them a certain amount of pleasure in misleading and annoying his hearer. The latter then damps down his annoyance by determining to tell them himself later on.

V

THE MOTIVES OF JOKES – JOKES
AS A SOCIAL PROCESS

IT might seem superfluous to talk about the motives of jokes, since the aim of getting pleasure must be recognized as a sufficient motive for the joke-work. But on the one hand the possibility cannot be excluded of other motives as well having a share in the production of jokes, and on the other hand, bearing in mind some familiar experiences, we must raise the general question of the subjective determinants of jokes.

Two facts in particular make this necessary. Although the joke-work is an excellent method of getting pleasure out of psychical processes, it is nevertheless evident that not everyone is equally capable of making use of that method, the joke-work is not at everyone's command, and altogether only a few people have a plentiful amount of it; and these are distinguished by being spoken of as having 'wit' [*Witz*].[1] 'Wit' appears in this connection as a special capacity – rather in the class of the old mental 'faculties'; and it seems to emerge fairly independently of the others, such as intelligence, imagination, memory, etc. We must therefore presume the presence in these 'witty' people of special inherited dispositions or psychical determinants which permit or favour the joke-work.

I fear that we shall not get very far in exploring this question. We can only succeed here and there in advancing from an understanding of a particular joke to a knowledge of the subjective determinants in the mind of the person who made it. It is a remarkable coincidence that precisely the example of the joke on which we began our investigations of the technique of jokes also gives us a glimpse into the subjective determinants

1. [See the Editor's Introduction, p. 35.]

of jokes. I refer to Heine's joke, which has also been considered by Heymans and Lipps [p. 47]:

'. . . I sat beside Salomon Rothschild and he treated me quite as his equal – quite famillionairely.' ('Bäder von Lucca.')

Heine puts this remark into the mouth of a comic character, Hirsch-Hyacinth, a Hamburg lottery-agent, extractor of corns and professional valuer, the valet of the aristocratic Baron Cristoforo Gumpelino (formerly Gumpel). The poet evidently takes the greatest satisfaction in this creation of his, for he makes Hirsch-Hyacinth into a great talker and gives him the most amusing and plain-spoken speeches, and even lets him display the practical philosophy of a Sancho Panza. It is a pity that Heine, who seems to have had no taste for dramatic construction, dropped this delightful character so soon. There are not a few passages in which the poet himself seems to be speaking, under a thin disguise, through the mouth of Hirsch-Hyacinth, and it soon becomes a certainty that this character is only a self-parody. Hirsch explains his reasons for having given up his former name and why he now calls himself 'Hyacinth'. He goes on: 'There's the further advantage that I already have an "H" on my signet, so that I don't need to have a new one cut.' But Heine himself effected the same economy when, at his baptism,[1] he changed his first name from 'Harry' to 'Heinrich'. Everyone, too, who is familiar with the poet's biography, will recall that Heine had an uncle of the same name in Hamburg (a place which provides another connection with the figure of Hirsch-Hyacinth) who, as the rich man of the family, played a large part in his life. This uncle was also called 'Salomon', just like the old Rothschild who treated Hirsch so famillionairely. What seemed in Hirsch-Hyacinth's mouth no more than a jest soon reveals a background of serious bitterness if we ascribe it to the nephew, Harry-Heinrich. After all, he was one of the family, and we know that he had a burning wish to marry a daughter of this uncle's; but his cousin rejected him, and his

1. [Heine was baptized a Christian at the age of 27.]

uncle always treated him a little famillionairely, as a poor relation. His rich cousins in Hamburg never took him seriously. I recall a story told by an old aunt of my own, who had married into the Heine family, of how one day, when she was an attractive young woman, she found sitting next her at the family dinner-table a person who struck her as uninviting and whom the rest of the company treated contemptuously. She herself felt no reason to be any more affable towards him. It was only many years later that she realized that this negligent and neglected cousin had been the poet Heinrich Heine. There is not a little evidence to show how much Heine suffered both in his youth and later from this rejection by his rich relations. It was from the soil of this subjective emotion that the 'famillionairely' joke sprang.

The presence of similar subjective determinants may be suspected in some other of the great scoffer's jokes; but I know of no other one in which this can be demonstrated so convincingly. For this reason it is not easy to try to make any more definite statement about the nature of these personal determinants. Indeed, we shall be disinclined in general to claim such complicated determinants for the origin of every individual joke. Nor are the jokes produced by other famous men any more easily accessible to our examination. We get an impression that the subjective determinants of the joke-work are often not far removed from those of neurotic illness – when we learn, for instance, of Lichtenberg that he was a severely hypochrondriacal man, with all kinds of eccentricities. The great majority of jokes, and especially those that are constantly being newly produced in connection with the events of the day, are circulated anonymously; one would be curious to learn from what sort of people such productions originate. If one has occasion as a doctor to make the acquaintance of one of those people who, though not remarkable in other ways, are well known in their circle as jokers and the originators of many viable jokes, one may be surprised to discover that the joker is a disunited personality, disposed to neurotic disorders. The insufficiency of documentary evidence, however, will certainly prevent our setting up a hypothesis that a psychoneurotic constitution of this kind is a habitual or necessary subjective condition for the construction of jokes.

A more transparent case is offered, once more, by the Jewish jokes, which, as I have already mentioned (p. 157), are ordinarily made by Jews themselves, while the anecdotes about them from other sources scarcely ever rise above the level of comic stories or of brutal derision. What determines their participating in the jokes themselves seems to be the same as in the case of Heine's 'famillionairely' joke; and its significance seems to lie in the fact that the person concerned finds criticism or aggressiveness difficult so long as they are direct, and possible only along circuitous paths.

Other subjective factors which determine or favour the joke-work are less wrapped in obscurity. The motive force for the production of innocent jokes is not infrequently an ambitious urge to show one's cleverness, to display oneself – an instinct that may be equated with exhibitionism in the sexual field. The presence of numerous inhibited instincts, whose suppression has retained a certain degree of instability, will provide the most favourable disposition for the production of tendentious jokes. Thus individual components of a person's sexual constitution, in particular, can appear as motives for the construction of a joke. A whole class of obscene jokes allows one to infer the presence of a concealed inclination to exhibitionism in their inventors; aggressive tendentious jokes succeed best in people in whose sexuality a powerful sadistic component is demonstrable, which is more or less inhibited in real life.

The second fact which makes an inquiry into the subjective determination of jokes necessary[1] is the generally recognized experience that no one can be content with having made a joke for himself alone. An urge to tell the joke to someone is in-

1. [Cf. above, p. 191.]

extricably bound up with the joke-work; indeed, this urge is so strong that often enough it is carried through in disregard of serious misgivings. In the case of the comic as well, telling it to someone else produces enjoyment; but the demand is not peremptory. If one comes across something comic, one can enjoy it by oneself. A joke, on the contrary, *must* be told to someone else. The psychical process of constructing a joke seems not to be completed when the joke occurs to one: something remains over which seeks, by communicating the idea, to bring the unknown process of constructing the joke to a conclusion.

We cannot in the first instance guess what the basis may be of this urge to communicate the joke. But we can see another peculiarity in jokes which distinguishes them from the comic. If I come across something comic, I myself can laugh heartily at it, though it is true that I am also pleased if I can make someone else laugh by telling it to him. But I myself cannot laugh at a *joke* that has occurred to me, that I have made, in spite of the unmistakable enjoyment that the joke gives me. It is possible that my need to communicate the joke to someone else is in some way connected with the laughter produced by it, which is denied to me but is manifest in the other person.

Why is it, then, that I do not laugh at a joke of my own? And what part is played in this by the other person?

Let us take the second question first. In the case of the comic, two persons are in general concerned: besides myself, the person in whom I find something comic. If inanimate things seem to me comic, that is on account of a kind of personification which is not of rare occurrence in our ideational life. The comic process is content with these two persons: the self and the person who is the object; a third person may come into it, but is not essential. Joking as a *play* with one's own words and thoughts is to begin with without a person as an object. But already at the preliminary stage of the *jest*, if it has succeeded in making play and nonsense safe from the protests of reason, it demands another person to whom it can communicate its result. But this second person in the case of jokes does not correspond to the person who is the object, but to the *third* person, the 'other' person in the case of the comic. It seems as though in the case of a jest the other person has the decision passed over to him on whether the joke-work has succeeded in its task – as though the self did not feel certain in its judgement on the point. Innocent jokes, too, jokes that serve to reinforce a thought, require another person to test whether they have attained their aim. If a joke enters the service of the purpose of exposing or of a hostile purpose, it may be described as a psychical process between three persons, who are the same as in the case of the comic, though the part played by the third person is different; the psychical process in jokes is accomplished between the first person (the self) and the third (the outside person) and not, as in the case of the comic, between the self and the person who is the object.

Jokes are confronted by subjective determinants in the case of the third person too, and these may make their aim of producing pleasurable excitation unattainable. As Shakespeare (*Love's Labour's Lost*, Act V, Scene 2) reminds us:

> A jest's prosperity lies in the ear
> Of him that hears it, never in the tongue
> Of him that makes it . . .

A person who is dominated by a mood concerned with serious thoughts is not fitted to confirm the fact that a jest has succeeded in rescuing the verbal pleasure. He must himself be in a cheerful or at least in an indifferent state of feeling in order to act as the jest's third person. The same obstacle applies to innocent and to tendentious jokes; but in the latter there is a further obstacle in the form of opposition to the purpose which the joke is trying to serve. The third person cannot be ready to laugh at an excellent obscene joke if the exposure applies to a highly respected relative of his own; before a gathering of priests and ministers no one would venture to produce Heine's comparison of catholic and protestant clerics to retail tradesmen and employees of a wholesale business [p. 128 f.]; and an audience composed of my opponent's devoted friends would receive my most successful pieces of joking invective against him not as jokes but as invective, and would meet them with indignation and not with pleasure. Some degree of benevolence or a kind of neutrality, an absence of any factor that could provoke feelings opposed to the purpose of the joke, is an indispensable condition if the third person is to collaborate in the completion of the process of making the joke.

Where there are no such obstacles to the operation of the joke, the phenomenon which is now the subject of our inquiry emerges: the pleasure which the joke has produced is more evident in the third person than in the creator of the joke. We must be content to say more '*evident*' where we should be inclined to ask whether the hearer's pleasure is not more '*intense*' than that of the maker of the joke, since we naturally have no means of measuring and comparing. We see, however, that the hearer gives evidence of his pleasure with a burst of laughter, after the first person has as a rule produced the joke with a tensely serious look. If I repeat a joke that I have heard myself, I must, if I am not to spoil its effect, behave in telling it exactly like the person who made it. The question now arises whether we can draw any conclusions about the psychical process of constructing jokes from this factor of laughing at jokes.

It cannot be our design to consider at this point all that has been propounded and published on the nature of laughter. We may well be deterred from any such plan by the remarks with which Dugas, a pupil of Ribot's, prefaces his book *La psychologie du rire* (1902, 1): 'Il n'est pas de fait plus banal et plus étudié que le rire; il n'en est pas qui ait eu le don d'exciter davantage la curiosité du vulgaire et celle des philosophes; il n'en est pas sur lequel on ait receuilli plus d'observations et bâti plus de théories, et avec cela il n'en est pas qui demeure plus inexpliqué. On serait tenté de dire avec les sceptiques qu'il faut être content de rire et de ne pas chercher à savoir pourquoi on rit, d'autant que peut-être la réflexion tue le rire, et qu'il serait alors contradictoire qu'elle en découvrît les causes.'[1]

On the other hand we shall not miss the opportunity of making use for our purposes of an opinion on the mechanism of laughter which fits in excellently with our own line of thought. I have in mind the attempt at an explanation made by Herbert Spencer in his essay on 'The Physiology of Laughter' (1860). According to Spencer, laughter is a phenomenon of the discharge of mental excitation and a proof that the psychical employment of this excitation has suddenly come up against an obstacle. He describes the psychological situation which ends in laughter in the following words: 'Laughter naturally results only when consciousness is unawares transferred from great things to small – only when there is what we may call a *descending* incongruity.'[2]

1. ['There is no action that is more commonplace or that has been more widely studied than laughter. There is none that has succeeded more in exciting the curiosity both of ordinary people and of philosophers. There is none on which more observations have been collected and more theories built. But at the same time there is none that remains more unexplained. It would be tempting to say with the sceptics that we must be content to laugh and not try to know why we laugh, since it may be that reflection kills laughter and it would thus be a contradiction to think that it could discover its causes.']

2. Various points in this definition would call for detailed examination in an investigation of comic pleasure; this has already been undertaken by other authors and in any case does not concern us here. – I do not think Spencer has been happy in his explanation of why the discharge takes the particular paths whose excitation produces the somatic picture of laughter. The theme of the physiological explanation of laughter – that is, the tracing back or interpretation of the muscular actions characteristic of laughter – has been treated at length both before and since Darwin, but has still not been finally cleared up. I have one contribution to make to this theme. So far as I know, the

In a quite similar sense French authors (e.g. Dugas) describe laughter as a '*détente*', a phenomenon of relaxation of tension. So too the formula proposed by Bain [1865, 250] – 'laughter a release from constraint'[1] – seems to me to diverge from Spencer's view much less than some authorities would have us believe.

Nevertheless, we feel a need to modify Spencer's notion, in part to give a more definite form to the ideas contained in it and in part to change them. We should say that laughter arises if a quota of psychical energy which has earlier been used for the cathexis of particular psychical paths has become unusable, so that it can find free discharge. We are well aware what 'evil looks' we are inviting with such a hypothesis; but we will venture to quote in our defence an apposite sentence from Lipps's book *Komik und Humor* (1898, 71) from which illumination is to be derived on more subjects than that of the comic and humour: 'Finally, specific psychological problems always lead fairly deep into psychology, so that at bottom no psychological problem can be treated in isolation.' The concepts of 'psychical energy' and 'discharge' and the treatment of psychical energy as a quantity have become habitual in my thoughts since I began to arrange the facts of psychopathology philosophically; and already in my *Interpretation of Dreams* (1900a) I tried (in the same sense as Lipps) to establish the fact that what are 'really psychically effective' are psychical processes which are unconscious in themselves, not the contents of

---

grimace characteristic of smiling, which twists up the corners of the mouth, appears first in an infant at the breast when it is satisfied and satiated and lets go of the breast as it falls asleep. Here it is a genuine expression of the emotions, for it corresponds to a decision to take no more nourishment, and represents as it were an 'enough' or rather a 'more than enough'. This original meaning of pleasurable satiety may have brought the smile, which is after all the basic phenomenon of laughter, into its later relation with pleasurable processes of discharge.

1. [Misquoted by Freud: '. . . a relief from restraint'. The slight difference in meaning is immaterial to the present argument.]

consciousness.[1] It is only when I speak of the 'cathexis of psychical paths' that I seem to depart from the analogies commonly used by Lipps. My experiences of the displaceability of psychical energy along certain paths of association, and of the almost indestructible persistence of the traces of psychical processes, have in fact suggested to me an attempt at picturing the unknown in some such way. To avoid misunderstanding, I must add that I am making no attempt to proclaim that the cells and nerve fibres, or the systems of neurones which are taking their place today, are these psychical paths,[2] even though it would have to be possible in some manner which cannot yet be indicated to represent such paths by organic elements of the nervous system.

In laughter, therefore, on our hypothesis, the conditions are present under which a sum of psychical energy which has hitherto been used for cathexis is allowed free discharge. And since laughter – not all laughter, it is true, but certainly laughter at a joke – is an indication of pleasure, we shall be inclined to relate this pleasure to the lifting of the cathexis which has previously been present. If we see that the hearer of a joke laughs but that its creator cannot laugh, this may amount to telling us

1. Cf. the sections 'On Psychical Force', etc. in Chapter VIII of Lipps's book quoted above. 'Thus the following general statement holds good: The factors of psychical life are not the contents of consciousness but the psychical processes which are in themselves unconscious. The task of psychology, if it does not merely wish to describe the contents of consciousness, must therefore consist in inferring the nature of these unconscious processes from the character of the contents of consciousness and their temporal connections. Psychology must be a theory of these processes. But a psychology of this kind will very soon find that there are quite a number of characteristics of these processes which are not represented in the corresponding contents of consciousness' (Lipps, ibid., 123[-4]). See also Chapter VII of my *Interpretation of Dreams* [P.F.L., 4, 771-5].

2. [Some ten years earlier Freud had in fact made an elaborate but abortive attempt to prove precisely this in his posthumously published 'Project for a Scientific Psychology' (Freud, 1950a).]

that in the hearer a cathectic expenditure has been lifted and discharged, while in the construction of the joke there have been obstacles either to the lifting or to the possibility of discharge. The psychical process in the hearer, the joke's third person, can scarcely be more aptly described than by stressing the fact that he has bought the pleasure of the joke with very small expenditure on his own part. He might be said to have been presented with it. The words of the joke he hears necessarily bring about in him the idea or train of thought to the construction of which great internal inhibitions were opposed in him too. He would have had to make an effort of his own in order to bring it about spontaneously as the first person, he would have had to use at least as much psychical expenditure on doing so as would correspond to the strength of the inhibition, suppression or repression of the idea. He has saved this psychical expenditure. On the basis of our earlier discussions (p. 166) we should say that his pleasure corresponds to this economy. Our insight into the mechanism of laughter leads us rather to say that, owing to the introduction of the proscribed idea by means of an auditory perception, the cathectic energy used for the inhibition has now suddenly become superfluous and has been lifted, and is therefore now ready to be discharged by laughter. The two ways of expressing the facts amount to the same thing in essentials, since the expenditure economized corresponds exactly to the inhibition that has become superfluous. But the second method of expression is the more illuminating, since it allows us to say that the hearer of the joke laughs with the quota of psychical energy which has become free through the lifting of the inhibitory cathexis; we might say that he laughs this quota off.

If the person in whom the joke is formed cannot laugh, this, as we have already said [p. 200], points to a divergence from what happens in the third person that lies either in the lifting of the inhibitory cathexis or in the possibility of its discharge. But the first of these alternatives will not meet the case, as we shall see at once. The inhibitory cathexis must have been lifted in the first person as well, or otherwise no joke would have come about, since its formation was precisely in order to overcome a resistance of that kind; otherwise, too, it would be impossible for the first person to feel the pleasure in the joke which we have been obliged to trace back precisely to the lifting of the inhibition. All that remains, then, is the other alternative, namely that the first person cannot laugh, although he feels pleasure, because there is an interference with the possibility of discharge. An interference of this kind with the possibility of discharge, which is a necessary precondition of laughter, may arise from the liberated cathectic energy being immediately applied to some other endopsychic use. It is a good thing that our attention has been drawn to that possibility; and our interest in it will very soon be further engaged. Another condition, however, leading to the same result, may be realized in the first person of a joke. It is possible that no quota of energy at all that is capable of being manifested may be liberated, in spite of the lifting of the inhibitory cathexis. In the first person of a joke the joke-work is performed, which must correspond to a certain quota of new psychical expenditure. Thus the first person himself produces the force which lifts the inhibition. This no doubt results in a yield of pleasure for him, and even, in the case of tendentious jokes, a very considerable one, since the fore-pleasure obtained by the joke-work itself takes over the lifting of *further* inhibitions; but the expenditure on the joke-work is in every case deducted from the yield resulting from the lifting of the inhibition – an expenditure which is the same as the one which the hearer of the joke avoids. What I have just said may be confirmed by observing that a joke loses its effect of laughter even in the third person as soon as he is required to make an expenditure on intellectual work in connection with it. The allusions made in a joke must be obvious and the omissions easy to fill; an awakening of conscious intellectual interest usually makes the effect of the joke impossible. There is an important distinction here between jokes and riddles. Perhaps the psychical constellation during the joke-work is in general not favourable to the free discharge of what has been gained. We are not, it seems, in a position to see further on this point; we have been more successful in throwing light on one part of our problem – on which the third person laughs – than on its other part – on why the first person does *not* laugh.

Nevertheless, if we firmly accept these views on the determinants of laughter and on the psychical process in the third person, we are now in a position to give a satisfactory explanation of a whole number of peculiarities which jokes have been known to possess but which have not been understood. If a quota of cathectic energy capable of discharge is to be liberated in the third person, there are several conditions which must be fulfilled or which are desirable in order to act as encouragements: (1) It must be ensured that the third person is really making this cathectic expenditure. (2) It is necessary to guard against the cathectic expenditure, when it is liberated, finding some other psychical use instead of offering itself for motor discharge. (3) It cannot but be an advantage if the cathexis which is to be liberated in the third person is intensified beforehand, raised to a greater height. All these aims are served by particular methods of the joke-work, which may be classed together as secondary or auxiliary techniques: –

[1] The first of these conditions lays down one of the necessary qualifications of the third person as hearer of the joke. It is essential that he should be in sufficient psychical accord with the first person to possess the same internal inhibitions, which the joke-work has overcome in the latter. A person who is responsive to smut will be unable to derive any pleasure from witty jokes of exposure; Herr N.'s attacks will not be understood by uneducated people who are accustomed to give free play to their desire to insult. Thus every joke calls for a public of its own and laughing at the same jokes is evidence of far-

reaching psychical conformity. Here moreover we have arrived at a point which enables us to guess still more precisely what takes place in the third person. He must be able as a matter of habit to erect in himself the same inhibition which the first person's joke has overcome, so that, as soon as he hears the joke, the readiness for this inhibition will compulsively or automatically awaken. This readiness for inhibition, which I must regard as a real expenditure, analogous to mobilization in military affairs, will at the same moment be recognized as superfluous or too late, and so be discharged *in statu nascendi* by laughter.[1]

[2] The second condition for making free discharge possible – that the liberated energy shall be prevented from being used in any other way – seems very much the more important. It provides the theoretical explanation of the uncertainty of the effect of jokes when the thoughts expressed in a joke arouse powerfully exciting ideas in the hearer; in that case the question whether the purposes of the joke agree with or contradict the circle of thoughts by which the hearer is dominated will decide whether his attention will remain with the joking process or be withdrawn from it. Of still greater theoretical interest, however, are a class of auxiliary techniques which clearly serve the end of entirely detaching the hearer's attention from the joking process, and of allowing that process to run its course automatically. I deliberately say 'automatically' and not 'unconsciously', because the latter description would be misleading. It is only a question here of holding back an increased cathexis of attention from the psychical process when the joke is heard; and the usefulness of these auxiliary techniques rightly leads us to suspect that precisely the cathexis of attention has a great share in the supervision and fresh employment of liberated cathectic energy.

It appears to be far from easy to avoid the endopsychic employment of cathexes that have become superfluous, for in

1. The notion of the *status nascendi* has been used by Heymans (1896) in a somewhat different connection.

our thought-processes we are constantly in the habit of displacing such cathexes from one path to another without losing any of their energy by discharge. Jokes make use of the following methods with that aim in view. Firstly, they try to keep their expression as short as possible, so as to offer fewer points of attack to the attention. Secondly, they observe the condition of being easy to understand (see above [p. 202]); as soon as they call for intellectual work which would demand a choice between different paths of thought, they would endanger their effect not only by the unavoidable expenditure of thought but also by the awakening of attention. But besides this they employ the device of distracting attention by putting forward something in the joke's form of expression which catches it, so that in the meantime the liberation of the inhibitory cathexis and its discharge may be completed without interruption. This aim is already fulfilled by the omissions in the joke's wording; they offer an incitement to filling up the gaps and in that way succeed in withdrawing the joking process from attention. Here the technique of riddles, which attract the attention [p. 203], is, as it were, brought into the service of the joke-work. Far more effective even are the façades which we have found especially in some groups of tendentious jokes (p. 150 ff.). The syllogistic façades admirably fulfil the aim of holding the attention by setting it a task. While we are beginning to wonder what was wrong with the reply, we are already laughing; our attention has been caught unawares and the discharge of the liberated inhibitory cathexis has been completed. The same is true of jokes with a *comic* façade, in which the comic comes to the help of the joke-technique. A comic façade encourages the effectiveness of a joke in more than one way; not only does it make the automatism of the joking process possible, by holding the attention, but it also facilitates the discharge by the joke, by sending on ahead a discharge of a comic kind. The comic is here operating exactly like a bribing fore-pleasure, and we can in this way understand how some jokes are able to renounce entirely the fore-pleasure produced by the ordinary methods of joking and make use only of the comic for fore-pleasure. Among the joke-techniques proper, it is in particular displacement and representation by something absurd which, apart from their other qualifications, give rise, too, to a distraction of the attention which is desirable for the automatic course of the joking process.[1]

As we can already guess, and as we shall see more clearly later on, we have discovered in the condition of distracting the

1. I should like to discuss yet another interesting characteristic of joke-technique, in connection with an example of a displacement joke. Once when Gallmeyer, that actress of genius, was asked [in the course of an official examination] the unwelcome question 'Your age?' she is said to have replied 'in the tone of voice of a Gretchen and with her eyes bashfully cast down: "at Brünn".' This is a model displacement. When she was asked her age she replied by giving the place of her birth. She was thus anticipating the next question and was letting it be understood that she would be glad to know that this one question had been passed over. Yet we feel that in this instance the characteristic of jokes is not expressed in all its purity. It is too clear that the question is being evaded, the displacement is too obvious. Our attention understands at once that what is in question is an intentional displacement. In the other displacement jokes the displacement is disguised; our attention is held by the effort to detect it. In the displacement joke recorded on p. 91, in the reply made to a recommendation of a riding-horse 'What should I be doing in Pressburg at half-past six?' the displacement is also prominent. But to make up for this it has a confusing effect on the attention through its nonsensical nature, whereas in the actress's examination we are able to recognize her displacement-reply immediately. – [*Added* 1912:] What are known as '*Scherzfragen* [facetious questions]' deviate from jokes in another direction, though apart from this they may make use of the best techniques. Here is an example of one of them, which uses the technique of displacement: 'What is a cannibal who has eaten his father and his mother?' – 'An orphan.' – 'And if he has eaten all his other relations as well?' – 'The sole heir.' – 'And where will a monster of that kind find sympathy?' – 'In the dictionary under "S".' 'Facetious questions' of this kind are not proper jokes because the joking answers that they call for cannot be guessed in the same way as are the allusions, omissions, etc. of jokes. – [Josefine Gallmeyer (1838–84) was a soubrette actress, extremely popular in Vienna.]

attention a by no means unessential feature of the psychical process in the hearer of a joke.[1] In connection with this there are still other things that we can understand. Firstly, there is the question why we scarcely ever know what we are laughing at in a joke, though we can discover it by an analytic investigation. The laughter is in fact the product of an automatic process which is only made possible by our conscious attention's being kept away from it. Secondly, we are able to understand the peculiar fact about jokes that they only produce their full effect on the hearer if they are new to him, if they come as a surprise to him. This characteristic of jokes (which determines the shortness of their life and stimulates the constant production of new jokes) is evidently due to the fact that the very nature of surprising someone or taking him unawares implies that it cannot succeed a second time. When a joke is repeated, the attention is led back to the first occasion of hearing it as the memory of it arises. And from this we are carried on to an understanding of the urge to tell a joke one has heard to other people who have not yet heard it. One probably recovers from the impression the joke makes on a newcomer some of the possibility of enjoyment that has been lost owing to its lack of novelty. And it may be that it was an analogous motive that drove the creator of the joke in the first instance to tell it to someone else.

1. [Freud remarked elsewhere that many functions are actually performed better in the absence of conscious attention. Cf. for instance the second of the *Introductory Lectures* (1916–17), *P.F.L.*, **1**, 55. He also pointed out later that the device of distracting the attention is a technique that is also used in hypnotic suggestion. Cf. Chapter X of his *Group Psychology* (1921c). He expressed his opinion, too, in a posthumously published paper on 'Psycho-Analysis and Telepathy' (1941d [1921]), that the same procedure was at work in certain cases of thought-reading. A first hint at the idea of the device is probably to be seen in Freud's technical contribution to the *Studies on Hysteria* (1895d), *P.F.L.*, **3**, 354–5, in his explanation of the mechanism of his own 'pressure' technique.]

[3] In the third place I shall bring forward – but this time not as necessary conditions but only as encouragements to the process of joking – the auxiliary technical methods of the joke-work which are calculated to increase the quota which obtains discharge and in that way intensify the effect of the joke. These, it is true, also for the most part increase the attention that is paid to the joke, but they make this effect innocuous once more by simultaneously holding it and inhibiting its mobility. Anything that provokes interest and bewilderment works in these two directions – thus, in particular, nonsense, and contradiction, too, the 'contrast of ideas' [p. 41 f.] which some authorities have tried to make into the essential characteristic of jokes, but which I can only regard as a means of intensifying their effect. Anything that bewilders calls up in the hearer the state of distribution of energy which Lipps has called 'psychical damming-up' [p. 166]; and he is no doubt also correct in supposing that the 'discharge' is the more powerful, the higher was the preceding damming-up. Lipps's account, it is true, does not relate specifically to jokes but to the comic in general; but we may regard it as most probable that in jokes, too, the discharge of an inhibitory cathexis is similarly increased by the height of the damming-up.

It now begins to dawn on us that the technique of jokes is in general determined by two sorts of purposes – those that make the construction of the joke possible in the first person and those that are intended to guarantee the joke the greatest possible pleasurable effect on the third person. The Janus-like, two-way-facing character of jokes, which protects their original yield of pleasure from the attacks of critical reason, and the mechanism of fore-pleasure belong to the first of these purposes; the further complication of the technique by the conditions that have been enumerated in the present chapter takes place out of regard for the joke's third person. A joke is thus a double-dealing rascal who serves two masters at once. Everything in jokes that is aimed at gaining pleasure is calculated with an eye to the third person, as though there were internal and unsurmountable obstacles to it in the first person. And this gives us a full impression of how indispensable this third person is for the completion of the joking process. But whereas we have been able to obtain a fairly good insight into the nature of this process in the third person, the corresponding process in the first person seems still to be veiled in obscurity. Of the two questions we asked [p. 194–195], 'Why are we unable to laugh at a joke we have made ourselves' and 'Why are we driven to tell our own joke to someone else?', the first has so far evaded our reply. We can only suspect that there is an intimate connection between the two facts that have to be explained: that we are compelled to tell our joke to someone else *because* we are unable to laugh at it ourselves. Our insight into the conditions for obtaining and discharging pleasure which prevail in the *third* person enables us to infer as regards the *first* person that in him the conditions for discharge are lacking and those for obtaining pleasure only incompletely fulfilled. That being so, it cannot be disputed that we supplement our pleasure by attaining the laughter that is impossible for us by the roundabout path of the impression we have of the person who has been made to laugh. As Dugas has put it, we laugh as it were '*par ricochet* [on the rebound]'. Laughter is among the highly infectious expressions of psychical states. When I make the other person laugh by telling him my joke, I am actually making use of him to arouse my own laughter; and one can in fact observe that a person who has begun by telling a joke with a serious face afterwards joins in the other person's laughter with a moderate laugh. Accordingly, telling my joke to another person would seem to serve several purposes: first, to give me objective certainty that the joke-work has been successful; secondly, to complete my own pleasure by a reaction from the other person upon myself; and thirdly – where it is a question of repeating a joke that one has not produced oneself – to make up for the loss of pleasure owing to the joke's lack of novelty.

At the conclusion of these discussions of the psychical processes in jokes in so far as they take place between two persons, we may glance back at the factor of economy, which has been in our mind as being of importance in arriving at a psychological view of jokes ever since our first explanation of their technique. We have long since abandoned the most obvious but simplest view of this economy – that it is a question of an avoidance of psychical expenditure in general, such as would be involved by the greatest possible restriction in the use of words and in the establishment of chains of thought. Even at that stage we told ourselves that being concise or laconic was not enough to make a joke [p. 79]. A joke's brevity is of a peculiar kind – 'joking' brevity. It is true that the original yield of pleasure, produced by playing with words and thoughts, was derived from mere economy in expenditure; but with the development of play into a joke the tendency to economy too must alter its aims, for the amount that would be saved by the use of the same word or the avoidance of a new way of joining ideas together would certainly count for nothing as compared with the immense expenditure on our intellectual activity. I may perhaps venture on a comparison between psychical economy and a business enterprise. So long as the turnover in the business is very small, the important thing is that outlay in general shall be kept low and administrative costs restricted to the minimum. Economy is concerned with the absolute height of expenditure. Later, when the business has expanded, the importance of the administrative cost diminishes; the height reached by the amount of expenditure is no longer of significance provided that the turnover and profits can be sufficiently increased. It would be niggling, and indeed positively detrimental, to be conservative over expenditure on the administration of the business. Nevertheless it would be wrong to assume that when expenditure was absolutely great there would be no room left for the tendency to economy. The mind of the manager, if it is inclined to economy, will now turn to economy over details. He will feel satisfaction if a piece of work can be carried out at smaller cost than previously, however small the saving may seem to be in comparison with the size of the total expenditure. In a quite analogous fashion, in our complex psychical business too, economy in detail remains a source of pleasure, as may be seen from everyday happenings. Anyone who used to have his room lighted by gas and has now had electricity installed will for quite a time be aware of a definite feeling of pleasure when he switches on the electric light; he will feel it as long as the memory is revived in him at that moment of the complicated manoeuvres that were necessary for lighting the gas. Similarly, the economies in psychical inhibitory expenditure brought about by a joke – though they are small in comparison with our total psychical expenditure – will remain a source of pleasure for us because they save us a particular expenditure which we have been accustomed to make and which we were already prepared to make on this occasion as well. The factor of the expenditure's being one that was expected and prepared for moves unmistakably into the foreground.

A localized economy, such as we have just been considering, will not fail to give us momentary pleasure; but it will not bring a lasting relief so long as what has been saved at this point can be put to use elsewhere. It is only if this disposal elsewhere can be avoided that this specialized economy is transformed into a general relief of psychical expenditure. Thus, as we come to a better understanding of the psychical processes of jokes, the factor of relief takes the place of economy. It is obvious that the former gives a greater feeling of pleasure. The process in the joke's first person produces pleasure by lifting inhibition and diminishing local expenditure; but it seems not to come to rest until through the intermediary of the interpolated third person, it achieves general relief through discharge.

C. THEORETIC PART

VI

THE RELATION OF JOKES TO
DREAMS AND TO THE
UNCONSCIOUS

At the end of the chapter in which I was concerned with discovering the technique of jokes, I remarked (p. 129 f.) that the
processes of condensation, with or without the formation of
substitutes, of representation by nonsense and by the opposite,
of indirect representation, and so on, which, as we found, play a
part in producing jokes, show a very far-reaching agreement
with the processes of the 'dream-work'. I further promised on
the one hand that we would study these similarities more
closely and on the other hand that we would examine the common element in jokes and dreams which seems to be thus suggested. It would be much easier for me to carry out this
comparison if I could assume that one of the two objects of
comparison – the 'dream-work' – was already familiar to my
readers. But it will probably be wiser not to make that assumption. I have an impression that my *Interpretation of Dreams*,
published in 1900, provoked more 'bewilderment' than 'enlightenment' among my fellow-specialists; and I know that
wider circles of readers have been content to reduce the contents of the book to a catch-word ('wish-fulfilment') which can
be easily remembered and conveniently misused.

Continued concern with the problems treated there – for
which my medical practice as a psychotherapist has given me
abundant opportunity – has not brought me up against anything that might have called for alterations or improvements
in my lines of thought; I can therefore wait quietly till my
readers' understanding catches up with me or till judicious
criticism has shown me the fundamental errors in my view. For

the purpose of making the comparison with jokes, I will now repeat, briefly and concisely, the most essential information about dreams and the dream-work.

We know a dream from what seems as a rule a fragmentary memory of it which we have after waking. It appears as a mesh-work of sense-impressions, mostly visual but also of other kinds, which have simulated an experience, and with which thought-processes ('knowledge' in the dream) and expressions of affect may be mingled. What we thus remember of the dream I call *the dream's manifest content*. It is often entirely absurd and confused – sometimes only the one or the other. But even if it is quite coherent, as it is in the case of some anxiety-dreams, it confronts our mental life as something alien, for whose origin one cannot in any way account. The explanation of these characteristics of dreams has hitherto been looked for in dreams themselves, by regarding them as indications of a disordered, dissociated and so to say 'sleepy' activity of the nervous elements.

I have on the contrary shown that this strange 'manifest' content of the dream can regularly be made intelligible as a mutilated and altered transcript of certain rational psychical structures which deserve the name of *latent dream-thoughts*. We arrive at a knowledge of these by dividing the dream's manifest content into its component parts, without considering any apparent meaning it may have [as a whole], and then by following the associative threads which start from each of what are now isolated elements. These interweave with one another and finally lead to a tissue of thoughts which are not only per-fectly rational but can also be easily fitted into the known con-text of our mental processes. In the course of this 'analysis', the content of the dream will have cast off all the peculiarities that puzzled us. But if the analysis is to succeed, we must, while it proceeds, firmly reject the critical objections which will un-ceasingly arise to the reproduction of the various intermediary associations.

A comparison of the recollected manifest content of the dream with the latent dream-thoughts thus discovered gives rise to the concept of the 'dream-work'. The dream-work is the name of the whole sum of transforming processes which have converted the dream-thoughts into the manifest dream. The surprise with which we formerly regarded the dream now attaches to the dream-work.

The achievements of the dream-work can, however, be described as follows. A tissue of thoughts, usually a very complicated one, which has been built up during the day and has not been completely dealt with – 'a day's residue' – continues during the night to retain the quota of energy – the 'interest' – claimed by it, and threatens to disturb sleep. This 'day's residue' is transformed by the dream-work into a dream and made innocuous to sleep. In order to provide a fulcrum for the dream-work, the 'day's residue' must be capable of constructing a wish – which is not a very hard condition to fulfil. The wish arising from the dream-thoughts forms the preliminary stage and later the core of the dream. Experience derived from analyses – and not the theory of dreams – informs us that in children any wish left over from waking life is sufficient to call up a dream, which emerges as connected and ingenious but usually short, and which is easily recognized as a 'wish-fulfilment'. In the case of adults it seems to be a generally binding condition that the wish which creates the dream shall be one that is alien to conscious thinking – a repressed wish – or will possibly at least have reinforcements that are unknown to consciousness. Without assuming the existence of the unconscious in the sense explained above [p. 199 f.], I should not be able to develop the theory of dreams further or to interpret the material met with in dream-analyses. The action of this unconscious wish upon the consciously rational material of the dream-thoughts produces the dream. While this happens, the dream is, as it were, dragged down into the unconscious, or, more precisely, is submitted to a treatment such as is met with at the level of unconscious thought-processes and is characteristic of that level. Hitherto it is only from the results of the 'dream-work' that we are in fact acquainted with the characteristics of unconscious thinking and its differences from thinking that is capable of becoming conscious – 'preconscious' thinking.

A theory which is novel, which lacks simplicity and which runs counter to our habits of thought, can scarcely gain in clarity from a concise presentation. All I can aim at in these remarks, therefore, is to draw attention to the fuller treatment of the unconscious in my *Interpretation of Dreams* and to the writings of Lipps, which seem to me of the highest importance. I am aware that anyone who is under the spell of a good academic philosophical education, or who takes his opinions at long range from some so-called system of philosophy, will be opposed to the assumption of an 'unconscious psychical' in the sense in which Lipps and I use the term, and will prefer to prove its impossibility on the basis of a definition of the psychical. But definitions are a matter of convention and can be altered. I have often found that people who dispute the unconscious as being something absurd and impossible have not formed their impressions from the sources from which I at least was brought to the necessity of recognizing it. These opponents of the unconscious had never witnessed the effect of a post-hypnotic suggestion, and when I have told them examples from my analyses with non-hypnotized neurotics they have been filled with the greatest astonishment. They had never realized the idea that the unconscious is something which we really do not know, but which we are obliged by compelling inferences to supply; they had understood it as being something capable of becoming conscious but which was not being thought of at the moment, which did not occupy 'the focal point of attention'. Nor had they ever tried to convince themselves of the existence in their own minds of unconscious thoughts like these by analysing one of their own dreams; and when I attempted to do so with them they could only greet their own associations with surprise and confusion. I have also formed an impression that fundamental emotional resistances stand in the way of accepting the 'unconscious', and that these are based on the fact that no one wants to get to know his unconscious and that the most convenient plan is to deny its possibility altogether.

The dream-work, then – to which I return after this digression – submits the thought-material, which is brought forward in the optative mood, to a most strange revision. First, it takes the step from the optative to the present indicative; it replaces 'Oh! if only . . .' by 'It is'. The 'It is' is then given a hallucinatory representation; and this I have called the 'regression' in the dream-work – the path that leads from thoughts to perceptual images, or, to use the terminology of the still unknown topography of the mental apparatus (which is not to be taken anatomically), from the region of thought-structures to that of sensory perceptions. On this path, which is in the reverse direction to that taken by the course of development of mental complications, the dream-thoughts are given a pictorial character; and eventually a plastic situation is arrived at which is the core of the manifest 'dream-picture'. In order for it to be possible for the dream-thoughts to be represented in sensory form, their expression has to undergo far-reaching modifications. But while the thoughts are being changed back into sensory images still further alterations occur in them, some of which can be seen to be necessary while others are surprising. We can understand that, as a subsidiary result of regression, almost all the internal relations between the thoughts which linked them together will be lost in the manifest dream. The dream-work, as we might say, only undertakes to represent the raw material of the ideas and not the logical relations in which they stand to one another; or at all events it reserves the liberty to disregard the latter. On the other hand, there is another part of the dream-work which we cannot attribute to regression, to the change back into sensory images; and it is precisely this part which has an important bearing on our analogy with the formation of jokes. In the course of the dream-work the material of the dream-thoughts is subjected to a quite extraordinary compression or *condensation*. A starting point for it is provided by any common elements that may be present in the dream-thoughts, whether by chance or from the nature of their content. Since these are not as a rule sufficient for any considerable condensation, new artificial and transient common elements are created in the dream-work, and to this end there is actually a preference for the use of words the sound of which expresses different meanings. The newly-created common elements of condensation enter the manifest content of the dream as representatives of the dream-thoughts, so that an element in the dream corresponds to a nodal point or junction in the dream-thoughts, and, as compared with these latter, must quite generally be described as 'overdetermined'. The fact of condensation is the piece of the dream-work which can be most easily recognized; it is only necessary to compare the text of a dream as it is noted down with the record of the dream-thoughts arrived at by analysis in order to get a good impression of the extensiveness of dream-condensation.

It is less easy to convince oneself of the second great modification of the dream-thoughts that is brought about by the dream-work – the process that I have named 'dream-*displacement*'. This is exhibited in the fact that things that lie on the periphery of the dream-thoughts and are of minor importance occupy a central position and appear with great sensory intensity in the manifest dream, and *vice versa*. This gives the dream the appearance of being displaced in relation to the dream-thoughts, and this displacement is precisely what brings it about that the dream confronts waking mental life as something alien and incomprehensible. In order that a displacement of this kind may occur, it must be possible for the cathectic energy to pass over uninhibited from the important ideas to the unimportant ones – which, in normal thought that is capable of being conscious, can only give an impression of 'faulty reasoning'.

Transformation with a view to the possibility of representation, condensation and displacement are the three major achievements that may be ascribed to the dream-work. A fourth, which was perhaps too shortly considered in *The Interpretation of Dreams*, is not relevant for our present purposes.[1] If the ideas of a 'topography of the mental apparatus' and of 'regression' are consistently followed up (and only in that way could these working hypotheses come to have any value), we must attempt to determine the stages of regression at which the various transformations of the dream-thoughts take place. This attempt has not yet been seriously undertaken; but it can at least be stated with certainty that displacement must take place in the thought-material while it is at the stage of the unconscious processes, while condensation must probably be pictured as a process stretching over the whole course of events till the perceptual region is reached. But in general we must be content to assume that all the forces which take part in the formation of dreams operate simultaneously. Though one must, as will be realized, exercise reserve in dealing with such problems, and though there are fundamental doubts, which cannot be entered into here, as to whether the question should be framed in this manner,[2] yet I should like to venture on the assertion that the process of the dream-work preparatory to the dream must be located in the region of the unconscious. Thus, speaking roughly, there would in all be three stages to be distinguished in the formation of a dream: first, the transplanting of the pre-

1. [The allusion is to 'secondary revision', the subject of Chapter VI (I) of *The Interpretation of Dreams* (1900a), P.F.L., 4, 628 ff. Elsewhere, however, Freud considers that this is *not* part of the dream-work: cf. the first of the 'Two Encyclopaedia Articles' (1923a), P.F.L., 15.]

2. [This is probably a reference to the inadequacy of a purely topographical account of mental processes. A full discussion of these doubts followed much later, in the paper on 'The Unconscious' (1915e), Sections II and VII.]

conscious day's residues into the unconscious, in which the conditions governing the state of sleep must play a part; then, the dream-work proper in the unconscious; and thirdly, the regression of the dream-material, thus revised, to perception, in which form the dream becomes conscious.

The following forces may be recognized as having a share in the formation of dreams: the wish to sleep, the cathexis of energy that still remains in the day's residues after it has been lowered by the state of sleep, the psychical energy of the dream-constructing unconscious wish and the opposing force of the 'censorship', which dominates daytime life and is not completely lifted during sleep. The task of dream-formation is above all to overcome the inhibition from the censorship; and it is precisely this task which is solved by the displacements of psychical energy within the material of the dream-thoughts.

Let us now recall what it was during our investigation of jokes that gave us occasion to think of dreams. We found that the characteristics and effects of jokes are linked with certain forms of expression or technical methods, among which the most striking are condensation, displacement and indirect representation. Processes, however, which lead to the same results – condensation, displacement and indirect representation – have become known to us as peculiarities of the dream-work. Does not this agreement suggest the conclusion that joke-work and dream-work must, at least in some essential respect, be identical? The dream-work has, I think, been revealed to us as regards its most important characteristics. Of the psychical processes in jokes the part that is hidden from us is precisely the one that may be compared to the dream-work – namely, what happens during the formation of a joke in the first person. Shall we not yield to the temptation to construct that process on the analogy of the formation of a dream? A few of the characteristics of dreams are so alien to jokes that the part of the dream-work corresponding to those characteristics cannot be transferred to the formation of jokes. There is no doubt that the regression of the train of thought to perception is absent in jokes. But the other two stages of dream-formation, the sinking of a preconscious thought into the unconscious and its unconscious revision, if they could be supposed to occur in joke-formation, would present the precise outcome that we can observe in jokes. Let us decide, then, to adopt the hypothesis that thts is the way in which jokes are formed in the first person: *a preconscious thought is given over for a moment to unconscious revision and the outcome of this is at once grasped by conscious perception.*

Before we examine this hypothesis in detail, we will consider an objection which might threaten our premiss. We have started from the fact that the techniques of jokes indicate the same processes that are known to us as peculiarities of the dream-work. Now it is easy to argue against this that we should not have described the techniques of jokes as condensation, displacement, etc., and should not have arrived at such far-reaching conformities between the methods of representation in jokes and dreams, if our previous knowledge of the dream-work had not prejudiced our view of the technique of jokes; so that at bottom we are only finding in jokes a confirmation of the expectations with which we approached them from dreams. If this was the basis of the conformity, there would be no certain guarantee of its existence apart from our prejudice. Nor indeed have condensation, displacement and indirect representation been taken by any other author as explaining the forms of expression of jokes. This would be a possible objection, but not on that account a just one. It would be equally possible that it was indispensable for our views to be sharpened by a knowledge of the dream-work before we could recognize the real conformity. A decision will after all depend only on whether a critical examination can prove on the basis of individual examples that this view of the technique of jokes is a forced one in whose favour other more plausible and deeper-going views have been suppressed, or whether such an examination is obliged to admit that the expectations derived from dreams can really be confirmed in jokes. I am of the opinion that we have nothing to fear from such criticism and that our procedure of 'reduction' (p. 55) has shown us reliably in what forms of expression to look for the techniques of jokes. And if we gave those techniques names which already anticipated the discovery of the conformity between joke-technique and dream-work, we had a perfect right to do so and it was in fact nothing more than an easily justifiable simplification.

There is another objection which would not affect our case so seriously but which is also not so open to a fundamental disproof. It might be said that, while it is true that these techniques of joking which fit in so well with our scheme deserve to be recognized, they are nevertheless not the only possible techniques of joking nor the only ones used in practice. It might be argued that under the influence of the model of the dream-work we have only looked for techniques of joking which fitted in with it, while others, overlooked by us, would have proved that this conformity was not invariably present. I really cannot venture to assert that I have succeeded in elucidating the technique of every joke in circulation; and I must therefore leave open the possibility that my enumeration of joke-techniques will show some incompleteness. But I have not intentionally excluded from discussion any kind of technique that was clear to me, and I can declare that the commonest, most important and most characteristic methods of joking have not escaped my attention.

Jokes possess yet another characteristic which fits satisfactorily into the view of the joke-work which we have derived from dreams. We speak, it is true, of 'making' a joke; but we are aware that when we do so our behaviour is different from what it is when we make a judgement or make an objection. A joke has quite outstandingly the characteristic of being a notion that has occurred to us 'involuntarily'. What happens is not that we know a moment beforehand what joke we are going to make, and that all it then needs is to be clothed in words. We have an indefinable feeling, rather, which I can best compare with an *'absence'*,[1] a sudden release of intellectual tension, and then all at once the joke is there – as a rule ready-clothed in words. Some of the techniques of jokes can be employed apart from them in the expression of a thought – for instance, the techniques of analogy or allusion. I can deliberately decide to make an allusion. In such a case I begin by having a direct expression of my thought in my mind (in my inner ear); I inhibit myself from expressing it owing to a misgiving related to the external situation, and can almost be said to make up my mind to replace the direct expression by another form of indirect expression; and I then produce an allusion. But the allusion which arises in this way and which is formed under my continuous supervision is never a joke, however serviceable it may be in other ways. A joking allusion, on the other hand, emerges without my being able to follow these preparatory stages in my thoughts. I will not attach too much importance to this behaviour; it is scarcely decisive, though it agrees well with our hypothesis that in the formation of a joke one drops a train of thought for a moment and that it then suddenly emerges from the unconscious as a joke.

Jokes show a special way of behaving, too, in regard to association. Often they are not at the disposal of our memory when we want them; but at other times, to make up for this, they appear involuntarily, as it were, and at points in our train of thought where we cannot see their relevance. These, again, are only small features, but nevertheless indicate their origin from the unconscious.

Let us now bring together those characteristics of jokes which can be referred to their formation in the unconscious. First and foremost there is the peculiar brevity of jokes – not, indeed, an essential, but an extremely distinctive feature. When we first

1. [The French term.]

came across it, we were inclined to regard it as an expression of the tendency to economy, but abandoned this view ourselves owing to obvious objections [p. 79]. It now seems to us rather a mark of the unconscious revision to which the joke-thought has been subjected. For we cannot connect what corresponds to it in dreams, condensation, with any factor other than localization in the unconscious; and we must suppose that the determinants for such condensations, which are absent in the preconscious, are present in the unconscious thought-process.[1] It is to be expected that in the process of condensation a few of the elements subjected to it will be lost, while others, which take over the cathectic energy of the former, will become intensified or over-intensified through the condensation. Thus the brevity of jokes, like that of dreams, would be a necessary concomitant of the condensations which occur in both of them – in both cases a result of the process of condensation. This origin would also account for the special character of the brevity of jokes, a character that cannot be further defined but which is felt as a striking one.

In an earlier passage (p. 173) we regarded one of the outcomes of condensation – multiple use of the same material, play upon words, and similarity of sound – as a localized economy, and the pleasure produced by an (innocent) joke as derived from that economy, and later [p. 177 f.] we inferred that the original intention of jokes was to obtain a yield of pleasure of this kind from words – a thing which had been permitted at

---

1. Apart from the dream-work and the technique of jokes, there is another kind of mental event in which I have been able to show that condensation is a regular and important process: namely the mechanism of normal (non-tendentious) *forgetting*. Unique impressions offer difficulties to forgetting; those that are analogous in any way are forgotten by being condensed in regard to their points of resemblance. Confusion between analogous impressions is one of the preliminary stages of forgetting. [Freud enlarged on this in a footnote added in 1907 to Section F of Chapter XII of *The Psychopathology of Everyday Life* (1901b), *P.F.L.*, 5, 339.]

the stage of play but had been dammed up by rational criticism in the course of intellectual development. We have now adopted the hypothesis that condensations of this kind, such as serve the technique of jokes, arise automatically, without any particular intention, during thought-processes in the unconscious. Have we not before us here two different views of the same fact which seem incompatible with each other? I do not think so. It is true that they are two different views, and that they need to be brought into harmony with each other; but they are not contradictory. One of them is merely foreign to the other; and when we have established a connection between them, we shall probably have made some advance in knowledge. The fact that such condensations are sources for a yield of pleasure is far from incompatible with the hypothesis that conditions for their production are easily found in the unconscious. We can, on the contrary, see a reason for the plunge into the unconscious in the circumstance that the pleasure-yielding condensations of which jokes are in need arise there easily. There are, moreover, two other factors which at a first glance seem to be completely foreign to each other and to have come together as though by some undesired chance, but which on deeper investigation turn out to be intimately linked and indeed essentially one. I have in mind the two assertions that, on the one hand, jokes during their development at the stage of play (that is, during the childhood of reason) are able to bring about these pleasurable condensations and that, on the other hand, at higher stages they accomplish the same effect by plunging the thought into the unconscious. For the infantile is the source of the unconscious, and the unconscious thought-processes are none other than those – the one and only ones – produced in early childhood. The thought which, with the intention of constructing a joke, plunges into the unconscious is merely seeking there for the ancient dwelling-place of its former play with words. Thought is put back for a moment to the stage of childhood so as once more to gain possession of the childish source of pleasure. If we did not already know it from research into the psychology of the neuroses, we should be led by jokes to a suspicion that the strange unconscious revision is nothing else than the infantile type of thought-activity. It is merely that it is not very easy for us to catch a glimpse in children of this infantile way of thinking, with its peculiarities that are retained in the unconscious of adults, because it is for the most part corrected, as it were, *in statu nascendi*. But in a number of cases we succeed in doing so, and we then laugh at the children's 'silliness'. Any uncovering of unconscious material of this kind strikes us in general as 'comic'.[1]

It is easier to perceive the characteristics of these unconscious thought-processes in the remarks made by sufferers from certain mental diseases. We should most probably be able (as Griesinger suggested long ago[2]) to understand the deliria of the insane and to make use of them as pieces of information, if we ceased to apply the demands of conscious thinking to them and if we treated them, like dreams, with our interpretative technique.[3] Indeed we have confirmed the fact that 'there is a return of the mind in dreams to an embryonic point of view'.[4]

We have entered so closely, in connection with the processes of condensation, into the importance of the analogy between

1. Many of my neurotic patients who are under psychoanalytic treatment are regularly in the habit of confirming the fact by a laugh when I have succeeded in giving a faithful picture of their hidden unconscious to their conscious perception; and they laugh even when the content of what is unveiled would by no means justify this. This is subject, of course, to their having arrived close enough to the unconscious material to grasp it after the doctor has detected it and presented it to them.

2. [W. Griesinger (1817–68) had pointed out the wish-fulfilling character of both dreams and psychoses. One particular passage of his (Griesinger, 1845, 89) is referred to several times by Freud. Cf., for example, *The Interpretation of Dreams*, P.F.L., 4, 163, 214 and 326*n*.]

3. In doing so we should not forget to take into account the distortion due to the censorship which is still at work even in psychoses.

4. *The Interpretation of Dreams*. [P.F.L., 4, 749. The phrase occurs there as a quotation; but its source is not specified.]

jokes and dreams that we may be briefer in what follows. As we know, the displacements in the dream-work point to the operation of the censorship of conscious thinking, and accordingly, when we come across displacement among the techniques of jokes, we shall be inclined to suppose that an inhibitory force plays a part in the formation of jokes as well. And we already know that this is quite generally the case. The effort made by jokes to recover the old pleasure in nonsense or the old pleasure in words finds itself inhibited in normal moods by objections raised by critical reason; and in every individual case this has to be overcome. But the manner in which the joke-work accomplishes this task shows a sweeping distinction between jokes and dreams. In the dream-work it is habitually accomplished by displacements, by the selection of ideas which are sufficiently remote from the objectionable one for the censorship to allow them to pass, but which are nevertheless derivatives of that idea and have taken over its psychical cathexis by means of a complete transference.[1] For this reason displacements are never absent in a dream and are far more comprehensive.

Among displacements are to be counted not merely diversions from a train of thought but every sort of indirect representation as well, and in particular the replacement of an important but objectionable element by one that is indifferent and that appears innocent to the censorship, something that seems like a very remote allusion to the other one – substitution by a piece of symbolism, or an analogy, or something small. It cannot be disputed that portions of such indirect representation are already present in the dream's preconscious thoughts – for instance, representation by symbols or analogies – because otherwise the thought would not have reached the stage of preconscious expression at all. Indirect representations of this kind, and allusions whose reference to the thing intended is easy

1. ['Transference' is not, of course, used here in the commoner sense in which it is used of a phenomenon in psychotherapy.]

to discover, are indeed permissible and much-used methods of expression in our conscious thinking as well. The dream-work, however, exaggerates this method of indirect expression beyond all bounds. Under the pressure of the censorship, any sort of connection is good enough to serve as a substitute by allusion, and displacement is allowed from any element to any other. Replacement of internal associations (similarity, causal connection, etc.) by what are known as external ones (simultaneity in time, contiguity in space, similarity of sound) is quite specially striking and characteristic of the dream-work.

All these methods of displacement appear too as techniques of joking. But when they appear, they usually respect the limits imposed on their employment in conscious thinking; and they may be altogether absent, although jokes too have invariably a task to accomplish of dealing with an inhibition. We can understand the subordinate place taken by displacements in the joke-work when we recall that jokes always have another technique at their command for keeping off inhibition and indeed that we have found nothing more characteristic of them than precisely this technique. For jokes do not, like dreams, create compromises; they do not evade the inhibition, but they insist on maintaining play with words or with nonsense unaltered. They restrict themselves, however, to a choice of occasions in which this play or this nonsense can at the same time appear allowable (in jests) or sensible (in jokes), thanks to the ambiguity of words and the multiplicity of conceptual relations. Nothing distinguishes jokes more clearly from all other psychical structures than this double-sidedness and this duplicity in speech. From this point of view at least the authorities come closest to an understanding of the nature of jokes when they lay stress on 'sense in nonsense' [p. 42].

In view of the universal predominance in jokes of this peculiar technique for overcoming their inhibitions, it might be thought superfluous for them ever to make use in particular cases of the technique of displacement. But, on the one hand, certain species of that technique remain of value to jokes as aims and as sources of pleasure – for instance, displacement proper (diversion of thoughts), which indeed partakes of the nature of nonsense. On the other hand, it should not be forgotten that the highest stage of jokes, tendentious jokes, often have to over-come two kinds of inhibitions, those opposed to the joke itself and those opposed to its purpose (p. 145), and that allusions and displacements are well qualified to make this latter task possible.

The abundant and unrestrained use in the dream-work of indirect representation, of displacements, and especially of allusions, has a result which I mention not for its own import-ance but because it became my subjective reason for taking up the problem of jokes. If one gives an account to an uninformed or unaccustomed person of a dream-analysis, in which are set out, therefore, the strange processes of allusions and displace-ments – processes so obnoxious to waking life – of which the dream-work has made use, the reader receives an uncomfort-able impression and declares that these interpretations are 'in the nature of a joke'. But he clearly does not regard them as *successful* jokes, but as forced, and in some way violating the rules of jokes. It is easy to explain this impression. It arises from the fact that the dream-work operates by the same methods as jokes, but in its use of them it transgresses the limits that are respected by jokes.[1] We shall presently [p. 238] learn that, as a result of the part played by the third person, jokes are bound by a certain condition which does not apply to dreams.

Among the techniques common to jokes and dreams, representation by the opposite and the use of nonsense claim some amount of our interest. The former is one of the more effective methods employed in jokes, as may be seen among others by the examples of 'overstatement jokes' (p. 111 f.). In-

1. [This question had in fact first been raised by Fliess, in connection with *The Interpretation of Dreams*. Cf. the Editor's Introduction, p. 31f. above.]

cidentally, representation by the opposite is not able, like most other joke-techniques, to escape conscious attention. A person who tries to bring the joke-work into operation in himself as deliberately as possible – a professional wag – soon discovers as a rule that the easiest way of replying to an assertion by a joke is by asserting its contrary and by leaving it to the inspiration of the moment to get rid of the objection which his contradiction is likely to provoke, by giving what he has said a fresh interpretation. It may be that representation by the opposite owes the favour it enjoys to the fact that it forms the core of another pleasurable way of expressing a thought, which can be understood without any need for bringing in the unconscious. I am thinking of *irony*, which comes very close to joking [see p. 113 above] and is counted among the sub-species of the comic. Its essence lies in saying the opposite of what one intends to convey to the other person, but in sparing him contradiction by making him understand – by one's tone of voice, by some accompanying gesture, or (where writing is concerned) by some small stylistic indications – that one means the opposite of what one says. Irony can only be employed when the other person is prepared to hear the opposite, so that he cannot fail to feel an inclination to contradict. As a result of this condition, irony is exposed particularly easily to the danger of being misunderstood. It brings the person who uses it the advantage of enabling him readily to evade the difficulties of direct expression, for instance in invectives. It produces comic pleasure in the hearer, probably because it stirs him into a contradictory expenditure of energy which is at once recognized as being unnecessary. A comparison like this between jokes and a closely related type of the comic may confirm our assumption that what is peculiar to jokes is their relation to the unconscious and that this may perhaps distinguish them from the comic as well.[1]

1. The characteristic of the comic which is described as its 'dryness' depends likewise on the distinction between a statement and the gestures (in the widest sense of the word) accompanying it.

In the dream-work, representation by the opposite plays a far greater part even than in jokes. Dreams are not merely fond of representing two contraries by one and the same composite structure, but they so often change something in the dream-thoughts into its opposite that this leads to a great difficulty in the work of interpretation. 'There is no way of deciding at a first glance whether any element that admits of a contrary is present in the dream-thoughts as a positive or as a negative.'[1]

I must state emphatically that this fact has not up to now met with any recognition. But it seems to point to an important characteristic of unconscious thinking, in which in all probability no process that resembles 'judging' occurs. In the place of rejection by a judgement, what we find in the unconscious is 'repression'. Repression may, without doubt, be correctly described as the intermediate stage between a defensive reflex and a condemning judgement.[2]

Nonsense, absurdity, which appears so often in dreams and has brought them into so much undeserved contempt, never arises by chance through the ideational elements being jumbled together, but can always be shown to have been admitted by the dream-work intentionally and to be designed to represent embittered criticism and contemptuous contradiction in the dream-thoughts. Thus the absurdity in the content of the dream takes the place of the judgement 'this is a piece of nonsense' in the dream-thoughts.[3] I laid great stress on the evidence of

1. *The Interpretation of Dreams.* [*P.F.L.*, 4, 429f.]

2. The highly remarkable and still insufficiently appreciated behaviour of the relation between contraries in the unconscious is no doubt likely to help our understanding of 'negativism' in neurotic and insane patients. (Cf. the last two works on the subject: Bleuler, 1904 and Gross, 1904. [*Added* 1912:] See also my review of 'The Antithetical Meaning of Primal Words' (1910e).) – [The statement that repression is an earlier form of a negative judgement seems to occur here for the first time. It is often repeated later and the whole question is discussed more fully in the much later paper on 'Negation' (1925h).]

3. [Cf. the first part of Section G of Chapter VI of *The Interpretation of Dreams*, *P.F.L.*, 4, 554ff.]

this in my *Interpretation of Dreams* because I thought that in this way I could make the most forcible attack on the error of believing that the dream is not a psychical phenomenon at all – an error which blocks the way to a knowledge of the unconscious. We have now learned, in the course of solving certain tendentious jokes (p. 94 ff.), that nonsense in jokes is made to serve the same aims of representation. We know too that a senseless façade to a joke is particularly well suited to increase the hearer's psychical expenditure and so to raise the quota liberated for discharge by laughing [p. 205]. But besides this, it must not be forgotten that the nonsense in a joke is an end in itself, since the intention of recovering the old pleasure in nonsense is among the joke-work's motives. There are other ways of recovering the nonsense and of deriving pleasure from it: caricature, exaggeration, parody and travesty make use of them and so create 'comic nonsense'. If we submit these forms of expression to an analysis similar to the one we have applied to jokes, we shall find that in none of these cases is there any occasion for bringing in unconscious processes in our sense in order to explain them. We can now understand too how it is that the characteristic of being a joke can come as an extra addition to a caricature, exaggeration or parody; what makes this possible is a difference in the 'psychical scene of action'.[1]

The assignment of the joke-work to the system of the unconscious has, I think, become of considerably greater importance to us now that it has enabled us to understand the fact that the techniques to which jokes admittedly cling are, on the other hand, not their exclusive property. Some doubts which we were obliged to hold over until later in our original ex-

1. An expression used by Fechner [1889, 2, 520–21] which has acquired importance for me as a support for my views. [Fechner's idea that 'the scene of action in dreams is different from that of waking ideational life' had been quoted by Freud in *The Interpretation of Dreams* (P.F.L., 4, 684) as supporting the topographical distinction between unconscious and preconscious mental processes.]

amination of these techniques now find a comfortable solution.[1] For that very reason another doubt that arises is all the more deserving of our consideration. This suggests that the undeniable relation of jokes to the unconscious is in fact only valid for certain categories of tendentious jokes, whereas *we* are prepared to extend it to every species and every developmental stage of jokes. We must not evade an examination of this objection.

It can be assumed with certainty that jokes are formed in the unconscious when it is a question of jokes in the service of unconscious purposes or of purposes reinforced by the unconscious – that is, of most 'cynical' jokes [p. 157 f.]. For in such cases the unconscious purpose drags the preconscious thought down into the unconscious and there gives it a new shape – a process to which the study of the psychology of the neuroses has taught us numerous analogies. In the case, however, of tendentious jokes of other kinds, of innocent jokes and of jests, this downward-dragging force seems absent and the relation of jokes to the unconscious is accordingly called in question.

But let us now consider the case in which a thought, not worthless in itself, arises in the course of a train of thought and is expressed as a joke. In order to enable this thought to be turned into a joke, it is clearly necessary to select from among the possible forms of expression the precise one which brings along with it a yield of verbal pleasure. We know from self-observation that this selection is not made by conscious attention; but it will certainly help the selection if the cathexis of the preconscious thought is reduced to an unconscious one, for, as we have learnt from the dream-work, the connecting paths which start out from *words* are in the unconscious treated in the same way as connections between *things*. An unconscious cathexis offers far more favourable conditions for selecting the expression. Moreoever, we can immediately assume that the possible form of expression that involves a yield of verbal

1. [See, for instance, pp. 99 and 122 f.]

pleasure exercises the same downward drag on the still un-settled wording of the preconscious thought as did the un-conscious purpose in the earlier case. To meet the simpler case of the jest, we may suppose that an intention which is all the time on the look-out to achieve a yield of verbal pleasure grasps the occasion offered in the preconscious for dragging the cathectic process down into the unconscious according to the familiar pattern.

I should be very glad if it were possible for me on the one hand to give a clearer exposition of this single decisive point in my view of jokes and on the other hand to reinforce it with conclusive arguments. But in fact what I am faced with here is not a two-fold failure but one and the same failure. I cannot give a clearer exposition because I have no further proof of my view. I arrived at it on the basis of a study of the technique [of jokes] and of a comparison with the dream-work, and on no other basis; and I then found that on the whole it fits in excel-lently with the characteristics of jokes. Thus this view has been arrived at by inference; and if from an inference of this kind one is led, not to a familiar region, but on the contrary, to one that is alien and new to one's thought, one calls the inference a 'hypothesis' and rightly refuses to regard the relation of the hypothesis to the material from which it was inferred as a 'proof' of it. It can only be regarded as 'proved' if it is reached by another path as well and if it can be shown to be the nodal point of still other connections. But proof of this sort is not to be had, in view of the fact that our knowledge of unconscious processes has scarcely begun. In the realization that we are standing upon ground which has never before been trodden, we are thus content, from our point of observation, to take one single, short and uncertain step forward into the unexplored region.

On such a foundation we cannot build a great deal. If we bring the various stages of the joke into relation with the mental states that are favourable to them we can perhaps proceed as follows. The *jest* springs from a cheerful mood, which seems to be characterized by an inclination to diminish mental cathexes. It already employs all the characteristic techniques of jokes and already fulfils their fundamental condition by selecting verbal material or connections of thoughts which will meet both the demands for a yield of pleasure and those made by rational criticism. We shall conclude that the lowering of the thought-cathexis to the unconscious level, facilitated by the cheerful mood, is present already in jests. In the case of *innocent jokes* that are linked to the expression of a valuable thought, the encouraging effect of mood no longer applies. Here we must presume the occurrence of a special *personal aptitude*, which is manifested in the ease with which the preconscious cathexis is dropped and exchanged for a moment for the unconscious one. A purpose that is all the time on the watch for renewing the original yield of pleasure from jokes exercises a downward drag on the still unsettled preconscious expression of the thought. No doubt most people are capable of producing jests when they are in a cheerful mood; the aptitude for making *jokes* is present in only a few people independently of their mood. Lastly, the joke-work receives its most powerful stimulus when strong purposes reaching down into the unconscious are present, which represent a special aptitude for the production of jokes and which may explain to us how it is that the subjective determinants of jokes are so often fulfilled in neurotic people. Under the influence of strong purposes even those who otherwise have the least aptitude for it become capable of making jokes.

With this last contribution, however, which explains, even though still only hypothetically, the joke-work in the first person, our interest in jokes is, strictly speaking, at an end. It remains for us to make a further short comparison between jokes and the better-known dream; and we may expect that, apart from the single conformity we have already considered, two such dissimilar mental functions will only reveal differences. The most important difference lies in their social behaviour. A dream is a completely asocial mental product; it has nothing to communicate to anyone else; it arises within the subject as a compromise between the mental forces struggling in him, it remains unintelligible to the subject himself and is for that reason totally uninteresting to other people. Not only does it not need to set any store by intelligibility, it must actually avoid being understood, for otherwise it would be destroyed; it can only exist in masquerade. For that reason it can without hindrance make use of the mechanism that dominates unconscious mental processes, to the point of a distortion which can no longer be set straight. A joke, on the other hand, is the most social of all the mental functions that aim at a yield of pleasure. It often calls for three persons and its completion requires the participation of someone else in the mental process it starts. The condition of intelligibility is, therefore, binding on it; it may only make use of possible distortion in the unconscious through condensation and displacement up to the point at which it can be set straight by the third person's understanding. Moreoever, jokes and dreams have grown up in quite different regions of mental life and must be allotted to points in the psychological system far remote from each other. A dream still remains a wish, even though one that has been made unrecognizable; a joke is developed play. Dreams, in spite of all their practical nonentity, retain their connection with the major interests of life; they seek to fulfil needs by the regressive détour of hallucination, and they are permitted to occur for the sake of the one need that is active during the night – the need to sleep. Jokes, on the other hand, seek to gain a small yield of pleasure from the mere activity, untrammelled by needs, of our mental apparatus. Later they try to catch hold of that pleasure as a by-product during the activity of that apparatus and thus arrive *secondarily* at not unimportant functions directed to the external world. Dreams serve predominantly for the avoidance of unpleasure, jokes for the attainment of pleasure; but all our mental activities converge in these two aims.

VII

JOKES AND THE SPECIES OF
THE COMIC

[1]

WE have approached the problems of the comic in an unusual way. It seemed to us that jokes, which are ordinarily regarded as a sub-species of the comic, offer enough peculiarities to be attacked directly; thus we have avoided their relation to the more inclusive category of the comic so long as that was possible, though we have not failed to pick out *en passant* a few hints that might throw light on the comic. We have had no difficulty in discovering that socially the comic behaves differently from jokes [p. 196 f.]. It can be content with two persons: a first who finds what is comic and a second in whom it is found. The third person, to whom the comic thing is told, intensifies the comic process but adds nothing new to it. In a joke this third person is indispensable for the completion of the pleasure-producing process; but on the other hand the second person may be absent, except where a tendentious, aggressive joke is concerned. A joke is made, the comic is found – and first and foremost in people, only by a subsequent transference in things, situations, and so on, as well. As regards jokes, we know that the sources of the pleasure that is to be fostered lie in the subject himself and not in outside people. We have seen, too, that jokes can sometimes re-open sources of the comic which have become inaccessible [p. 147], and that the comic often serves as a façade for a joke and replaces the fore-pleasure which has otherwise to be produced by the familiar technique (p. 205). None of this precisely suggests that the relations between jokes and the comic are very simple. On the other hand, the problems of the comic have proved so complicated and all the efforts of the philosophers at solving them have been so unsuccessful that we cannot hold out any prospect that we shall be able to master them in a sudden onslaught, as it were, by approaching them from the direction of jokes. Moreover, for our investigation of jokes we brought with us an instrument of which no one else had hitherto made use – a knowledge of the dream-work. We have no similar advantage at our command to help us to understand the comic, and we must therefore expect that we shall discover no more about the nature of the comic than what we have already found in jokes, in so far as they form part of the comic and possess in their own nature certain of its features unchanged or merely modified.

The type of the comic which stands nearest to jokes is the *naïve*. Like the comic in general, the naïve is 'found' and not, like a joke, 'made'. Indeed, the naïve cannot be made at all, whereas alongside the pure comic we have to take into account the case in which something is made comic – an evocation of the comic. The naïve must arise, without our taking any part in it, in the remarks and actions of other people, who stand in the position of the *second* person in the comic or in jokes. The naïve occurs if someone completely disregards an inhibition because it is not present in him – if, therefore, he appears to overcome it without any effort. It is a condition for the naïve's producing its effect that we should know that the person concerned does not possess the inhibition; otherwise we call him not naïve but impudent. We do not laugh at him but are indignant at him. The effect produced by the naïve is irresistible, and seems simple to understand. An inhibitory expenditure which we usually make suddenly becomes unutilizable owing to our hearing the naïve remark, and it is discharged by laughter. There is no need here for the attention to be distracted [p. 205], probably because the lifting of the inhibition occurs directly and not through the intermediary of an operation that has been provoked. In this we are behaving like the third person in a joke, who is presented with the economy in inhibition without any effort on his own part [p. 200].

In view of the insight we have gained into the genesis of inhibitions from following the course of development from play to jokes, it will not surprise us to find that the naïve occurs far the most often in children, and is then carried over to un-educated adults, whom we may regard as childish so far as their intellectual development is concerned. Naïve *remarks* are, of course, better suited for comparison with jokes than naïve actions, since remarks and not actions are the usual form in which jokes are expressed. It is illuminating to find that naïve remarks like those made by children may also be described as 'naïve jokes'. The conformity between jokes and *naïveté*, as well as the reasons for their dissimilarity, will be made clearer to us by a few examples.

A three-and-a-half-year-old girl gave this warning to her brother: 'I say, don't eat so much of that pudding or you'll get ill and have to have some *"Bubizen"*.' '"*Bubizen*"?' asked her mother, 'What's that?' 'When I was ill,' answered the child in self-justification, 'I had to have some *Medizin.*' The child thought that what the doctor prescribed was called '*Mädi-zin*' when it was for a '*Mädi*' [little girl] and concluded that if it was for a '*Bubi*' [little boy] it would be called '*Bubi-zin*'. This is constructed like a verbal joke working with the technique of similarity of sound, and indeed it might have occurred as a real joke, in which case we should have greeted it, half-unwillingly, with a smile. As an example of *naïveté* it strikes us as quite excellent and it raises a laugh. What is it that makes the differ-ence here between a joke and something naïve? Evidently not the wording or the technique, which would be the same for both possibilities, but a factor, rather, which at first sight seems quite remote from both of them. It is merely a question of whether we assume that the speaker has intended to make a joke or whether we suppose that he – the child – has tried in good faith to draw a serious conclusion on the basis of his uncorrected ignorance. Only the latter case is one of *naïveté*. Here for the first time our attention is drawn to the other person putting himself into the psychical process that occurs in the person who produces the remark.

This view will be confirmed if we examine another example. A brother and sister – a twelve-year-old girl and a ten-year-old boy – were performing a drama composed by themselves before an audience of uncles and aunts. The scene represented a hut by the sea-shore. In the first act the two author-actors, a poor fisherman and his honest wife, are complaining about the hard times and their small earnings. The husband decides to cross the wide seas in his boat to seek his fortune elsewhere, and, after tender farewells between the two of them, the curtain falls. The second act takes place a few years later. The fisherman has returned a wealthy man with a big bag of money; and he tells his wife, who awaits his arrival outside the hut, what good fortune he has met with in foreign lands. His wife interrupts him proudly: 'I too have not been idle.' And thereupon she opens the door of the hut and reveals to his eyes twelve large dolls lying asleep on the floor . . . At this point in the drama the actors were interrupted by a storm of laughter from the audience, which they were unable to understand. They stared disconcerted at their fond relatives, who had behaved properly till then and had listened with eager attention. The laughter is explained on the supposition that the audience assumed that the young authors still knew nothing of the conditions governing the origin of children and were therefore able to believe that a wife could boast of the offspring born during her husband's long absence and that a husband could rejoice with her over them. What the authors produced on the basis of this ignorance might be described as nonsense or absurdity.[1]

1. [This anecdote is told, with a different setting, of the children of the 1st Earl of Lytton. Cf. G. W. E. Russell's *Collections and Recollections*, 1898, Chapter 32.]

A third example will show us yet another technique, the acquaintance of which we have made in jokes, in the service of the naïve. A 'Frenchwoman'[1] was engaged as governess for a little girl, but did not meet with her personal approval. Scarcely had the newcomer left the room when the little girl gave voice to loud criticism: '*That* a Frenchwoman? She may *call* herself one because she once lay beside a Frenchman!' This might have been a joke – even a tolerably good one – (double meaning or allusion, with *double entendre*) if the child had had the slightest notion of the possibility of the double meaning. In fact she had merely transferred to the stranger she disliked a facetious way of describing a thing as ungenuine which she had often heard: '*That* genuine gold? It may once have lain beside gold.' Owing to the child's ignorance, which so completely altered the psychical process in her understanding hearers, her remark became a naïve one. In consequence of this condition [that the child must really be ignorant], there is the possibility of a *misleading naïveté*. We may assume in the child an ignorance that no longer exists; and children often represent themselves as naïve, so as to enjoy a liberty that they would not otherwise be granted.

We can illustrate from these examples the position occupied by the naïve between jokes and the comic. The naïve (in speech) agrees with jokes as regards wording and content: it brings about a misuse of words, a piece of nonsense, or a piece of smut. But the psychical process in the first person, who produces it, which raised so many interesting and puzzling questions for us in regard to jokes, is here completely absent. A naïve person thinks he has used his means of expression and trains of thought normally and simply, and he has no *arrière pensée* in mind; nor does he derive any yield of pleasure from producing something naïve. None of the characteristics of the naïve exist except in the apprehension of the person who hears it – a person who coincides with the third person in jokes. Moreover the person

1. ['*Französin*.' The ordinary term for a French governess in Austria.]

who produces it does so without any effort. The complicated technique, which in jokes is designed to paralyse the inhibition arising from rational criticism, is absent in him; he does not possess this inhibition as yet, so that he can produce nonsense and smut directly and without compromise. In that respect the naïve is a marginal case of the joke; it arises if in the formula for the construction of jokes we reduce the value of the censorship to zero.

Whereas it was a condition for the effectiveness of a joke that both persons should be subject to approximately the same inhibitions or internal resistances [p. 204], it will be seen that it is a condition for the naïve that the one person should possess inhibitions which the other is without. The apprehension of the naïve lies with the person provided with inhibitions, and he alone obtains the yield of pleasure which the naïve brings about. We have come near to guessing that that pleasure arises from the lifting of inhibitions. Since the pleasure from jokes has the same origin – a core of verbal pleasure and pleasure from nonsense, and a casing of pleasure in the lifting of inhibitions or in the relief of psychical expenditure [p. 189n.] – this similar relation to inhibition explains the internal kinship between the naïve and jokes. In both of them the pleasure arises through the lifting of internal inhibition.

The psychical process in the receptive person, however, is as much more complicated in the case of the naïve as it is simplified in comparison with jokes in the productive person. (In the case of the naïve, incidentally, our own self invariably coincides with the receptive person, while in the case of jokes we may equally occupy the position of the productive one.) When the receptive person hears something naïve, it must on the one hand affect him like a joke – and our examples give evidence precisely of this – for, as with a joke, the lifting of the censorship is made possible for him by no more than the effort of listening. But only a part of the pleasure created by the naïve can be explained in this way; and even this might be endangered in certain instances – for example, at hearing a naïve piece of smut. We might react to this at once with the same indignation that might be felt against a real piece of smut, if it were not that another factor spares us this indignation and at the same time offers us the more important part of our pleasure in the naïve. This other factor is the condition already mentioned [p. 240] that, in order to recognize the naïve, we must know that the internal inhibition is absent in the producing person. Only when this is certain do we laugh instead of being indignant. Thus we take the producing person's psychical state into consideration, put ourselves into it and try to understand it by comparing it with our own. It is these processes of empathy and comparison that result in the economy in expenditure which we discharge by laughing.

It would be possible to prefer a simpler account – that our indignation is made superfluous by the fact that the other person has had no need to overcome a resistance; in that case the laughter would occur at the cost of the economy in indignation. In order to discourage this view, which is on the whole misleading, I will make a sharper distinction between two cases which I have treated together above. The naïve which we come across can either be in the nature of a joke, as it was in our examples, or in the nature of smut (or of what is in general objectionable); and the latter will occur especially when it is expressed not in speech but in action. This second alternative is really misleading: one could suppose, as far as it is concerned, that the pleasure arises from the economized and transformed indignation. But the first alternative throws more light on things. A naïve remark – e.g. *'Bubizin'* [p. 241] – can in itself act like a minor joke and give no cause for indignation. This alternative is certainly the less frequent; but it is the purer and by far the more instructive. In so far as what we are concerned with is the fact that the child has seriously and without *arrière pensée* believed that the syllable *'Medi'* in *'Medizin'* is identical with her own name *'Mädi'*, our pleasure in what we hear receives an increase which has no longer anything to do with pleasure in a joke. We now look at what has been said from two points of view – once in the way it happened in the child and once in the way it would have happened to us; and in making this comparison we see that the child has found an identity[1] and that she has overcome a barrier that exists for us; and we then seem to go further and say to ourselves: 'If you choose to understand what you've heard, you can economize the expenditure on keeping up this barrier.' The expenditure liberated in a comparison like this is the source of pleasure in the naïve and it is discharged by laughter; and it is, incidentally, the same pleasure that we should otherwise have transformed into indignation, if this had not been excluded by our understanding of the producing person and, in this case, by the nature of what was said as well. But if we take the instance of a naïve joke as a model for the other alternative, of something naïve that is objectionable, we shall see that there too the economy in inhibition can arise directly from the comparison, that there is no necessity for us to assume an indignation that begins and is then stifled, and that this indignation in fact only corresponds to using the liberated expenditure in another way – against which in the case of jokes complicated protective arrangements were necessary [p. 204 f.].

This comparison, and this economy in expenditure by putting oneself into the mental process of the producing person, can only claim to be of significance for the naïve, however, if it is not in it alone that they are found. A suspicion occurs to us, in fact, that this mechanism, which is wholly alien to jokes, may be a part and perhaps an essential part of the psychical process in the comic. Looked at from this point of view – and this is undoubtedly the most important aspect of the naïve – the naïve thus presents itself as a species of the comic. The extra element in our examples of naïve speeches that is added to the pleasure of a joke is 'comic' pleasure. We should be inclined to assume

1. [I.e. the identity between *Medi* and *Mädi*.]

of it quite generally that it arises from expenditure economized in a comparison of someone else's remarks with our own. But since this leads us to far-reaching considerations, we will first conclude our discussion of the naïve. The naïve, then, would be a species of the comic in so far as its pleasure springs from the difference[1] in expenditure which arises in trying to understand someone else; and it would approach the joke in being subject to the condition that the expenditure economized in the comparison must be an inhibitory expenditure.[2]

Let us hastily add a few points of agreement and of difference between the concepts that we have just reached and those which have long been familiar in the psychology of the comic. The putting of oneself in the other person's place and trying to understand him is clearly nothing other than the 'comic lending' which since Jean Paul has played a part in the analysis of the comic; the 'comparing' of someone else's mental process with one's own corresponds to the 'psychological contrast' which we can at last find a place for here, after not knowing what to do with it in jokes [p. 41 f.]. But we differ in our explanation of comic pleasure from many authorities who regard it as arising from the oscillation of attention backwards and forwards between contrasting ideas. A mechanism of pleasure like this would seem incomprehensible to us;[3] but we may

1. [The German word here (and regularly in this connection throughout the rest of the book) is 'Differenz', not the usual 'Unterschied'. It is the term used in mathematics and means a *quantitative* not a qualitative difference. The English word has to cover both meanings.]

2. In what I have written, I have all the time identified the naïve with the naïve-comic, which is certainly not in every case admissible. But it is enough for our purposes to study the character of the naïve in 'naïve jokes' and in 'naïve smut'. Any further investigation would imply an intention on my part of using this as a basis for my explanation of the comic.

3. Bergson, too, rejects the idea of comic pleasure having any such derivation, which is evidently influenced by an effort to establish an analogy with the laughter caused by tickling; and he supports his view with some good arguments (1900, 99). – The explanation of comic

point out that in a comparison between contrasts a difference in expenditure occurs which, if it is not used for some other purpose, becomes capable of discharge and may thus become a source of pleasure.

It is only with misgivings that I venture to approach the problem of the comic itself. It would be presumptuous to expect that my efforts would be able to make any decisive contribution to its solution when the works of a great number of eminent thinkers have failed to produce a wholly satisfactory explanation. My intention is in fact no more than to pursue the lines of thought that have proved valuable with jokes a short distance further into the sphere of the comic.

The comic arises in the first instance as an unintended discovery derived from human social relations. It is found in people – in their movements, forms, actions and traits of character, originally in all probability only in their physical characteristics but later in their mental ones as well or, as the case may be, in the expression of those characteristics. By means of a very common sort of personification, animals become comic too, and inanimate objects. At the same time, the comic is capable of being detached from people, in so far as we recognize the conditions under which a person seems comic. In this way the comic of situation comes about, and this recognition affords the possibility of making a person comic at one's will by putting him in situations in which his actions are subject to these comic conditions. The discovery that one has it in one's power to make someone else comic opens the way to an undreamt-of yield of comic pleasure and is the origin of a highly developed technique. One can make *oneself* comic, too, as

---

pleasure given by Lipps is on a quite different plane: in accordance with his view of the comic, he would regard it as something that is 'unexpectedly small'. [In the German this footnote is attached at the *end* of the paragraph.]

easily as other people. The methods that serve to make people comic are: putting them in a comic situation, mimicry, disguise, unmasking, caricature, parody, travesty, and so on. It is obvious that these techniques can be used to serve hostile and aggressive purposes. One can make a person comic in order to make him become contemptible, to deprive him of his claim to dignity and authority. But even if such an intention habitually underlies making people comic, this need not be the meaning of what is comic spontaneously.

This irregular survey of the occurrences of the comic will already show us that a very extensive field of origin is to be ascribed to it and that such specialized conditions as we found, for instance, in the naïve are not to be expected in it. In order to get on the track of the determining condition that is valid for the comic, the most important thing is the choice of an introductory case. We shall choose the comic of movement, because we recollect that the most primitive kind of stage performance – the pantomime – uses that method for making us laugh. The answer to the question of why we laugh at the clown's movements is that they seem to us extravagant and inexpedient. We are laughing at an expenditure that is too large. Let us look now for the determining condition outside the comic that is artificially constructed – where it can be found unintended. A child's movements do not seem to us comic, although he kicks and jumps about. On the other hand, it *is* comic when a child who is learning to write follows the movements of his pen with his tongue stuck out; in these associated motions we see an unnecessary expenditure of movement which we should spare ourselves if we were carrying out the same activity. Similarly, other such associated motions, or merely exaggerated expressive movements, seem to us comic in adults too. Pure examples of this species of the comic are to be seen, for instance, in the movements of someone playing skittles who, after he has released the ball, follows its course as though he could still continue to direct it. Thus, too, all grimaces are comic which exaggerate the normal expression of the emotions, even if they are produced involuntarily as in sufferers from St Vitus's dance (chorea). And in the same way, the passionate movements of a modern conductor seem comic to any unmusical person who cannot understand their necessity. Indeed, it is from this comic of movement that the comic of bodily shapes and facial features branches off; for these are regarded as though they were the outcome of an exaggerated or pointless movement. Staring eyes, a hooked nose hanging down to the mouth, ears sticking out, a humpback – all such things probably only produce a comic effect in so far as movements are imagined which would be necessary to bring about these features; and here the nose, the ears and other parts of the body are imagined as more movable than they are in reality. There is no doubt that it is comic if someone can 'waggle his ears', and it would certainly be still more comic if he could move his nose up and down. A good deal of the comic effect produced on us by animals comes from our perceiving in them movements such as these which we cannot imitate ourselves.

But how is it that we laugh when we have recognized that some other person's movements are exaggerated and inexpedient? By making a comparison, I believe, between the movement I observe in the other person and the one that I should have carried out myself in his place. The two things compared must of course be judged by the same standard, and this standard is my expenditure of innervation, which is linked to my idea of the movement in both of the two cases. This statement calls for elucidation and expansion.

What we are here comparing is on the one hand the psychical expenditure while we are having a certain idea and on the other hand the content of the thing that we are having the idea of. Our statement says that the former is not in general and in theory independent of the latter, the content of the idea, and in particular that the idea of something large demands more expenditure than the idea of something small. So long as it is only a matter of the idea of different large *movements*, there should be no difficulties over the theoretical grounds for our statement or over proving it by observation. We shall see that in this case an attribute of the idea in fact coincides with an attribute of what we have an idea of, though psychology warns us as a rule against such a confusion.

I have acquired the idea of a movement of a particular size by carrying the movement out myself or by imitating it, and through this action I have learnt a standard for this movement in my innervatory sensations.[1]

When, now, I perceive a movement like this of greater or lesser size in someone else, the securest way to an understanding (an apperception) of it will be for me to carry it out by imitation, and I can then decide from the comparison on which of the movements my expenditure was the greater. An impulsion of this kind to imitation is undoubtedly present in perceptions of movements. But actually I do not carry the imitation through, any more than I still spell words out if I learnt to read by spelling. Instead of imitating the movement with my muscles, I have an idea of it through the medium of my memory-traces of expenditures on similar movements. Ideation or 'thinking' differs from acting or performing above all in the fact that it displaces far smaller cathectic energies and holds back the main expenditure from discharge.[2]

1. The memory of this innervatory expenditure will remain the essential part of my idea of this movement, and there will always be modes of thinking in my mental life in which the idea will be represented by nothing else than this expenditure. In other circumstances, indeed, this element may be replaced by another – for instance, by visual images of the aim of the movement or by a verbal image; and in certain kinds of abstract thinking a token will suffice instead of the full content of the idea.

2. [This important principle had been expressed by Freud in *The Interpretation of Dreams* (1900a), *P.F.L.*, 4, 758–9, though perhaps less clearly than here. He had discussed it earlier (in 1895) in quasi-

But how is the *quantitative* factor – the greater or lesser size – of the perceived movement to be given expression in the idea? And if there can be no representation of quantity in the idea, which is made up of qualities, how can I distinguish the ideas of movements of different sizes? – how can I make the comparison on which everything here depends? The way is pointed out by physiology, for it teaches us that even during the process of ideation innervations run out to the muscles, though these, it is true, correspond to a very modest expenditure of energy.[1] Now it becomes very plausible to suppose that this innervatory energy that accompanies the process of ideation is used to represent the quantitative factor of the idea: that it is larger when there is an idea of a large movement than when it is a question of a small one. Thus the idea of the larger movement would in this case in fact be the larger one – that is, it would be the idea accompanied by the larger expenditure of energy.

Direct observation shows that human beings are in the habit of expressing the attributes of largeness and smallness in the contents of their ideas by means of a varying expenditure in a kind of *ideational mimetics*. If a child or a man from the common people, or a member of certain races, narrates or describes something, it is easy to see that he is not content to make his idea plain to the hearer by the choice of clear words, but that he also represents its subject-matter in his expressive movements: he combines the mimetic and the verbal forms of representation. And he especially demonstrates quantities and intensities: 'a high mountain' – and he raises his hand over his

---

neurological terms in Section 18 of Part I of his posthumously published 'Project' (1950a). The point is once more brought out very plainly in the paper on 'The Two Principles of Mental Functioning' (1911b), and recurs in many later passages – e.g. in Lecture XXXII of the *New Introductory Lectures* (1933a), P.F.L., **2**, 122.]

1. [Some approach to the ideas contained in this passage may perhaps be traced in Sections 17 and 18 of Part I of Freud's 'Project' (see last footnote).]

head, 'a little dwarf' – and he holds it near the ground. He may have broken himself of the habit of painting with his hands, yet for that reason he will do it with his voice; and if he exercises self-control in this too, it may be wagered that he will open his eyes wide when he describes something large and squeeze them shut when he comes to something small. What he is thus expressing is not his affects but actually the content of what he is having an idea of.

Are we to suppose, then, that this need for mimetics is only aroused by the requirements of communicating something, in spite of the fact that a good part of this method of representation altogether escapes the hearer's attention? On the contrary, I believe that these mimetics exist, even if with less liveliness, quite apart from any communication, that they occur as well when the subject is forming an idea of something for his own private benefit and is thinking of something pictorially, and that he then expresses 'large' and 'small' in his own body just as he does in speech, at all events by a change in the innervation of his features and sense organs. I can even believe that the somatic innervation which is commensurate with the content of what he is having an idea of may have been the beginning and origin of mimetics for purposes of communication; it only needed to be intensified and made noticeable to other people in order to be able to serve that end. If I support the view that to the 'expression of the emotions', which is well known as the physical concomitant of mental processes, there should be added the 'expression of the ideational content', I can see quite clearly that my remarks relating to the category of large and small do not exhaust the subject. I might myself add a variety of points even before arriving at the phenomena of tension by which a person indicates somatically the concentration of his attention and the level of abstraction at which his thinking is at the moment proceeding. I regard the matter as a really important one, and I believe that if ideational mimetics are followed up, they may be as useful in other branches of aesthetics as they are here for an understanding of the comic.

To return now to the comic of movement. When, I repeat, a particular movement is perceived, the impulsion is given to forming an idea of it by means of a certain expenditure of energy. In 'trying to understand', therefore, in apperceiving this movement, I make a certain expenditure, and in this portion of the mental process I behave exactly as though I were putting myself in the place of the person I am observing. But at the same moment, probably, I bear in mind the aim of this movement, and my earlier experience enables me to estimate the scale of expenditure required for reaching that aim. In doing so I disregard the person whom I am observing and behave as though I myself wanted to reach the aim of the movement. These two possibilities in my imagination amount to a comparison between the observed movement and my own. If the other person's movement is exaggerated and inexpedient, my increased expenditure in order to understand it is inhibited *in statu nascendi*, as it were in the act of being mobilized [p. 204]; it is declared superfluous and is free for use elsewhere or perhaps for discharge by laughter. This would be the way in which, other circumstances being favourable, pleasure in a comic movement is generated – an innervatory expenditure which has become an unusable surplus when a comparison is made with a movement of one's own.

It will be seen that our discussions must proceed in two different directions: first, to establish the conditions governing the discharge of the surplus, and second, to examine whether the other cases of the comic can be looked at in the same way as the comic of movement.

We will take the second question first and will turn from the comic of movement and action to the comic which is found in the intellectual functions and the character traits of other people.

As a sample of this class we may choose comic nonsense, as it is produced by ignorant candidates in an examination; it is no doubt more difficult to give a simple example of character traits. We should not be confused if we find that nonsense and stupidity, which so often produce a comic effect, are nevertheless not felt as comic in every case, just as the same characters which on one occasion can be laughed at as comic may on another occasion strike one as contemptible or hateful. This fact, of which we must not lose sight, merely points out that other factors are concerned in producing the comic effect besides the comparison we know about – factors which we may be able to trace out in another connection. [See p. 280 ff.]

The comic that is found in someone else's intellectual and mental characteristics is evidently once again the outcome of a comparison between him and my own self, though, curiously enough, a comparison which has as a rule produced the opposite result to that in the case of a comic movement or action. In this latter case it was comic if the other person had made a greater expenditure than I thought I should need. In the case of a mental function, on the contrary, it becomes comic if the other person has spared himself expenditure which I regard as indispensable (for nonsense and stupidity are inefficiencies of function). In the former case I laugh because he has taken too much trouble, in the latter because he has taken too little. The comic effect apparently depends, therefore, on the *difference*[1] between the two cathectic expenditures – one's own and the other person's as estimated by 'empathy' – and not on which of the two the difference favours. But this peculiarity, which at first sight confuses our judgement, vanishes when we bear in mind that a restriction of our muscular work and an increase of our intellectual work fit in with the course of our personal development towards a higher level of civilization. By raising our intellectual expenditure we can achieve the same result with a diminished expenditure on our movements. Evidence of this cultural success is provided by our machines.[2]

1. [See footnote 1, p. 247 above.]
2. As the proverb says: 'Was man nicht im Kopfe hat, muss man in den Beinen haben.' [Literally: 'What one hasn't in one's head one must have in one's legs.']

Thus a uniform explanation is provided of the fact that a person appears comic to us if, in comparison with ourselves, he makes too great an expenditure on his bodily functions and too little on his mental ones; and it cannot be denied that in both these cases our laughter expresses a pleasurable sense of the superiority which we feel in relation to him. If the relation in the two cases is reversed – if the other person's physical expenditure is found to be less than ours or his mental expenditure greater – then we no longer laugh, we are filled with astonishment and admiration.[1]

The origin of comic pleasure which has been discussed here – its derivation from a comparison of another person with ourself, from the difference between our own psychical expenditure and the other person's as estimated by empathy – is probably the most important genetically. It is certain, however, that it has not remained the only one. We have learnt at one time or other to disregard this comparison between the other person and ourself and to derive the pleasurable difference from the one side only, whether from the empathy or from the processes in ourself – which proves that the feeling of superiority bears no essential relation to comic pleasure. A comparison is [nevertheless] indispensable for the generation of this pleasure. We find that it is made between two cathectic expenditures that occur in rapid succession and are concerned with the same function, and these expenditures are either brought about in us through empathy into someone else or, without any such relation, are discovered in our own mental processes.

The first of these cases – in which, therefore, the other person still plays a part, though no longer in comparison with our own

1. The contradictoriness with which the determining conditions of the comic are pervaded – the fact that sometimes an excess and sometimes an insufficiency seems to be the source of comic pleasure – has contributed no little to the confusion of the problem. Cf. Lipps (1898, 47).

self – arises when the pleasurable difference in cathectic expenditures is brought about by external influences, which we may sum up as a 'situation'. For that reason, this species of the comic is also known as 'the comic of situation'. The characteristics of the person who provides the comic effect do not in this case play an essential part: we laugh even if we have to confess that *we* should have had to do the same in that situation. We are here extracting the comic from the relation of human beings to the often over-powerful external world; and so far as the mental processes of a human being are concerned, this external world also comprises social conventions and necessities and even his own bodily needs. A typical instance of the latter kind is provided if, in the middle of an activity which makes demands on a person's mental powers, he is suddenly interrupted by a pain or an excretory need. The contrast which, through empathy, offers us the comic difference is that between the high degree of interest taken by him *before* the interruption and the minimal one that he has left over for his mental activity when the interruption has occurred. The person who offers us this difference becomes comic to us once again for his inferiority; but he is inferior only in comparison with his earlier self and not in comparison with *us*, for we know that in the same circumstances we could not have behaved otherwise. But it is noteworthy that we only find someone's being put in a position of inferiority comic where there is empathy – that is, where someone else is concerned: if we ourselves were in similar straits we should be conscious only of distressing feelings. It is probably only by keeping such feelings away from ourselves that we are able to enjoy pleasure from the difference arising out of a comparison between these changing cathexes.

The other source of the comic, which we find in the transformations of *our own* cathexes, lies in our relations with the future, which we are accustomed to anticipate with our expectant ideas. I assume that a quantitatively definite expenditure underlies each of our ideas – an expenditure which, in the event of a disappointment, is therefore diminished by a definite difference. Here I may once again recall the remarks I made earlier [p. 252 f.] on 'ideational mimetics'. But it seems to me to be easier to prove a real mobilization of cathectic energy in the case of expectation. It is quite obviously true of a number of cases that motor preparations are what form the expression of expectation – above all in all cases in which the expected event makes demands on my motility – and that these preparations can be at once determined quantitatively. If I am expecting to catch a ball which is being thrown to me, I put my body into tensions which will enable it to meet the impact of the ball; and, should the ball when it is caught turn out to be too light, my superfluous movements make me comic to the spectators. I have let myself be enticed by my expectation into an exaggerated expenditure of movement. The same is true if, for instance, I lift a fruit which I have judged to be heavy out of a basket, but which, to my disappointment, turns out to be a sham one, hollow and made of wax. My hand, by jumping up, betrays the fact that I had prepared an innervation too large for the purpose – and I am laughed at for it. There is at least one case in which the expenditure on expectation can be directly demonstrated measurably by physiological experiments on animals. In Pavlov's experiments on salivary secretions, various kinds of food are set before dogs in whom a salivary fistula has been opened; the amounts of saliva secreted then vary according to whether the experimental conditions confirm or disappoint the dogs' expectations of being fed with the food set before them.

Even when what is expected makes demands on my sense organs and not on my motility, I may assume that the expectation is expressed in a certain motor expenditure towards making the senses tense and towards holding back other impressions that are not expected; and, in general, I may regard an attitude of attention as being a motor function equivalent to a certain expenditure. I may further take it as a premiss that the preparatory activity of expectation will not be independent of the magnitude of the impression that is expected, but that I shall represent its largeness or smallness mimetically by a larger or smaller preparatory expenditure, as in the case of making a communication and in the case of thinking unaccompanied by expectation. The expenditure on expectation is, however, put together from several components, and in the case of my disappointment, too, various points will be involved – not only whether what happens is perceptually greater or smaller than what is expected, but also whether it is worthy of the great interest which I had expended on the expectation. In this way I shall perhaps be led to take into account, besides the expenditure on the representation of large and small (the ideational mimetics), the expenditure on tightening the attention (the expenditure on expectation), and beyond this in other cases the expenditure on abstraction. But these other kinds of expenditure can easily be traced back to that on large and small, since what is more interesting, more sublime and even more abstract are only special cases, with particular qualities, of what is larger. If we consider in addition that, according to Lipps and other writers, *quantitative* (and not qualitative) contrast is to be regarded primarily as the source of comic pleasure, we shall on the whole feel glad that we chose the comic of movement as the starting-point of our inquiry.

Lipps, in the volume which has been so often quoted in these pages, has attempted, as an amplification of Kant's statement[1] that the comic is 'an expectation that has turned to nothing', to derive comic pleasure quite generally from expectation. [Lipps, 1898, 50 ff.] In spite, however, of the many instructive and valuable findings which this attempt has brought to light, I should like to support the criticism made by other authorities that Lipps has taken the field of origin of the comic far too narrowly and has been obliged to use great violence in order to bring its phenomena within the scope of his formula.

1. [Cf. footnote, p. 43.]

[2]

Mankind have not been content to enjoy the comic where they have come upon it in their experience; they have also sought to bring it about intentionally, and we can learn more about the nature of the comic if we study the means which serve to *make* things comic. First and foremost, it is possible to produce the comic in relation to oneself in order to amuse other people – for instance, by making oneself out clumsy or stupid. In that way one produces a comic effect exactly as though one really were these things, by fulfilling the condition of the comparison which leads to the difference in expenditure. But one does not in this way make oneself ridiculous or contempt-ible, but may in some circumstances even achieve admiration. The feeling of superiority does not arise in the other person if he knows that one has only been pretending; and this affords fresh evidence of the fundamental independence of the comic from the feeling of superiority [p. 256].

As regards making *other people* comic, the principal means is to put them in situations in which a person becomes comic as a result of human dependence on external events, particularly on social factors, without regard to the personal characteristics of the individual concerned – that is to say, by employing the comic of situation. This putting of someone in a comic situation may be a *real* one (a practical joke[1]) – by sticking out a leg so that someone trips over it as though he were clumsy, by making him seem stupid by exploiting his credulity, or trying to con-vince him of something nonsensical, and so on – or it may be simulated by speech or play. The aggressiveness, to which making a person comic usually ministers, is much assisted by the fact that the comic pleasure is independent of the reality of the comic situation, so that everyone is in fact exposed, without any defence, to being made comic.

But there are yet other means of making things comic which

1. [In English in the original.]

deserve special consideration and also indicate in part fresh sources of comic pleasure. Among these, for instance, is *mimicry*, which gives quite extraordinary pleasure to the hearer and makes its object comic even if it is still far from the exaggeration of a caricature. It is much easier to find a reason for the comic effect of *caricature* than for that of mere mimicry. Caricature, parody and travesty (as well as their practical counterpart, unmasking) are directed against people and objects which lay claim to authority and respect, which are in some sense '*sublime*'.[1] They are procedures for *Herabsetzung*, as the apt German expression has it.[2] What is sublime is something large in the figurative, psychical sense; and I should like to suggest, or rather to repeat my suggestion [cf. p. 259], that, like what is somatically large, it is represented by an increased expenditure. It requires little observation to establish that when I speak of something sublime I innervate my speech in a different way, I make different facial expressions, and I try to bring the whole way in which I hold myself into harmony with the dignity of what I am having an idea of. I impose a solemn restraint upon myself – not very different from what I should adopt if I were to enter the presence of an exalted personality, a monarch, or a prince of science. I shall hardly be wrong in assuming that this different innervation in my ideational mimetics corresponds to an increased expenditure. The third instance[3] of an increased expenditure of this kind is no doubt to be found when

1. [The German word here is '*erhaben*', for which the accepted English translation in aesthetics is 'sublime'. As, however, it is difficult to apply this rendering in the case of people, we have, where necessary, used the word 'exalted' instead.]

2. 'Degradation' [in English in the original]. Bain (1865, 248) writes: 'The occasion of the Ludicrous is the Degradation of some person or interest, possessing dignity, in circumstances that excite no other strong emotion.' [The English word 'degradation' has accordingly been used in all that follows as a translation of '*Herabsetzung*'.]

3. [The other two being presumably the somatically large and the sublime.]

I proceed in abstract trains of thought instead of in the habitual concrete and plastic ones. When, therefore, the procedures that I have discussed for the degradation of the sublime allow me to have an idea of it as though it were something commonplace, in whose presence I need not pull myself together but may, to use the military formula, 'stand easy', I am being spared the increased expenditure of the solemn restraint; and the comparison between this new ideational method (instigated by empathy) and the previously habitual one, which is simultaneously trying to establish itself – this comparison once again creates the difference in expenditure which can be discharged by laughter.

Caricature, as is well known, brings about degradation by emphasizing in the general impression given by the exalted object a single trait which is comic in itself but was bound to be overlooked so long as it was only perceivable in the general picture. By isolating this, a comic effect can be attained which extends in our memory over the whole object. This is subject to the condition that the actual presence of the exalted object himself does not keep us in a reverential attitude. If a comic trait of this kind that has been overlooked is lacking in reality, a caricature will unhesitatingly create it by exaggerating one that is not comic in itself; and the fact that the effect of the caricature is not essentially diminished by this falsification of reality is once again an indication of the origin of comic pleasure [p. 261].

Parody and *travesty* achieve the degradation of something exalted in another way: by destroying the unity that exists between people's characters as we know them and their speeches and actions, by replacing either the exalted figures or their utterances by inferior ones. They are distinguished from caricature in this, but not in the mechanism of their production of comic pleasure. The same mechanism is also used for *unmasking*, which only applies when someone has seized dignity and authority by a deception and these have to be taken from him in reality. We have already met with a few examples of the comic effect of unmasking in jokes – for instance, in the story of the aristocratic lady who, at the first onset of her labour-pains, exclaimed 'Ah! mon Dieu!' but whom the doctor would not assist till she cried out 'Aa-ee, aa-ee!' [p. 122]. Having come to know the characteristics of the comic, we can no longer dispute that this anecdote is in fact an example of comic unmasking and has no justifiable claim to be called a joke. It only recalls jokes by its setting and by the technical method of 'representation by something very small' [loc.cit.] – in this case the patient's cry, which is found sufficient to establish the indication for treatment. It nevertheless remains true that our linguistic sense, if we call on it for a decision, raises no objection to our calling a story like this a joke. We may explain this by reflecting that linguistic usage is not based on the scientific insight into the nature of jokes that we have arrived at in this laborious investigation. Since one of the functions of jokes is to make hidden sources of comic pleasure accessible once more (p. 147), any device that brings to light something that is not manifestly comic may, by a loose analogy, be termed a joke. This applies preferably, however, to unmasking as well as to other methods of making people comic.[1]

Under the heading of 'unmasking' we may also include a procedure for making things comic with which we are already acquainted [p. 256 f.] – the method of degrading the dignity of individuals by directing attention to the frailties which they share with all humanity, but in particular the dependence of their mental functions on bodily needs. The unmasking is equivalent here to an admonition: such and such a person, who is admired as a demigod, is after all only human like you and me. Here, too, are to be placed the efforts at laying bare the monotonous psychical automatism that lies behind the wealth

1. 'Thus every conscious and ingenious evocation of the comic (whether the comic of contemplation or of situation) is in general described as a joke. We, of course, cannot here make use of this concept of the joke either' (Lipps, 1898, 78).

and apparent freedom of psychical functions. We came across examples of 'unmasking' of this kind in the marriage-broker jokes, and felt a doubt at the time whether these anecdotes have a right to be counted as jokes [p. 104]. We are now able to decide with greater certainty that the anecdote of the echo [p. 102] who reinforced all the assertions of the marriage-broker and finally confirmed his admission that the bride had a hump with the exclamation 'And *what* a hump!' – that this anecdote is essentially a *comic* story, an example of the unmasking of a psychical automatism. Here, however, the comic story is only serving as a façade. For anyone who will attend to the hidden meaning of the marriage-broker anecdotes, the whole thing remains an admirably staged joke [p. 149 ff.]; anyone who does not penetrate so far is left with a comic story. The same thing applies to the other joke, about the marriage-broker who, in order to answer an objection, ended by confessing the truth with a cry of 'But I ask you, who would lend such people anything?' [p. 103.]. Here again we have a comic unmasking as the façade for a joke, though in this instance the characteristic of a joke is much more unmistakable, since the marriage-broker's remark is at the same time a representation by the opposite. In trying to prove that the people are rich he at the same time proves that they are *not* rich, but very poor. Here a joke and the comic are combined, and teach us that the same remark can be both things at once.

We are glad to seize the opportunity of returning to jokes from the comic of unmasking, since our true problem is not to determine the nature of the comic but to throw light on the relation between jokes and the comic. We have discussed the uncovering of psychical automatism, in a case in which our feeling as to whether something is comic or a joke left us in the lurch. And we will now add another case in which there is a similar confusion between jokes and the comic – the case of nonsensical jokes. But our investigation will show us in the end that as regards this second case the convergence between jokes and the comic can be theoretically accounted for. [Cf. p. 268.]

In discussing the techniques of jokes we found that giving free play to modes of thought which are usual in the unconscious but which can only be judged as examples of 'faulty reasoning' in the conscious is the technical method adopted in many jokes; and about these, once again, we felt doubts whether they possessed the true character of jokes, so that we were inclined to classify them simply as comic stories [p. 98 f.]. We were unable to reach a decision about our doubts because at the time we were ignorant of the essential characteristic of jokes. Subsequently, led by an analogy with the dream-work, we discovered that it lay in the compromise effected by the joke-work between the demands of reasonable criticism and the urge not to renounce the ancient pleasure in words and nonsense [p. 188 f.]. What came about in this way as a compromise, when the preconscious start of the thought was left for a moment to unconscious revision, satisfied both claims in every instance, but presented itself to criticism in various forms and had to put up with various judgements at its hands. Sometimes a joke would succeed in slipping on the appearance of an insignificant but nevertheless permissible assertion, another time it would smuggle itself in as the expression of a valuable thought. But, in the marginal case of effecting a compromise, it would give up attempting to satisfy criticism. Boasting of the sources of pleasure at its command, it would appear before criticism as sheer nonsense and not be afraid to provoke contradiction from it; for the joke could reckon on the hearer straightening out the disfigurement in the form of its expression by unconscious revision and so giving it back its meaning.

In what instances, then, will a joke appear before criticism as nonsense? Particularly when it makes use of the modes of thought which are usual in the unconscious but are proscribed in conscious thought – faulty reasoning, in fact. For certain modes of thought proper to the unconscious have also been retained by the conscious – for instance, some kinds of indirect representation, allusion, and so on – even though their conscious employment is subject to considerable restrictions. When a joke makes use of these techniques it will raise little or no objection on the part of criticism; objections will only appear if it also makes use for its technique of the methods with which conscious thought will have nothing more to do. A joke can still avoid objection, if it conceals the faulty reasoning it has used and disguises it under a show of logic, as happened in the anecdotes of the cake and the liqueur [p. 98], of the salmon mayonnaise [p. 86.], and similar ones. But if it produces the faulty reasoning undisguised, then the objections of criticism will follow with certainty.

In such cases the joke has another resource. The faulty reasoning, which it uses for its technique as one of the modes of thought of the unconscious, strikes criticism – even though not invariably so – as being *comic*. Consciously giving free play to unconscious modes of thought (which have been rejected as faulty) is a means of producing comic pleasure; and it is easy to understand this, since it certainly requires a greater expenditure of energy to establish a preconscious cathexis than to give free play to an unconscious one. When, on hearing a thought which has, as it were, been formed in the unconscious, we compare it with its correction, a difference in expenditure emerges for us from which comic pleasure arises. A joke which makes use of faulty reasoning like this for its technique, and therefore appears nonsensical, can thus produce a comic effect at the same time. If we fail to detect the joke, we are once again left with only the comic or funny story.

The story of the borrowed kettle which had a hole it in when it was given back (p. 100) is an excellent example of the purely comic effect of giving free play to the unconscious mode of thought. It will be recalled that the borrower, when he was questioned, replied firstly that he had not borrowed a kettle at all, secondly that it had had a hole in it already when he borrowed it, and thirdly that he had given it back undamaged and without a hole. This mutual cancelling-out by several thoughts, each of which is in itself valid, is precisely what does not occur in the unconscious. In dreams, in which the modes of thought of the unconscious are actually manifest, there is accordingly no such thing as an 'either – or',[1] only a simultaneous juxtaposition. In the example of a dream, which, in spite of its complication, I chose in my *Interpretation of Dreams* as a specimen of the work of interpretation, I tried to rid myself of the reproach of having failed to relieve a patient of her pains by psychical treatment. My reasons were: (1) that she herself was responsible for her illness because she would not accept my solution, (2) that her pains were of organic origin and were therefore no concern of mine, (3) that her pains were connected with her widowhood, for which I was evidently not responsible and (4) that her pains were due to an injection from a contaminated syringe, which had been given her by someone else. All these reasons stood side by side, as though they were not mutually exclusive. I was obliged to replace the 'and' of the dream by an 'either – or' in order to escape a charge of nonsense.[2]

There is a similar comic story of a Hungarian village in which the blacksmith had been guilty of a capital offence. The burgomaster, however, decided that as a penalty a *tailor* should be hanged and not the blacksmith, because there were two tailors in the village but no second blacksmith, and the crime must be expiated.[3] A displacement of this kind from the figure of the guilty person to another naturally contradicts every law of conscious logic but by no means the mode of thought of the unconscious. I do not hesitate to call this story comic, and yet I have included the one about the kettle among the jokes. I will

1. At the most, it is introduced by the narrator by way of interpretation. [See *The Interpretation of Dreams* (1900*a*), P.F.L., 4, 427–9.]

2. [See *The Interpretation of Dreams*, ibid., 196–7, where the story of the borrowed kettle also appears again.]

3. [This story reappeared many years later in Lecture 11 of *Introductory Lectures* (1916–17), P.F.L., 1, 209, and again in Chapter IV of *The Ego and the Id* (1923*b*).]

now admit that this latter story too is far more correctly described as 'comic' rather than as a joke. But I now understand
how it is that my feeling, which is as a rule so sure, can leave me
in doubt as to whether this story is comic or a joke. This is a case
in which I cannot come to a decision on the basis of my feeling
– when, that is, the comic arises from the uncovering of a mode
of thought that is exclusively proper to the unconscious. A
story like this may be comic and a joke at the same time; but it
will give me the impression of being a joke, even if it is merely
comic, because the use of the faulty reasoning of the unconscious reminds me of jokes, just as did the manoeuvres for
uncovering what is not manifestly comic (p. 202).

I set great store by clarifying this most delicate point in my
arguments – the relation of jokes to the comic; and I will therefore supplement what I have said with a few negative statements. I may first draw attention to the fact that the instance of
the convergence of jokes and the comic which I am dealing
with here is not identical with the former one (p. 202). It is true
that the distinction is a rather narrow one, but it can be made
with certainty. In the earlier case the comic arose from the
uncovering of psychical automatism. This, however, is by no
means peculiar to the unconscious alone, nor does it play any
striking part in the technique of jokes. Unmasking only comes
into relation with jokes accidentally, when it serves some other
joke-technique, such as representation by the opposite. But in
the case of giving free play to unconscious modes of thought the
convergence of jokes and the comic is a *necessary* one, since the
same method which is used here by the first person of the joke
as a technique for releasing pleasure must from its very nature
produce comic pleasure in the third person.

One might be tempted to generalize from this last case and
look for the relation of jokes to the comic in the notion that the
effect of jokes on the third person takes place according to the
mechanism of comic pleasure. But there is no question of this
being so. Contact with the comic is by no means to be found

in all jokes or even in the majority of them; in most cases, on the contrary, a clear distinction is to be made between jokes and the comic. Whenever a joke succeeds in escaping the appearance of nonsense – that is, in most jokes accompanied by double meaning and allusion – there is no trace to be found in the hearer of any effect resembling the comic. This may be tested on the examples I have given earlier, or on a few new ones that I can bring up:

Telegram of congratulations to a gambler on his seventieth birthday: '*Trente et quarante*.' (Dividing-up [pp. 64 and 77] with allusion.)

Hevesi somewhere describes the process of tobacco manufacture: 'The bright yellow leaves . . . were dipped in a sauce and were sauced in this dip.'[1] (Multiple use of the same material.)

Madame de Maintenon was known as 'Madame de *Maintenant*'. (Modification of a name.)

Professor Kästner [cf. p. 179] said to a prince who stood in front of a telescope during a demonstration: 'Your Highness, I know quite well that you are "*durchläuchtig* (illustrious)",[2] but you are not "*durchsichtig* (transparent)".'

Count Andrássy was known as 'Minister of the Fine Exterior'.[3]

It might further be thought that at any rate all jokes with a façade of nonsense will seem comic and must produce a comic effect. But I must recall that jokes of this kind very often affect the hearer in another way and provoke bewilderment and a tendency to repudiation (see p. 189*n*.). Thus it evidently depends on whether the nonsense of a joke appears as comic or as sheer ordinary nonsense – and we have not yet investigated

1. ['Saucing' (German '*tunken*') used to be part of the technical process for preparing tobacco.]

2. [An adjective derived from '*Durchlaucht*', a title applied to minor royalty: 'Serene Highness'.]

3. [Count Gyula Andrássy (1823–90) was for many years the Austro-Hungarian Minister for Foreign Affairs (for 'the Exterior'). He was something of a dandy.]

what determines this. We therefore stick to our conclusion that jokes are from their nature to be distinguished from the comic and only converge with it, on the one hand in certain special cases, and on the other hand in their aim of obtaining pleasure from intellectual sources.

During these inquiries into the relations between jokes and the comic the distinction has become plain to us which we must emphasize as the most important and which points at the same time to a main psychological characteristic of the comic. We found ourselves obliged to locate the pleasure in jokes in the unconscious; no reason is to be found for making the same localization in the case of the comic. On the contrary, all the analyses we have hitherto made have pointed to the source of comic pleasure being a comparison between two expenditures both of which must be ascribed to the preconscious. Jokes and the comic are distinguished first and foremost in their psychical localization; *the joke, it may be said, is the contribution made to the comic from the realm of the unconscious.*

[3]

There is no need to apologize for this digression, since the relation of jokes to the comic was the reason for our being forced into an investigation of the comic. But it is certainly time we returned to our previous topic – the discussion of the methods which serve for making things comic. We considered caricature and unmasking first, because we can derive some indications from these two for the analysis of the comic of *mimicry.* As a rule, no doubt, mimicry is permeated with caricature – the exaggeration of traits that are not otherwise striking [p. 262] –, and it also involves the characteristic of degradation. But this does not seem to exhaust its nature. It cannot be disputed that it is in itself an extraordinarily fertile source of comic pleasure, for we laugh particularly at the *faithfulness* of a piece of mimicry. It is not easy to give a satisfactory explanation of this unless one is prepared to adopt the view held by Bergson (1900), which approximates the comic of mimicry to the comic due to the discovery of psychical automatism. Bergson's opinion is that everything in a living person that makes one think of an inanimate mechanism has a comic effect. His formula for this runs '*mécanisation de la vie*'. He explains the comic of mimicry by starting out from a problem raised by Pascal in his *Pensées* of why it is that one laughs when one compares two similar faces neither of which has a comic effect by itself. 'What is living should never, according to our expectation, be repeated exactly the same. When we find such a repetition we always suspect some mechanism lying behind the living thing.' [Bergson, 1900, 35.] When one sees two faces that resemble each other closely, one thinks of two impressions from the same mould or of some similar mechanical procedure. In short, the cause of laughter in such cases would be the divergence of the living from the inanimate, or, as we might say, the degradation of the living to the inanimate (ibid., 35). If, moreover, we were to accept these plausible suggestions of Bergson's, we should not find it difficult to include his view under our own formula. Experience has taught us that every living thing is different from every other and calls for a kind of expenditure by our understanding; and we find ourselves disappointed if, as a result of complete conformity or deceptive mimicry, we need make no fresh expenditure. But we are disappointed in the sense of a relief, and the expenditure on expectation which has become superfluous is discharged by laughter. The same formula would also cover all the cases which Bergson considers of comic rigidity ('*raideur*'), of professional customs, fixed ideas, and turns of speech repeated on every possible occasion. All these cases would go back to a comparison between the expenditure on expectation and the expenditure actually required for an understanding of something that has remained the same; and the larger amount needed for expectation would be based on observation of the multiplicity and plasticity of living things. In the case of mimicry, accordingly, the source of the comic pleasure would be not the comic of situation but of expectation [p. 257 f.].

Since we derive comic pleasure in general from a comparison, it is incumbent on us to examine the comic of comparison itself; and this, indeed, serves as a method of making things comic. Our interest in this question will be increased when we recall that in the case of analogies, too, we often found that our 'feeling' left us in the lurch as to whether something was to be called a joke or merely comic (p. 122 f.).

The subject would, it must be admitted, deserve more careful treatment than our interests can devote to it. The main attribute that we inquire after in an analogy is whether it is apt – that is, whether it draws attention to a conformity which is really present in two different objects. The original pleasure in rediscovering the same thing (Groos, 1899, 153 [and above, p. 170 f.]) is not the only motive that favours the use of analogies; there is the further fact that analogies are capable of a use which brings with it a relief of intellectual work – if, that is to say, one follows the usual practice of comparing what is less known with what is better known or the abstract with the concrete, and by the comparison elucidates what is more unfamiliar or more difficult. Every such comparison, especially of something abstract with something concrete, involves a certain degradation and a certain economy in expenditure on abstraction (in the sense of ideational mimetics) [p. 259], but this is of course not sufficient to allow the characteristic of the comic to come clearly into prominence. It does not emerge suddenly but gradually from the pleasure of the relief brought about by the comparison. There are plenty of cases which merely fringe on the comic and in which doubt might be felt whether they show the characteristic of the comic. The comparison becomes undoubtedly comic if there is a rise in the level of difference between the expenditure on abstraction in the two things that are being compared, if something serious and unfamiliar, especially if it is of an intellectual or moral nature, is brought into comparison with something commonplace and inferior. The previous pleasure of the relief and the contribution from the determinants of ideational mimetics may perhaps explain the gradual transition, conditioned by quantitative factors, from general pleasure to comic pleasure during the comparison. I shall no doubt avoid misunderstandings if I stress the fact that I do not trace the comic pleasure in analogies to the contrast between the two things compared but to the difference between the two expenditures on abstraction. When an unfamiliar thing that is hard to take in, a thing that is abstract and in fact sublime in an intellectual sense, is alleged to tally with something familiar and inferior, in imagining which there is a complete absence of any expenditure on abstraction, then that abstract thing is itself unmasked as something equally inferior. The comic of comparison is thus reduced to a case of degradation.

A comparison can, however, as we have already seen, be in the nature of a joke, without a trace of comic admixture – precisely, that is, when it avoids degradation. Thus the comparison of truth with a torch that cannot be carried through a crowd without singeing someone's beard [p. 123] is purely in the nature of a joke, because it takes a watered-down turn of speech ('the torch of truth') at its full value, and it is not comic, because a torch as an object, though it is a concrete thing, is not without a certain distinction. But a comparison can just as easily be a joke and comic as well, and can be each independently of the other, since a comparison can be of help to certain techniques of jokes, such as unification or allusion. In this way Nestroy's comparison of memory to a 'warehouse' (p. 127) is at once comic and a joke – the former because of the extraordinary degradation which the psychological concept has to put up with in being compared to a 'warehouse', and the latter because the person making use of the comparison is a clerk, who thus establishes in the comparison a quite unexpected unification between psychology and his profession. Heine's phrase 'till at last every button bursts on my breeches of patience' [p. 126] seems at first sight to be no more than a remarkable example of a comically degrading comparison; but on further consideration we must also allow it the characteristics of a joke, since the comparison, as a means of allusion, impinges on the region of the obscene and so succeeds in liberating pleasure in the obscene. The same material, by what is admittedly not an entirely chance coincidence, provides us with a yield of pleasure which is simultaneously comic and of the character of a joke. If the conditions of the one favour the generation of the other, their union has a confusing effect on the 'feeling' which is supposed to tell us whether we are being offered a joke or something comic, and a decision can only be arrived at by an attentive investigation that has been freed from any predisposition to a particular kind of pleasure.

However attractive it may be to follow up these more intimate determinants of the yield of comic pleasure, the author must bear in mind that neither his education nor his daily occupation justify his extending his inquiries far beyond the sphere of jokes; and he must confess that the topic of comic comparisons makes him particularly aware of his inability.

We therefore readily recall that many authorities do not recognize the sharp conceptual and material distinction between jokes and the comic to which we have found ourselves led, and that they regard jokes as simply 'the comic of speech' or 'of words'. In order to test this view we will choose one example each of something intentionally and of something involuntarily comic in words to compare with jokes. We have remarked earlier that we believe ourselves very well able to distinguish a comic remark from a joke:

> 'With a fork and much to-do
> His mother dragged him from the stew' [p. 108]

is merely comic; Heine's remark about the four castes among the inhabitants of Göttingen – 'professors, students, philistines and donkeys' [p. 108] is *par excellence* a joke.

For something intentionally comic I will take as a model Stettenheim's 'Wippchen'.[1] People speak of Stettenheim as 'witty' because he possesses to a special degree the gift of evoking the comic. This capacity does in fact aptly determine the 'wit' that one 'has' in contrast to the 'joke' that one 'makes'.[2] It cannot be disputed that the letters of Wippchen, the Correspondent from Bernau, are also 'witty' in so far as they are abundantly sprinkled with jokes of every kind, among them some that are genuinely successful (e.g. of a display by savages: 'in ceremonial undress'). But what gives these productions their peculiar character is not these separate jokes but the almost too abundant comic of speech which flows through them. 'Wippchen' was no doubt originally intended as a satirical figure, a modification of Gustav Freytag's 'Schmock',[3] one of those uneducated people who misuse and trade away the nation's store of culture; but the author's enjoyment of the comic effects achieved in his picture of this character has evidently pushed the satirical purpose little by little into the background. Wippchen's productions are for the most part 'comic nonsense'. The author has made use of the pleasurable mood brought about by the piling up of these successes to introduce (justifiably, it must be said), alongside perfectly permissible material, all kinds of insipidities which could not be tolerated on their own account. Wippchen's nonsense produces a specific effect on account of a peculiar technique. If one looks more closely at these 'jokes' one is specially struck by a few kinds which give the whole production its stamp. Wippchen

1. [Julius Stettenheim (1831–1916), Berlin journalist.]

2. [The same German word '*Witz*' is used here for both 'wit' and 'joke'. Cf. p. 191.]

3. [Gustav Freytag (1816–95), novelist and dramatist. 'Schmock' was an unscrupulous journalist in his comedy *Die Journalisten*.]

makes use predominantly of combinations (amalgamations,,
modifications of familiar turns of speech and quotations and
replacements of a few commonplace elements in them by more
pretentious and weighty forms of expression. This incidentally
is coming near to the techniques of jokes.

Here, for instance, are some amalgamations (taken from the
preface and the first pages of the whole series):

'Turkey has money *wie Heu am Meere* [like hay by the sea].'
This is made up of the two expressions: 'Money *wie Heu* [like
hay]' and 'Money *wie Sand am Meere* [like sand by the sea]'.[1]

Or, 'I am no more than a column stripped of its leaves,[2]
which bears witness to its vanished glory' – condensed from 'a
tree stripped of its leaves' and 'a column which . . . etc.'

Or, 'Where is the thread of Ariadne which will lead me from
the Scylla of this Augean stable?' to which three Greek legends
have each contributed an element.

The modifications and substitutions can be summarized
without much difficulty. Their nature can be seen from the
following examples, which are characteristic of Wippchen and
behind which we have, in each case, a glimpse of another, more
current and usually more commonplace wording, which has
been reduced to a *cliché*:

'*Mir Papier und Tinte höher zu hängen* [to hang paper and ink
higher for me].' We use the phrase '*einem den Brotkorb höher
hängen* [to hang his bread-basket higher for someone – to put
someone on short commons]' metaphorically for 'to put
someone in more difficult circumstances'. So why should not
the metaphor be extended to other material?

'Battles in which the Russians sometimes draw the shorter
[lot – i.e. come off second best] and sometimes the longer.'
Only the first of these expressions ['*den Kürzeren ziehen*', 'draw

1. [These are two common expressions in German, equivalent to
'money like dirt' or 'oceans of money'.]

2. ['*Eine entlaubte Säule*' – an echo of '*eine entleibte Seele*', 'a dis-
embodied spirit'.]

the shorter'] is in common use; but in view of its derivation there would be no absurdity in bringing the second into use as well.

'While I was still young, Pegasus stirred within me.' If we put back 'the poet' instead of 'Pegasus' we find an auto-biographical *cliché* well worn by frequent use. It is true that 'Pegasus' is not a suitable substitute for 'the poet', but it has a conceptual relation with it and is a high-sounding word.

'Thus I lived through the thorny shoes of childhood.' A simile instead of a simple statement. '*Die Kinderschuhe austreten*' ['to wear out the shoes of childhood', 'to leave the nursery behind'] is one of the images connected with the concept of childhood.

From the profusion of Wippchen's other productions some can be stressed as pure examples of the comic. For instance, as a comic disappointment: 'For hours the fight fluctuated, until at last it remained undecided.' Or, as a comic unmasking (of ignorance): 'Clio, the Medusa of History'. Or quotations such as: '*Habent sua fata morgana*.'[1] But our interest is more aroused by the amalgamations and modifications, because they repeat familiar joke-techniques. We may, for instance, compare with the modifications such jokes as 'he has a great future behind him' [p. 58], or '*er hat ein Ideal vor dem Kopf*' [p. 117], or Lich-tenberg's modification joke 'new spas cure well' [p. 115 f.], and so on. Are Wippchen's productions which have the same tech-nique now to be called jokes? or how do they differ from these?

It is not difficult to answer. Let us recall that jokes present a double face to their hearer, force him to adopt two different views of them. In a nonsense joke, like the ones last mentioned, the one view, which only takes the wording into account,

1. ['*Habent sua fata libelli* (books have their destinies)' is a Latin saying attributed to Terence. '*Fata Morgana* is the Italian name for a particular kind of mirage seen in the Straits of Messina: from Morgan le Fey (fairy), King Arthur's sister.]

regards it as nonsense; the other view, following the hints that are given, passes through the hearer's unconscious and finds an excellent sense in it. In Wippchen's joke-like productions one face of the joke is blank, as though it were rudimentary: a Janus head but with only one face developed on it. If we allow the technique to lure us into the unconscious, we come upon nothing. The amalgamations lead us to no instance in which the two things that are amalgamated really yield a new meaning; if we attempt an analysis, they fall completely apart. The modifications and substitutions lead, as they do in jokes, to a usual and familiar wording; but the modification or substitution itself tells us nothing fresh and as a rule, indeed, nothing possible or serviceable. So that only the one view of these 'jokes' is left over – that they are nonsense. We can merely decide whether we choose to call such productions, which have freed themselves from one of the most essential characteristics of jokes, 'bad' jokes or not jokes at all.

Rudimentary jokes of this kind undoubtedly produce a comic effect, which we can account for in more than one way. Either the comic arises from the uncovering of the modes of thought of the unconscious, as in cases we considered earlier [e.g. p. 266 f], or the pleasure comes from the comparison with a complete joke. Nothing prevents our supposing that both these ways of generating comic pleasure converge here. It is not impossible that here the inadequacy of support from a joke is precisely what makes the nonsense into comic nonsense.

For there are other easily intelligible cases in which inadequacy of this kind as compared with what ought to be effected makes the nonsense irresistibly comic. The counterpart of jokes – riddles [p. 105n.] – can perhaps offer us better examples of this than jokes themselves. For instance, here is a 'facetious question' [p. 206n.]: 'What is it that hangs on the wall and that one can dry one's hands on?' It would be a stupid riddle if the answer were 'a hand-towel'. But that answer is rejected. – 'No, a herring.' – 'But for heaven's sake,' comes the infuriated protest, 'a herring doesn't hang on the wall.' – 'You *can* hang it up there.' – 'But who in the world is going to dry his hands on a herring?' – 'Well,' is the soothing reply, 'you don't *have* to.' This explanation, given by means of two typical displacements, shows how far this question falls short of a genuine riddle; and on account of its absolute inadequacy it strikes us as being – instead of simply nonsensically stupid – irresistibly comic. In this way, by failing to comply with essential conditions, jokes, riddles, and other things, which do not produce comic pleasure in themselves, are made into sources of comic pleasure.

There is still less difficulty in understanding the case of the *involuntary* comic of speech, which we can find realized as often as we please in, for instance, the poems of Friederike Kempner (1891):

> *Against Vivisection*
> Ein unbekanntes Band der Seelen kettet
> Den Menschen an das arme Tier.
> Das Tier hat einen Willen – ergo Seele –
> Wenn auch 'ne kleinere als wir.[1]

Or a conversation between a loving married couple:

> *The Contrast*
> 'Wie glücklich bin ich,' ruft sie leise,
> 'Auch ich,' sagt lauter ihr Gemahl,
> 'Es macht mich deine Art und Weise
> Sehr stolz auf meine gute Wahl!'[2]

There is nothing here to make us think of jokes. But there is

1. [Between mankind and poor dumb beasts there stretches
   A chain of souls impossible to see.
   Poor dumb beasts have a will – *ergo* a soul too –
   E'en though they have a soul smaller than we.]
2. ['How fortunate am I!' she softly cried.
   'I too,' declared her husband's louder voice:
   'Your many qualities fill me with pride
   At having made so excellent a choice.']

no doubt that it is the inadequacy of these 'poems' that makes them comic – the quite extraordinary clumsiness of their expression, which is linked with the tritest or most journalistic turns of phrase, the simple-minded limitation of their thought, the absence of any trace of poetic matter or form. In spite of all this, however, it is not obvious why we find Kempner's poems comic. We find many similar products nothing but shockingly bad; they do not make us laugh but annoy us. But it is precisely the greatness of the distance that separates them from what we expect of a poem that imposes the comic view on us; if this difference struck us as smaller we should be more inclined to criticize than to laugh. Furthermore, the comic effect of Kempner's poems is assured by a subsidiary circumstance – the authoress's unmistakably good intentions and a peculiar sincerity of feeling which disarms our ridicule or our annoyance and which we sense behind her helpless phrases.

Here we are reminded of a problem whose consideration we have postponed. Difference in expenditure is undoubtedly the basic determining condition of comic pleasure; but observation shows that this difference does not invariably give rise to pleasure. What further conditions must be present or what disturbances must be kept back, in order that comic pleasure may actually arise from the difference in expenditure? Before we turn to answering this question, we will conclude this discussion with a clear assertion that the comic of speech does not coincide with jokes, and that jokes must therefore be something other than the comic of speech. [Cf. p. 275.]

[4]

Now that we are on the point of approaching an answer to our last question, as to the necessary conditions for the generating of comic pleasure from the difference in expenditure, we may allow ourselves a relief which cannot fail to give *us* pleasure. An accurate reply to the question would be identical with an exhaustive account of the nature of the comic, for which we can claim neither capacity nor authority. We shall once more be content to throw light on the problem of the comic only so far as it contrasts clearly with the problem of jokes.

Every theory of the comic is objected to by its critics on the score that its definition overlooks what is essential to the comic: 'The comic is based on a contrast between ideas.' 'Yes, in so far as the contrast has a comic and not some other effect.' 'The feeling of the comic arises from the disappointment of an expectation.' 'Yes, unless the disappointment is in fact a distressing one.' No doubt the objections are justified; but we shall be over-estimating them if we conclude from them that the essential feature of the comic has hitherto escaped detection. What impairs the universal validity of these definitions are conditions which are indispensable for the generating of comic pleasure; but we do not need to look for the essence of the comic in them. In any case, it will only become easy for us to dismiss the objections and throw light on the contradictions to the definitions of the comic if we suppose that the origin of comic pleasure lies in a comparison of the difference between two expenditures. Comic pleasure and the effect by which it is known – laughter – can only come about if this difference is unutilizable and capable of discharge. We obtain no pleasurable effect but at most a transient sense of pleasure in which the characteristic of being comic does not emerge, if the difference is put to another use as soon as it is recognized. Just as special contrivances have to be adopted in the case of jokes in order to prevent the use elsewhere of the expenditure that is recognized as superfluous [p. 204 ff.], so, too, comic pleasure can only appear in circumstances that guarantee this same condition. For this reason occasions on which these differences in expenditure occur in our ideational life are uncommonly numerous, but the occasions on which the comic emerges from those differences are relatively quite rare.

Two observations force themselves on anyone who studies

even cursorily the conditions for the generation of the comic from difference in expenditure. Firstly, there are cases in which the comic appears habitually and as though by force of necessity, and on the contrary others in which it seems entirely dependent on the circumstances and on the standpoint of the observer. But secondly, unusually large differences very often break through unfavourable conditions, so that the comic feeling emerges in spite of them. In connection with the first of these points it would be possible to set up two classes – the inevitably comic and the occasionally comic – though one must be prepared from the first to renounce the notion of finding the inevitability of the comic in the first class free from exceptions. It would be tempting to inquire into the determining conditions for the two classes.

The conditions, some of which have been brought together as the 'isolation'[1] of the comic situation, apply essentially to the second class. A closer analysis elicits the following facts:

(a) The most favourable condition for the production of comic pleasure is a generally cheerful mood in which one is 'inclined to laugh'. In a toxic mood of cheerfulness almost everything seems comic, probably by comparison with the expenditure in a normal state. Indeed, jokes, the comic and all similar methods of getting pleasure from mental activity are no more than ways of regaining this cheerful mood – this euphoria – from a single point of approach, when it is not present as a general disposition of the psyche.

(b) A similarly favourable effect is produced by an *expectation* of the comic, by being attuned to comic pleasure. For this reason, if an intention to make something comic is communicated to one by someone else, differences of such a low degree are sufficient that they would probably be overlooked if they occurred in one's experience unintentionally. Anyone who starts out to read a comic book or goes to the theatre to see a farce owes to this intention his ability to laugh at things which

1. [Some light is thrown on this by a passage on p. 289 f. below.]

would scarcely have provided him with a case of the comic in his ordinary life. In the last resort it is in the recollection of having laughed and in the expectation of laughing that he laughs when he sees the comic actor come on to the stage, before the latter can have made any attempt at making him laugh. For that reason, too, one admits feeling ashamed afterwards over what one was able to laugh at in the theatre.

(c) Unfavourable conditions for the comic arise from the kind of mental activity with which a particular person is occupied at the moment. Imaginative or intellectual work that pursues serious aims interferes with the capacity of the cathexes for discharge – cathexes which the work requires for its displacements – so that the only unexpectedly large differences in expenditure are able to break through to comic pleasure. What are quite specially unfavourable for the comic are all kinds of intellectual processes which are sufficiently remote from what is perceptual to bring ideational mimetics to a stop. There is no place whatever left for the comic in abstract reflection except when that mode of thought is suddenly interrupted.

(d) The opportunity for the release of comic pleasure disappears, too, if the attention is focused precisely on the comparison from which the comic may emerge. In such circumstances what would otherwise have the most certain comic effect loses its comic force. A movement or a function cannot be comic for a person whose interest is directed to comparing it with a standard which he has clearly before his mind. Thus the examiner does not find the nonsense comic which the candidate produces in his ignorance; he is annoyed by it, while the candidate's fellow students, who are far more interested in what luck he will have than in how much he knows, laugh heartily at the same nonsense. A gymnastic or dancing instructor seldom has an eye for the comic in his pupils' movements; and a clergyman entirely overlooks the comic in the human weaknesses which the writer of comedies can bring to light so effectively. The comic process will not bear being hypercathected

by attention; it must be able to take its course quite un-
observed – in this respect, incidentally, just like jokes [p. 204 ff.].
It would, however, contradict the nomenclature of the 'processes of consciousness' of which I made use, with good reason,
in my *Interpretation of Dreams* if one sought to speak of the comic
process as a necessarily unconscious one. It forms part, rather, of
the preconscious; and such processes, which run their course in
the preconscious but lack the cathexis of attention with which
consciousness is linked, may aptly be given the name of
'automatic'. The process of comparing expenditures must
remain automatic if it is to produce comic pleasure.

(*e*) The comic is greatly interfered with if the situation from
which it ought to develop gives rise at the same time to a release of strong affect. A discharge of the operative difference is
as a rule out of the question in such a case. The affects, disposition and attitude of the individual in each particular case
make it understandable that the comic emerges and vanishes
according to the standpoint of each particular person, and that
an absolute comic exists only in exceptional instances. The contingency or relativity of the comic is therefore far greater than
that of a joke, which never happens of its own accord but is
invariably *made*, and in which the condition under which it can
find acceptance can be observed at the time at which it is constructed. The generation of affect is the most intense of all the
conditions that interfere with the comic and its importance in
this respect has been nowhere overlooked.[1] For this reason it
has been said that the comic feeling comes easiest in more or
less indifferent cases where the feelings and interests are not
strongly involved. Yet precisely in cases where there is a release
of affect one can observe a particularly strong difference in expenditure bring about the automatism of release. When
Colonel Butler[2] answers Octavio's warnings by exclaiming

1. 'It is easy for you to laugh; it means nothing more to you.'
2. [In Schiller's tragedy *Wallensteins Tod* (II, 6). Colonel Butler, a
veteran Irish soldier in the Imperial army during the Thirty Years War,

'with a bitter laugh': '*Thanks* from the House of Austria!', his embitterment does not prevent his laughing. The laugh applies to his memory of the disappointment he believes he has suffered; and on the other hand the magnitude of the disappointment cannot be portrayed more impressively by the dramatist than by his showing it capable of forcing a laugh in the midst of the storm of feelings that have been released. I am inclined to think that this explanation would apply to every case in which laughter occurs in circumstances other than pleasurable ones and accompanied by intensely distressing or strained emotions.

(*f*) If we add to this that the generating of comic pleasure can be encouraged by any other pleasurable accompanying circumstance as though by some sort of contagious effect (working in the same kind of way as the fore-pleasure principle with tendentious jokes), we shall have mentioned enough of the conditions governing comic pleasure for our purposes, though certainly not all of them. We can then see that these conditions, as well as the inconstancy and contingency of the comic effect, cannot be explained so easily by any other hypothesis than that of the derivation of comic pleasure from the discharge of a difference which, under the most varying circumstances, is liable to be used in ways other than discharge.

[5]

The comic of sexuality and obscenity would deserve more detailed consideration; but we can only touch upon it here with a few comments. The starting-point would once more [as in the case of obscene jokes, p. 140] be exposure. A chance

---

believes that he has been snubbed by the Emperor and is preparing to desert to his enemies. Octavio Piccolomini, his superior officer, begs him to reconsider the position and reminds him of the thanks which Austria owes him for his forty years' loyalty, and to this Butler replies in the words quoted above.]

exposure has a comic effect on us because we compare the ease
with which we have enjoyed the sight with the great expenditure which would otherwise be required for reaching this end.
Thus the case approaches that of the naïvely comic, but is
simpler. Every exposure of which we are made the spectator
(or audience in the case of smut) by a third person is equivalent
to the exposed person being made comic. We have seen that it
is the task of jokes to take the place of smut and so once more to
open access to a lost source of comic pleasure. As opposed to
this, witnessing an exposure is not a case of the comic for the
witness, because his own effort in doing so does away with the
determining condition of comic pleasure: nothing is left but
the sexual pleasure in what is seen. If the witness gives an account to someone else, the person who has been witnessed
becomes comic once more, because there is a predominant sense
that the latter has omitted the expenditure which would have
been in place for concealing his secret. Apart from this, the
spheres of sexuality and obscenity offer the amplest occasions
for obtaining comic pleasure alongside pleasurable sexual excitement; for they can show human beings in their dependence
on bodily needs (degradation) or they can reveal the physical
demands lying behind the claim of mental love (unmasking).

[6]

An invitation to us to look for an understanding of the comic
in its psychogenesis is also to be found, surprisingly enough, in
Bergson's charming and lively volume *Le rire*. We have already
[p. 271] made the acquaintance of Bergson's formulas for
grasping the characteristics of the comic: '*mécanisation de la vie*',
'*substitution quelconque de l'artificiel au naturel*'.[1] He proceeds by a
plausible train of thought from automatism to automata, and
tries to trace back a number of comic effects to the faded re-

    1. ['Mechanization of life' – 'some kind of substitution of the artificial
for the natural'.]

collection of a children's toy. In this connection he reaches for
a moment a point of view, which, it is true, he soon abandons:
he endeavours to explain the comic as an after-effect of the joys
of childhood. 'Peut-être même devrions-nous pousser la
simplification plus loin encore, remonter à nos souvenirs les
plus anciens, chercher dans les jeux qui amusèrent l'enfant la
première ébauche des combinaisons qui font rire l'homme . . .
Trop souvent surtout nous méconnaissons ce qu'il y a d'encore
enfantin, pour ainsi dire, dans la plupart de nos émotions
joyeuses' (Bergson, 1900, 68 ff.).[1] Since we have traced back
jokes to children's play with words and thoughts which has
been frustrated by rational criticism [p. 177 ff.] we cannot help
feeling tempted to investigate the infantile roots which Bergson
suspects in the case of the comic as well.

And, in fact, if we examine the relation of the comic to the
child we come upon a whole number of connections which
seem promising. Children themselves do not strike us as in any
way comic, though their nature fulfils all the conditions which,
if we compare it with our own nature, yield a comic difference:[2] the excessive expenditure on movement as well as the
small intellectual expenditure, the domination of the mental
functions by the bodily ones, and other features. A child only
produces a comic effect on us when he conducts himself not as a
child but as a serious adult, and he produces it then in the same
way as other people who disguise themselves. But so long as he
retains his childish nature the perception of him affords us a
pure pleasure, perhaps one that reminds us slightly of the
comic. We call him naïve, in so far as he shows us his lack of
inhibition, and we describe as naïvely comic those of his utter-

    1. ['Perhaps we should even carry simplification further still, go back
to our oldest memories, and trace in the games that amused the child
the first sketch of the combinations which make the grown man laugh.
. . . Above all, we too often fail to recognize how much of childishness,
so to speak, there still is in most of our joyful emotions.']
    2. [Cf. footnote 1, p. 247.]

ances which in another person we should have judged obscenities or jokes.

On the other hand, children are without a feeling for the comic. This assertion seems to say no more than that the comic feeling, like such a number of other things, only starts at some point in the course of mental development; and this would be by no means surprising, especially as it has to be admitted that the feeling already emerges clearly at an age which has to be counted as part of childhood. But it can nevertheless be shown that the assertion that children lack the feeling of the comic contains more than something self-evident. In the first place, it is easy to see that it could not be otherwise if our view is correct which derives the comic feeling from a difference in expenditure that arises in the course of understanding another person. Let us once again take the comic of movement as an example. The comparison which provides the difference runs (stated in conscious formulas): 'That is how he does it' and 'This is how I should do it, how I did it'. But a child is without the standard contained in the second sentence; he understands simply by mimicry: he does it in just the same way. The child's upbringing presents him with a standard: 'this is how you ought to do it'. If he now makes use of this standard in making the comparison, he will easily conclude: 'he did not do it right' and 'I can do it better'. In this case he laughs at the other person, he laughs at him in the feeling of his own superiority. There is nothing to prevent our deriving this laughter too from a difference in expenditure; but on the analogy of the cases of laughing at people that we have come across we may infer that the comic feeling is not present in a child's superior laughter. It is a laughter of pure pleasure. In our own case when we have a clear judgement of our own superiority, we merely smile instead of laughing, or, if we laugh, we can nevertheless distinguish this becoming conscious of our superiority from the comic that makes us laugh [pp. 256 and 260].

It is probably right to say that children laugh from pure

pleasure in a variety of circumstances that we feel as 'comic' and cannot find the motive for, whereas a child's motives are clear and can be stated. For instance, if someone slips in the street and falls down we laugh because the impression – we do not know why – is comic. A child laughs in the same case from a feeling of superiority or from *Schadenfreude*: 'You've fallen down, I haven't.' Certain motives for pleasure in children seem to be lost to us adults, and instead in the same circumstances we have the 'comic' feeling as a substitute for the lost one.

If one might generalize, it would seem most attractive to place the specific characteristic of the comic which we are in search of in an awakening of the infantile – to regard the comic as the regained 'lost laughter of childhood'. One could then say: 'I laugh at a difference in expenditure between another person and myself, every time I rediscover the child in him.' Or, put more exactly, the complete comparison which leads to the comic would run: 'That is how he does it – I do it in another way – he does it as I used to do it as a child.'

Thus the laughter would always apply to the comparison between the adult's ego and the child's ego. Even the lack of uniformity in the comic difference – the fact that what seems to me comic is sometimes a greater and sometimes a smaller expenditure [p. 256n.] – would fit in with the infantile determinant; actually what is comic is invariably on the infantile side.

This is not contradicted by the fact that, when children themselves are the object of the comparison, they do not give me a comic impression but a purely pleasurable one; nor is it contradicted because the comparison with the infantile only produces a comic effect if any other use of the difference is avoided. For these are matters concerned with the conditions governing *discharge*. Whatever brings a psychical process into connection with others operates against the discharge of the surplus cathexis and puts it to some other use; whatever isolates a psychical act encourages discharge [cf. p. 282]. A conscious attitude to children as objects of comparison therefore makes impossible the discharge that is necessary for comic pleasure. Only when the cathexis is *preconscious* [p. 284] is there an approximation to an isolation such as, incidentally, we may ascribe to the mental processes in children as well. The addition to the comparison ('I did it like that as a child too') from which the comic effect is derived would thus only come into consideration, as far as differences of medium magnitude are concerned, if no other nexus could gain control over the liberated surplus.

If we pursue our attempt to discover the essence of the comic in a preconscious link with the infantile, we must go a step further than Bergson and admit that a comparison need not, in order to produce the comic, arouse old childish pleasures and childish play; it will be enough for it to touch upon childish nature in general, and perhaps even on childish suffering. Here we shall be parting from Bergson but remaining in agreement with ourselves if we connect comic pleasure not with recollected pleasure but once more with a comparison. It may be that cases of the former kind [those connected with recollected pleasure] may coincide with the invariably and irresistibly comic [p. 281 f.].

Let us at this point review the scheme which we drew up earlier [p. 256] of the various comic possibilities. We remarked that the comic difference was found either

(a) by a comparison between another person and oneself, or

(b) by a comparison entirely within the other person, or

(c) by a comparison entirely within oneself.

In the first of these cases the other person would appear to me as a child; in the second he would reduce himself to a child; and in the third I should discover the child in myself.

[a] The first case would include the comic of movement and form, of mental functioning and of character. The corresponding infantile factors would be the urge to movement and the child's inferior mental and moral development. So that, for

instance, a stupid person would be comic to me in so far as he reminded me of a lazy child and a bad person in so far as he reminded me of a naughty child. There could only be a question of a childish pleasure lost to adults in the single instance in which the child's own joy in movement was concerned.

[b] The second case, in which the comic depends entirely on 'empathy', includes the most numerous possibilities – the comic of situation, of exaggeration (caricature), of mimicry, of degradation and of unmasking. This is the case in which the introduction of the infantile point of view proves most useful. For the comic of situation is mostly based on embarrassments, in which we rediscover the child's helplessness. The worst of the embarrassments, the interference by the peremptory demands of natural needs with other functions, corresponds to the child's incomplete control over his bodily functions. Where the comic of situation operates by means of repetitions, it is based on the child's peculiar pleasure in constant repetition (of questions or of being told stories) which make him a nuisance to the adult. [Cf. p. 178n.] Exaggeration, which still gives pleasure to adults in so far as it can find justification with their critical faculty, is connected with the child's peculiar lack of a sense of proportion, his ignorance of all quantitative relations, which he comes to know later than qualitative ones. The use of moderation and restraint, even in the case of permitted impulses, is a late fruit of education and is acquired by the mutual inhibition of mental activities brought together in a combination. Where such combinations are weakened, as in the unconscious of dreams or in the mono-ideism of psychoneuroses, the child's lack of moderation re-emerges.

We found relatively great difficulties in understanding the comic of mimicry so long as we left the infantile factor out of account. But mimicry is the child's best art and the driving motive of most of his games. A child's ambition aims far less at excelling among his equals than at mimicking the grown-ups. The relation of children to adults is also the basis of the comic of degradation, which corresponds to the condescension shown by adults in their attitude to the life of children. There is little that gives children greater pleasure than when a grown-up lets himself down to their level, renounces his oppressive superiority and plays with them as an equal. This relief, which gives the child pure pleasure, becomes in adults, in the form of degradation, a means of making things comic and a source of comic pleasure. As regards unmasking, we know that it goes back to degradation.

[c] We come up against the most difficulties in finding the infantile basis of the third case, the comic of expectation, which no doubt explains why those authorities who have put this case first in their discussion of the comic have found no occasion for taking account of the infantile factor in the comic. The comic of expectation is no doubt the remotest in children; the capacity to grasp it is the latest to appear. In most of the instances which seem comic to an adult a child would probably feel only disappointment. We might, however, take the child's power of blissful expectation and credulity as a basis for understanding how we appear to ourselves comic 'as a child' when we meet with a comic disappointment.

What we have said would seem to suggest a certain probability for a translation of the comic feeling that might run: 'Those things are comic which are not proper for an adult.' Nevertheless I do not feel bold enough, in virtue of my whole attitude to the problem of the comic, to defend this last assertion with as much seriousness as my earlier ones. I am unable to decide whether degradation to being a child is only a special case of comic degradation, or whether everything comic is based fundamentally on degradation to being a child.[1]

1. The fact that comic pleasure has its source in the 'quantitative contrast' of a comparison between small and large, which after all also expresses the essential relation between a child and an adult – this would certainly be a strange coincidence if the comic had no other connection with the infantile.

[7]

An inquiry which deals with the comic, however cursorily, would be seriously incomplete if it did not find room for at least a few remarks about *humour*. The essential kinship between the two is so little open to doubt that an attempt at explaining the comic is bound to make at least some contribution to an understanding of humour. However much that is pertinent and impressive may have been brought forward in the appreciation of humour (which, itself one of the highest psychical achievements, enjoys the particular favour of thinkers), yet we cannot evade an attempt at giving expression to its nature by an approach to the formulas for jokes and for the comic.

We have seen [p. 284] that the release of distressing affects is the greatest obstacle to the emergence of the comic. As soon as the aimless movement does damage, or the stupidity leads to mischief, or the disappointment causes pain, the possibility of a comic effect is at an end. This is true, at all events, for a person who cannot ward off such unpleasure, who is himself its victim or is obliged to have a share in it; whereas a person who is not concerned shows by his demeanour that the situation involved contains everything that is required for a comic effect. Now humour is a means of obtaining pleasure in spite of the distressing affects that interfere with it; it acts as a substitute for the generation of these affects, it puts itself in their place. The conditions for its appearance are given if there is a situation in which, according to our usual habits, we should be tempted to release a distressing affect and if motives then operate upon us which suppress that affect *in statu nascendi*. In the cases that have just been mentioned the person who is the victim of the injury, pain, and so on, might obtain *humorous* pleasure, while the unconcerned person laughs from *comic* pleasure. The pleasure of humour, if this is so, comes about – we cannot say otherwise – at the cost of a release of affect that does not occur: it arises from *an economy in the expenditure of affect*.

Humour is the most easily satisfied among the species of the comic. It completes its course within a single person; another person's participation adds nothing new to it. I can keep to myself the enjoyment of the humorous pleasure that has arisen in me, without feeling obliged to communicate it. It is not easy to say what happens in a person when humorous pleasure is generated; but we can obtain some insight if we examine the cases in which humour is communicated or sympathized with, cases in which, by an understanding of the humorous person, we arrive at the same pleasure as his. The crudest case of humour – what is known as *Galgenhumor* [literally, 'gallows humour'] – may be instructive in this connection. A rogue who was being led out to execution on a Monday remarked: 'Well, this week's beginning nicely.'[1] This is actually a joke, since the remark is quite apt in itself, but on the other hand, is misplaced in a nonsensical way, since for the man himself there would be no further events that week. But humour is concerned in the *making* of such a joke – that is, in disregarding what it is that distinguishes the beginning of this week from others, in denying the distinction which might give rise to motives for quite special emotions. The case was the same when the rogue on his way to execution asked for a scarf for his bare throat so as not to catch cold – an otherwise laudable precaution but one which, in view of what lay in store so shortly for the neck, was remarkably superfluous and unimportant. It must be confessed that there is something like magnanimity in this *blague*, in the man's tenacious hold upon his customary self and his disregard of what might overthrow that self and drive it to despair. This kind of grandeur of humour appears unmistakably in cases in which our admiration is not inhibited by the circumstances of the humorous person.

In Victor Hugo's *Hernani*, the bandit who has become involved in a conspiracy against his King, Charles I of Spain (the

1. [The anecdote is discussed again in Freud's late paper on 'Humour' (1927*d*).]

Emperor Charles V), has fallen into the hands of this powerful enemy. He foresees that, convicted of high treason, it is his fate to lose his head. But this fore-knowledge does not prevent his letting himself be known as a Hereditary Grandee of Spain and declaring that he has no intention of renouncing any of the privileges that are his due. A Grandee of Spain might cover his head in the presence of his royal master. Very well, then:

> .... Nos têtes ont le droit
> De tomber couvertes devant de toi.[1]

This is humour on the grand scale, and if when we hear it we do not laugh, that is because our admiration covers the humorous pleasure. In the case of the rogue who refuses to catch cold on the way to execution we laugh heartily. The situation that ought to drive the criminal to despair might rouse intense pity in us; but that pity is inhibited because we understand that he, who is more closely concerned, makes nothing of the situation. As a result of this understanding, the expenditure on the pity, which was already prepared, becomes unutilizable and we laugh it off. We are, as it were, infected by the rogue's indifference – though we notice that it has cost him a great expenditure of psychical work.

An economy of pity is one of the most frequent sources of humorous pleasure. Mark Twain's humour usually works with this mechanism. In an account of his brother's life, for instance, he tells us how he was at one time employed on a great road-making enterprise. The premature explosion of a mine blew him up into the air and he came down again far away from the place where he had been working. We are bound to have feelings of sympathy for the victim of the accident and would like to ask whether he was injured by it. But when the story goes on to say that his brother had a half-day's wages deducted for being 'absent from his place of employment' we are entirely distracted from our pity and become almost as hard-hearted as

1. ['Our heads have the right to fall before you covered.']

the contractor and almost as indifferent to possible damage to the brother's health. On another occasion Mark Twain presents us with his family tree, which he traces back to one of Columbus's fellow-voyagers. He then describes this ancestor's character and how his baggage consisted entirely of a number of pieces of washing each of which had a different laundry-mark – here we cannot help laughing at the cost of an economy of the feeling of piety into which we were prepared to enter at the beginning of this family history. The mechanism of the humorous pleasure is not interfered with by our knowledge that this pedigree is a fictitious one and that the fiction serves the satirical purpose of exposing the embellishments in similar accounts by other people: it is as independent of the condition that it must be real as in the case of making things comic [p. 260 f.]. In yet another story, Mark Twain describes how his brother constructed a subterranean dwelling, into which he brought a bed, a table and a lamp and which he roofed over with a large piece of sailcloth with a hole in the middle. At night, however, after the hut was finished, a cow that was being driven home fell through the opening of the roof on to the table and put out the lamp. His brother patiently helped to get the beast out and put the establishment to rights again. Next night the same interruption was repeated and his brother behaved as before. And so it was every following night. Repetition makes the story comic, but Mark Twain ends it by reporting that on the forty-sixth night, when the cow fell through again, his brother finally remarked: 'The thing's beginning to get monotonous.' At this our humorous pleasure cannot be kept back, for what we had long expected to hear was that this obstinate set of misfortunes would make his brother *angry*. And indeed the small contributions of humour that we produce ourselves are as a rule made at the cost of anger – instead of getting angry.[1]

1. The grandiose humorous effect of a figure like that of the fat knight Sir John Falstaff rests on an economy in contempt and indignation.

The species of humour are extraordinarily variegated according to the nature of the emotion which is economized in favour of the humour: pity, anger, pain, tenderness, and so on. Their number seems to remain uncompleted becaues the kingdom of humour is constantly being enlarged whenever an artist or writer succeeds in submitting some hitherto unconquered emotions to the control of humour, in making them, by devices like those in the examples we have given, into sources of

---

We recognize him as an undeserving gormandizer and swindler, but our condemnation is disarmed by a whole number of factors. We can see that he knows himself as well as we do; he impresses us by his wit [see Editor's Introduction, p. 35], and, besides this, his physical misproportion has the effect of encouraging us to take a comic view of him instead of a serious one, as though the demands of morality and honour must rebound from so fat a stomach. His doings are on the whole harmless, and are almost excused by the comic baseness of the people he cheats. We admit that the poor fellow has a right to try to live and enjoy himself like anyone else, and we almost pity him because in the chief situations we find him a plaything in the hands of someone far his superior. So we cannot feel angry with him and we add all that we economize in indignation with him to the comic pleasure which he affords us apart from this. Sir John's own humour arises in fact from the superiority of an ego which neither his physical nor his moral defects can rob of its cheerfulness and assurance.

The ingenious knight Don Quixote de la Mancha is, on the contrary, a figure who possesses no humour himself but who with his seriousness offers us a pleasure which could be called humorous, though its mechanism shows an important divergence from that of humour. Don Quixote is originally a purely comic figure, a big child; the phantasies from his books of chivalry have gone to his head. It is well known that to begin with the author intended nothing else of him and that his creation gradually grew far beyond its creator's first intentions. But after the author had equipped this ridiculous figure with the deepest wisdom and the noblest purposes and had made him into the symbolic representative of an idealism which believes in the realization of its aims and takes duties seriously and takes promises literally, this figure ceased to have a comic effect. Just as in other cases humorous pleasure arises from the prevention of an emotion, so it does here from the interference with comic pleasure. But it is clear that these examples have already carried us a long way from the simple cases of humour.

humorous pleasure. The artists in *Simplicissimus*[1], for instance, have had astonishing results in achieving humour at the cost of horror and disgust. The forms in which humour is manifested are, moreover, determined by two peculiarities which are connected with the conditions under which it is generated. Humour may, in the first place, appear merged with a joke or some other species of the comic; in that case its task is to get rid of a possibility implicit in the situation that an affect may be generated which would interfere with the pleasurable outcome. In the second place, it may stop this generating of an affect entirely or only partially; this last is actually the common case since it is easier to bring about, and it produces the various forms of 'broken'[2] humour – the humour that smiles through tears. It withdraws a part of its energy from the affect and in exchange gives a tinge of humour.

The humorous pleasure derived from sympathy originates, as can be seen from the examples above, from a peculiar technique comparable to displacement, by means of which the release of affect that is already in preparation is disappointed and the cathexis diverted on to something else, often on to something of secondary importance. But this does not help us at all to understand the process by which the displacement away from the generating of affect takes place in the humorous person himself. We can see that the receiver imitates the creator of the humour in his mental processes, but this tells us nothing of the forces which make the process possible in the latter.

We can only say that if someone succeeds, for instance, in disregarding a painful affect by reflecting on the greatness of the interests of the world as compared with his own smallness, we do not regard this as an achievement of humour but of philosophical thought, and if we put ourselves into his train of thought, we obtain no yield of pleasure. Humorous displacement is thus just as impossible under the glare of conscious

1. [See footnote, p. 113.]
2. A term which is used in quite another sense in Vischer's aesthetics.

attention as is comic comparison [p. 284]; like the latter, it is tied to the condition of remaining preconscious or automatic.

We can gain some information about humorous displacement if we look at it in the light of a defensive process. Defensive processes are the psychical correlative of the flight reflex and perform the task of preventing the generation of unpleasure from internal sources. In fulfilling this task they serve mental events as an automatic regulation, which in the end, incidentally, turns out to be detrimental and has to be subjected to conscious thinking. I have indicated one particular form of this defence, repression that has failed, as the operative mechanism for the development of psychoneuroses. Humour can be regarded as the highest of these defensive processes. It scorns to withdraw the ideational content bearing the distressing affect from conscious attention as repression does, and thus surmounts the automatism of defence. It brings this about by finding a means of withdrawing the energy from the release of unpleasure that is already in preparation and of transforming it, by discharge, into pleasure. It is even conceivable that once again it may be a connection with the infantile that puts the means for achieving this at its disposal. Only in childhood have there been distressing affects at which the adult would smile today – just as he laughs, as a humorist, at his present distressing affects. The exaltation of his ego, to which the humorous displacement bears witness, and of which the translation would no doubt be 'I am too big (too fine) to be distressed by these things', might well be derived from his comparing his present ego with his childish one. This view is to some extent supported by the part played by the infantile in neurotic processes of repression.

On the whole humour is closer to the comic than to jokes. It shares with the former its psychical localization in the preconscious, whereas jokes, as we have had to suppose, are formed as a compromise between the unconscious and the preconscious. On the other hand humour does not participate in a peculiar characteristic common to jokes and the comic, on which we have perhaps not yet laid sufficient stress. It is a necessary condition for generating the comic that we should be obliged, *simultaneously or in rapid succession*, to apply to one and the same act of ideation two different ideational methods, between which the 'comparison' is then made and the comic difference emerges [p. 256]. Differences in expenditure of this kind arise between what belongs to someone else and to oneself, between what is as usual and what has been changed, between what is expected and what happens.[1] In the case of jokes, the difference between two simultaneous methods of viewing things, which operate with a different expenditure, applies to the process in the person who hears the joke. One of these two views, following the hints contained in the joke, passes along the path of thought through the unconscious; the other stays on the surface and views the joke like any other wording that has emerged from the preconscious and become conscious [p. 277 f.]. We should perhaps be justified in representing the pleasure from a joke that is heard as being derived from the difference between these two methods of viewing it.[2] Here we are saying of jokes what we described [p. 278] as their possessing a Janus head, while the relation between jokes and the comic had still to be cleared up.[3]

1. If we are prepared to do a little violence to the concept of 'expectation', we can, following Lipps, include a very large region of the comic under the comic of expectation. But what are probably the most basic instances of the comic, those arising from a comparison between someone else's expenditure and one's own, would be the very ones that fitted in least easily to this grouping.

2. We can accept this formula without question, since it leads to nothing that would contradict our earlier discussions. The difference between the two expenditures must in essence come down to the inhibitory expenditure that is saved. The lack of this economy in inhibition in the case of the comic, and the absence of quantitative contrast in the case of jokes, would determine the distinction between the comic feeling and the impression of a joke, in spite of their agreeing in the characteristic of using two kinds of ideational activity for the same view.

3. This peculiarity of the '*double face*' [in French in the original] has

In the case of humour the characteristic which we have just brought forward becomes effaced. It is true that we feel humorous pleasure when an emotion is avoided which we should have expected because it usually accompanies the situation, and to that extent humour too comes under the extended concept of the comic of expectation. But with humour it is no longer a question of two different methods of viewing the same subject-matter. The fact that the situation is dominated by the emotion that is to be avoided, which is of an unpleasurable character, puts an end to the possibility of comparing it with the characteristics of the comic and of jokes. Humorous displacement is in fact a case of a liberated expenditure being used elsewhere – a case which has been shown to be so perilous to a comic effect [p. 281].[1]

[8]

We are now at the end of our task, having reduced the mechanism of humorous pleasure to a formula analogous to those for

---

naturally not escaped the authorities. Mélinand (1895), from whom I have borrowed this phrase, states the determinants of laughter in the following formula: 'Ce qui fait rire c'est ce qui est à la fois, d'un côté, absurde et de l'autre, familier.' ['What makes one laugh is what is on the one hand absurd, and on the other familiar.'] This formula fits jokes better than the comic, but does not completely cover the former either. – Bergson (1900, 98) defines the comic situation by the 'interférence des séries': 'Une situation est toujours comique quand elle appartient en même temps à deux séries d'événements absolument indépendantes, et qu'elle peut s'interpréter à la fois dans deux sens tout différents.' ['A situation is always comic when it belongs at the same time to two series of events that are absolutely independent, and when it can be interpreted simultaneously in two quite different senses.'] – Lipps regards the comic as 'the bigness and smallness of the same thing'.

1. [Over twenty years after the publication of this book, Freud returned to the subject of humour in a short paper (1927d), reflecting his new views on mental structure.]

comic pleasure and for jokes. The pleasure in jokes has seemed to us to arise from an *economy in expenditure upon inhibition*, the pleasure in the comic from an *economy in expenditure upon ideation* (upon cathexis) and the pleasure in humour from an *economy in expenditure upon feeling*. In all three modes of working of our mental apparatus the pleasure is derived from an economy. All three are agreed in representing methods of regaining from mental activity a pleasure which has in fact been lost through the development of that activity. For the euphoria which we endeavour to reach by these means is nothing other than the mood of a period of life in which we were accustomed to deal with our psychical work in general with a small expenditure of energy – the mood of our childhood, when we were ignorant of the comic, when we were incapable of jokes and when we had no need of humour to make us feel happy in our life.

APPENDIX

FRANZ BRENTANO'S RIDDLES

THE account of Franz Brentano's riddles given by Freud in his footnote on p. 65 is so obscure that a further explanation is called for. In 1879 Brentano (under the pseudonym of 'Aenigmatias') published a booklet of some two hundred pages with the title *Neue Räthsel* (New Riddles). It included specimens of various different types of riddle, the last of which was described as '*Füllräthsel*' – 'fill-up riddles'. He gives an account of these in the introduction to the booklet. According to him, this type of riddle was a favourite pastime in the Main region of Germany, but had only recently reached Vienna. The booklet includes thirty examples of the 'fill-up riddles', among them the two quoted, not quite accurately, by Freud. A complete translation of these will be the simplest way of making their construction plain:

'XXIV.

'How our friend is plagued by his belief in premonitions! The other day when his mother was ill, I found him sitting under a tall tree. The wind was blowing through its branches, so that some of its large leaves came away, and one of them happened to fall in his lap. Thereupon he burst into tears. His mother, he moaned, was going to die: *das lasse ihn das herabgefallene* [literally: this he was led by the fallen] daldaldal – daldaldal.'

Answer: '*Platanenblatt ahnen*' [plane tree leaf to think].

'XXVIII.

'A man from Hindustan fell ill. His doctor was in the act of writing him out a prescription when he was suddenly called away by an urgent message. He finished writing out the prescription as quickly as possible and went off on the other call. Soon afterwards the news reached him that the Asian, hardly had he tasted the drug prepared for him, had died in convulsions. "Unhappy wretch!" the doctor said to himself in horror. "What have you done? Is it possible that you *indem du den Trank dem* [literally: when you the potion for the] daldaldaldaldaldal – daldaldaldaldaldal?"'

Answer: '*Inder hast verschrieben, in der Hast verschrieben*' [Indian prescribed, in your haste made a slip of the pen].

An English specimen may make things clearer still:

'Burglars had broken into a large furriers' store. But they were disturbed and went off without taking anything, though leaving the show-room in the greatest confusion. When the manager arrived in the morning, he gave instructions to his assistants: "Never mind about the cheaper goods. The urgent thing is to get the daldal – daldal."'

Answer: 'first-rate furs straight'.

BIBLIOGRAPHY
AND AUTHOR INDEX

Titles of books and periodicals are in italics, titles of papers are in inverted commas. Abbreviations are in accordance with the *World List of Scientific Periodicals* (London, 1963–5). Further abbreviations used in this volume will be found in the List at the end of this bibliography. Numerals in bold type refer to volumes, ordinary numerals refer to pages. The figures in round brackets at the end of each entry indicate the page or pages of this volume on which the work in question is mentioned.

In the case of the Freud entries, only English translations are given. The initial dates are those of the German original publications. (The date of writing is added in square brackets where it differs from the latter.) The letters attached to the dates of publication are in accordance with the corresponding entries in the complete bibliography of Freud's writings included in Volume **24** of the *Standard Edition*. Details of the original publication, including the original German title, are given in the editorial introduction to each work in the *Pelican Freud Library*.

For non-technical authors, and for technical authors where no specific work is mentioned, see the General Index.

ABRAHAM, K., and FREUD, S. (1965) *See* FREUD, S. (1965*a*)

'AENIGMATIAS' [F. BRENTANO] (1879) *Neue Räthsel*, Vienna. (303–4)

ANDREAS-SALOMÉ, L., and FREUD, S. (1966) *See* FREUD, S. (1966*a*)

BAIN, A. (1865) *The Emotions and the Will*, 2nd ed., London. (199, 261)

BERGSON, H. (1900) *Le rire: essai sur la signification du comique*, Paris. (247, 271–2, 286–7, 301)

  [*Trans.: Laughter, an Essay on the Meaning of the Comic,* by C. Brereton and F. Rothwell, London, 1911.]

BLEULER, E. (1904) 'Die negative Suggestibilität', *Psychiat.-neurol. Wschr.*, **6,** 249 and 261. (233)

BRENTANO, F. *See* 'AENIGMATIAS'

BREUER, J., and FREUD, S. (1895) *See* FREUD, S. (1895*d*)

BRILL, A. A. (1911) 'Freud's Theory of Wit', *J. abnorm. Psychol.*, **6**, 279. (53–4, 64, 66, 67)

DUGAS, L. (1902) *Psychologie du rire*, Paris. (197–8, 199, 209)

EHRENFELS, C. VON (1903) 'Sexuales Ober- und Unterbewusstsein', *Politisch-anthrop. Rev.*, **2.** (156)

FALKE, J. VON (1897) *Lebenserinnerungen*, Leipzig. (46, 98, 110)

FECHNER, G. T. (1889) *Elemente der Psychophysik* (2 vols.), 2nd ed., Leipzig. (1st ed., 1860.) (234)

  (1897) *Vorschule der Ästhetik* (2 vols.), 2nd ed., Leipzig. (1st ed., 1876.) 173, 185–6)

  (n.d.) *Rätselbüchlein von Dr Mises*, 4th ed., enlarged, Leipzig. (106–7)

FISCHER, K. (1889) *Über den Witz*, 2nd ed., Heidelberg. (39–41, 44, 49, 64, 71, 76, 82, 83, 105, 106, 107–8, 109, 135, 138)

FREUD, M. (1957) *Glory Reflected*, London. (22)

FREUD, S. (1891*b*) *On Aphasia*, London and New York, 1953. (14, 26, 168)

  (1893*a*) with BREUER, J., 'On the Psychical Mechanism of Hysterical Phenomena: Preliminary Communication', in *Studies on Hysteria*, Standard Ed., **2**, 3; P.F.L., **3**, 53. (26)

  (1895*d*) with BREUER, J., *Studies on Hysteria*, London, 1956; Standard Ed., **2**; P.F.L. **3.** (26, 32, 207)

  (1900*a*) *The Interpretation of Dreams*, London and New York, 1955; Standard Ed., **4–5**; P.F.L., **4.** (21, 26, 31–2, 33, 34, 36, 61, 131, 168, 173, 175, 182, 187, 199–200, 215, 218, 221, 228, 231, 233, 234, 251, 267)

  (1901*b*) *The Psychopathology of Everyday Life*, Standard Ed., **6**; P.F.L., **5.** (21, 26, 33, 34, 60, 136, 150, 226)

  (1905*d*) *Three Essays on the Theory of Sexuality*, London, 1962; Standard Ed., **7**, 130; P.F.L., **7.** (26, 33, 141, 188)

  (1905*e* [1901]) 'Fragment of an Analysis of a Case of Hysteria', Standard Ed., **7**, 7; P.F.L. **8**, (33)

  (1908*d*) ' "Civilized" Sexual Morality and Modern Nervous Illness', Standard Ed., **9**, 181; P.F.L. **12.** (156)

  (1908*e* [1907]) 'Creative Writers and Day-Dreaming', Standard Ed., **9**, 143; P.F.L. **14.** (188)

(1909*b*) 'Analysis of a Phobia in a Five-Year-Old Boy', *Standard Ed.*, **10**, 3; *P.F.L.* **8**. (27, 168)

(1909*d*) 'Notes upon a Case of Obsessional Neurosis' *Standard Ed.*, **10**, 155; *P.F.L.*, **9**. (118)

(1910*a* [1909]) *Five Lectures on Psycho-Analysis*, Standard Ed., **11**, 3; in *Two Short Accounts of Psycho-Analysis*, Penguin Books, Harmondsworth, 1962. (16, 27)

(1910*e*) 'The Antithetical Meaning of Primal Words', *Standard Ed.*, **11**, 155. (233)

(1911*b*) 'Formulations on the Two Principles of Mental Functioning', *Standard Ed.*, **12**, 218; *P.F.L.* **11**. (252)

(1911*c* [1910]) 'Psycho-Analytic Notes on an Autobiographical Account of a Case of Paranoia (Dementia Paranoides)', *Standard Ed.*, **12**, 9; *P.F.L.*, **9**. (27)

(1912–13) *Totem and Taboo*, London, 1950; New York, 1952; *Standard Ed.*, **13**, 1; *P.F.L.*, **13**. (27)

(1914*d*) 'On the History of the Psycho-Analytic Movement', *Standard Ed.*, **14**, 7; *P.F.L.* **15**. (27, 98)

(1915*e*) 'The Unconscious', *Standard Ed.*, **14**, 166; *P.F.L.* **11**. (168, 221)

(1916–17 [1915–17]) *Introductory Lectures on Psycho-Analysis*, New York, 1966; London, 1971; *Standard Ed.*, **15–16**; *P.F.L.*, **1**. (27, 33, 136, 207, 267)

(1918*b* [1914]) 'From the History of an Infantile Neurosis', *Standard Ed.*, **17**, 7; *P.F.L.*, **9**. (27)

(1920*g*) *Beyond the Pleasure Principle*, London, 1961; *Standard Ed.*, **18**, 7; *P.F.L.*, **11**. (27, 178)

(1921*c*) *Group Psychology and the Analysis of the Ego*, London and New York, 1959; *Standard Ed.*, **18**, 69; *P.F.L.*, **12**. (27, 207)

(1923*a*) 'Two Encyclopaedia Articles', *Standard Ed.*, **18**, 235; *P.F.L.*, **15**. (221)

(1923*b*) *The Ego and the Id*, London and New York, 1962; *Standard Ed.*, **19**, 12; *P.F.L.*, **11**. (27, 267)

(1925*d* [1924]) *An Autobiographical Study*, Standard Ed., **20**, 7; *P.F.L.*, **15**. (12, 33, 188)

(1925*h*) 'Negation', *Standard Ed.*, **19**, 235; *P.F.L.*, **11**. (233)

(1926*d* [1925]) *Inhibitions, Symptoms and Anxiety*, London, 1960; *Standard Ed.*, **20**, 87; *P.F.L.*, **10**. (28)

FREUD, S. (*cont.*)

(1927a) 'Postscript to *The Question of Lay Analysis*', *Standard Ed.*, **20**, 251; *P.F.L.* **15**. (12)

(1927c) *The Future of an Illusion*, London, 1962; *Standard Ed.*, **21**, 5; *P.F.L.*, **12**. (28)

(1927d) 'Humour', *Standard Ed.*, **21**, 159; *P.F.L.* **14**. (33, 294, 301)

(1930a) *Civilization and its Discontents*, New York, 1961; London, 1963; *Standard Ed.*, **21**, 64; *P.F.L.*, **12**. (28)

(1933a [1932]) *New Introductory Lectures on Psycho-Analysis*, New York, 1966; London, 1971; *Standard Ed.*, **22**; *P.F.L.*, **2**. (252)

(1933b [1932]) *Why War?*, Paris, 1933; *Standard Ed.*, **22**, 203; *P.F.L.*, **12**. (127)

(1935a) Postscript (1935) to *An Autobiographical Study*, new edition, London and New York; *Standard Ed.*, **20**, 71; *P.F.L.*, **15**. (12)

(1939a [1937–39]) *Moses and Monotheism*, *Standard Ed.*, **23**, 7; *P.F.L.*, **13**. (28)

(1940a [1938]) *An Outline of Psycho-Analysis*, New York, 1968; London, 1969; *Standard Ed.*, **23**, 141; *P.F.L.*, **15**. (28)

(1941d [1921]) 'Psycho-Analysis and Telepathy', *Standard Ed.*, **18**, 177. (207)

(1942a [1905–6]) 'Psychopathic Characters on the Stage', *Standard Ed.*, **7**, 305; *P.F.L.*, **14**. (188)

(1950a [1887–1902]) *The Origins of Psycho-Analysis*, London and New York, 1954. (Partly, including 'A Project for a Scientific Psychology', in *Standard Ed.*, **1**, 175.) (16, 24, 25, 26, 31–2, 200, 252)

(1960a) *Letters 1873–1939* (ed. E. L. Freud) (trans. T. and J. Stern), New York, 1960; London, 1961. (23, 24, 26)

(1963a [1909–39]) *Psycho-Analysis and Faith. The Letters of Sigmund Freud and Oskar Pfister* (ed. H. Meng and E. L. Freud) (trans. E. Mosbacher), London and New York, 1963. (24)

(1965a [1907–26]) *A Psycho-Analytic Dialogue. The Letters of Sigmund Freud and Karl Abraham* (ed. H. C. Abraham and E. L. Freud) (trans. B. Marsh and H. C. Abraham), London and New York, 1965. (24)

(1966a [1912–36]) *Sigmund Freud and Lou Andreas-Salomé: Letters* (ed. E. Pfeiffer) (trans. W. and E. Robson-Scott), London and New York, 1972. (24)

(1968a [1927–39]) *The Letters of Sigmund Freud and Arnold Zweig* (ed. E. L. Freud) (trans. W. and E. Robson-Scott), London and New York, 1970. (24)

(1970a [1919–1935]) *Sigmund Freud as a Consultant. Recollections of a Pioneer in Psychoanalysis* (Letters from Freud to Edoardo Weiss, including a Memoir and Commentaries by Weiss, with Foreword and Introduction by Martin Grotjahn), New York, 1970. (24)

(1974a [1906–23]) *The Freud/Jung Letters* (ed. W. McGuire) (trans. R. Manheim and R. F. C. Hull), London and Princeton, N.J., 1974. (24)

GRIESINGER, W. (1845) *Pathologie und Therapie der psychischen Krankheiten*, Stuttgart. (228)

GROOS, C. (1899) *Die Spiele der Menschen*, Jena. (170–71, 174, 178, 272)

GROSS, O. (1904) 'Zur Differentialdiagnostik negativistischen Phänomene', *Psychiat.-neurol. Wschr.*, **6.** (233)

HANSLICK, E. (1894) *Aus meinem Leben, Autobiographie* (2 vols.), Berlin. (4th ed., illustrated, Berlin, 1911.) (54)

HERMANN, W. (1904) *Das grosse Buch der Witze*, Berlin. (72)

HEVESI, L. (1888) *Almanaccando, Bilder aus Italien*, Stuttgart. (81)

HEYMANS, G. (1896) 'Ästhetische Untersuchungen in Anschluss an die Lippssche Theorie des Komischen', *Z. Psychol. Physiol. Sinnesorg.*, **11**, 31 and 333. (43, 47, 72, 204)

JONES, E. (1953) *Sigmund Freud: Life and Work*, Vol. 1, London and New York. (24)

JONES, E. (1955) *Sigmund Freud: Life and Work*, Vol. 2, London and New York. (Page reference is to the English edition.) (24, 33)

JONES, E. (1957) *Sigmund Freud: Life and Work*, Vol. 3, London and New York. (24)

JUNG, C. G., and FREUD, S. (1974) *See* FREUD, S. (1974a)

KANT, I. (1790) *Critik der Urtheilskraft*, Berlin. (43, 259)
[*Trans.: Kritik of Judgment*, by J. H. Bernard, London, 1892.]

KEMPNER, F. (1891) *Gedichte*, 6th ed., Berlin. (279–80)

KLEINPAUL, R. (1890) *Die Rätsel der Sprache*, Leipzig. (137, 179)

KRAEPELIN, E. (1885) 'Zur Psychologie des Komischen', *Philosophische Studien* (ed. W. Wundt), **2**, 128 and 327, Leipzig. (42)

LICHTENBERG, G. C. VON (The Elder) (1853) *Witzige und satirische Einfälle*, Vol. 2 of New Enlarged Edition, Göttingen. (123–6, 127–8)

LIPPS, T. (1883) *Grundtatsachen des Seelenlebens*, Bonn. (32)

(1897) 'Der Begriff des Unbewussten in der Psychologie', *Records of the Third Int. Congr. Psychol.*, Munich. (32)

(1898) *Komik und Humor*, Hamburg and Leipzig. (32, 39, 42, 43, 47–8, 49, 72–3, 108–9, 166, 199–200, 208, 248, 256, 259, 263)

LOUISA ANTOINETTE MARIA [OF TUSCANY] (1911) *My Own Story*, London. (172)

MÉLINAND, C. (1895) 'Pourquoi rit-on?', *Revue des deux mondes*, **127** (February), 612. (301)

MICHELET, J. (1860) *La femme*, Paris. (97)

MOLL, A. (1898) *Untersuchungen über die Libido sexualis*, Vol. 1, Berlin. (141)

PFISTER, O., and FREUD, S. (1963) See FREUD, S. (1963a)

RICHTER, JEAN PAUL (1804) *Vorschule der Aesthetik* (2 vols.), Hamburg. (41, 44, 60)

SAXONY, PRINCESS LOUISE OF. See LOUISA ANTOINETTE MARIA

SPENCER, H. (1860) 'The Physiology of Laughter', *Macmillan's Magazine*, March; in *Essays*, **2**, London, 1901. (198, 199)

SPITZER, D. (1912) *Wiener Spaziergänge, I, Gessammelte Schriften*, **1**, Munich. (66, 74)

ÜBERHORST, K. (1900) *Das Komische* (2 vols.), Leipzig. (107)

VISCHER, F. T. (1846–57) *Aesthetik* (3 vols. in 4), Leipzig and Stuttgart. (41, 64)

WEISS, E., and FREUD, S. (1970) See FREUD, S. (1970a)

ZWEIG, A., and FREUD, S. (1968) See FREUD, S. (1968a)

LIST OF ABBREVIATIONS

Gesammelte Werke = Freud, *Gesammelte Werke* (18 vols.), Vols. 1–17 London, 1940–52, Vol. 18 Frankfurt am Main, 1968. From 1960 the whole edition published by S. Fischer Verlag, Frankfurt am Main.

Standard Edition = *The Standard Edition of the Complete Psychological Works of Sigmund Freud* (24 vols), Hogarth Press and The Institute of Psycho-Analysis, London, 1953–74.

P.F.L. = *Pelican Freud Library* (15 vols.), Penguin Books, Harmondsworth, from 1973.

INDEX OF JOKES

GENERAL INDEX

This index includes the names of non-technical authors. It also includes the names of technical authors where no reference is made in the text to specific works. For references to specific technical works, the Bibliography should be consulted. The compilation of the index was undertaken by Mrs R. S. Partridge.

MORE ABOUT PENGUINS
AND PELICANS

Penguinews, which appears every month, contains details of all the new books issued by Penguins as they are published. From time to time it is supplemented by *Penguins in Print*, which is our complete list of almost 5,000 titles.

A specimen copy of *Penguinews* will be sent to you free on request. Please write to Dept EP, Penguin Books Ltd, Harmondsworth, Middlesex, for your copy.

In the U.S.A.: For a complete list of books available from Penguins in the United States write to Dept CS, Penguin Books, 625 Madison Avenue, New York, New York 10022.

In Canada: For a complete list of books available from Penguins in Canada write to Penguin Books Canada Ltd, 41 Steelcase Road West, Markham, Ontario.

Edited by Angela Richards for the general reader and based on James Strachey's Standard Edition this collection of fifteen volumes will be the first full paperback edition of Freud's works in English.

Virtually all Freud's major psychological writings will be included. As well as the more famous titles and the volumes of lectures and case histories, there will be numerous shorter works arranged by subject. Thus Freud's papers and essays on sexuality, the neuroses, society, religion, art and literature will be brought together into single volumes.

Volume 1

INTRODUCTORY LECTURES ON PSYCHOANALYSIS

Sigmund Freud

The *Introductory Lectures on Psychoanalysis* were delivered by Freud during the First World War. Never before, in the course of thirty years of lecturing at the University of Vienna, had he deliberately set down, with a view to publication, the full range of his theories and observations. This series, therefore, represents a stock-taking of psychoanalysis as it stood after the secession of Adler and Jung.

In common with the majority of profound thinkers Freud commanded an exceptionally simple and readable style of exposition: his conclusions about the unconscious mind, about dreams, phantasies, anxiety, symbolism, perversions, infantile sexuality and other aspects of psychoanalysis are summarized here with a telling and easy elegance.

Volume 2

NEW INTRODUCTORY LECTURES ON PSYCHOANALYSIS

Sigmund Freud

Freud published his *New Introductory Lectures on Psychoanalysis* in 1933, the year in which the Nazis publicly burned his books in Berlin. These (though never intended for delivery) are cast in the lively rhetorical manner of speech and in places they recapitulate his established views (as, for instance, about dreams). But Freud also develops very fully here his newer concepts of id, ego and super-ego as elements in the structure of the mind, and explains his more recent conclusions about anxiety and the instincts and about the psychology of women. In addition he applies his analytical method to such phenomena as telepathy and communism, among a number of subjects of indirect relevance to psychoanalysis.

Volume 3

STUDIES ON HYSTERIA

Sigmund Freud and Joseph Breuer

Psychoanalysis is bedded in the work on hysteria done by Sigmund Freud and Joseph Breuer, and this volume contains both their 'Preliminary Communication' of 1893 and the fuller publication of 1895, with its famous case histories of Anna O., Emmy von N., and other patients.

THE PELICAN FREUD LIBRARY

Volume 4

THE INTERPRETATION OF DREAMS

Sigmund Freud

The Interpretation of Dreams is generally agreed to be Freud's major and most original work. By a detailed investigation of these universal phenomena he discovered a way of exploring the unconscious, recognized that dreams, like neurotic symptoms, are products of a conflict and compromise between conscious and unconscious impulses and was able to classify the differences between the primary and secondary processes of thought – between the modes of functioning in the unconscious and conscious regions of the mind. In addition Freud was led to revise his methods of treatment for neurotic patients by introducing the valuable technical adjunct of dream-interpretation and to develop, largely based on this remarkable work, his revolutionary theories of the Oedipus Complex and of the profound importance of infantile life and sexuality for the development of adults.

Although depressed by its initially cool reception, Freud wrote in the Preface to the third English edition: 'It contains even according to my present day judgement, the most valuable of all the discoveries it has been my good fortune to make. Insight such as this falls to one's lot but once in a lifetime.'

THE PELICAN FREUD LIBRARY

Volume 5

THE PSYCHOPATHOLOGY OF EVERYDAY LIFE

Sigmund Freud

The Psychopathology of Everyday Life has possibly done more than any other book to popularize psychology. Freud wrote it deliberately for the ordinary reader at the turn of the century and, as fresh editions appeared, constantly added new illustrations and anecdotes without changing his basic theories. Though hardly any of his work has been so frequently printed and so widely read, it is a curious fact that this translation, made by Alan Tyson, contains the first full English text of Freud's book in its final and greatly expanded form.

Here, with brief examples that are endlessly intriguing, we have the simple but convincing explanations of things that are familiar to everybody: the sudden forgetting of proper names, of sets of words, impressions and intentions; childhood and 'screen' memories; bungled actions and other errors; and all those little, significant mistakes of tongue and pens that have come to be called 'Freudian slips'.

This volume also contains James Strachey's sketch of Freud's life and ideas.